FOSTER'S
MURRAY WALKER'S
1992 GRAND PRIX YEAR

D1330867

Photo: Diana Burnett

Photography
John Townsend

Murray Walker's 1992 Grand Prix Year is published by Hazleton Publishing, 3 Richmond Hill, Richmond, Surrey TW10 6RE, in association with FOSTER'S.
Typeset by Surrey Typesetters, Stoneleigh, Epsom, Surrey.
Colour reproduction by Masterlith Ltd, Mitcham, Surrey.
Printed in England by Fulmar Colour Printing, Croydon, Surrey.

DISTRIBUTORS
UK
Reed Illustrated Books
Michelin House, 81 Fulham Road,
London SW3 6RB

AUSTRALIA
Technical Book & Magazine Co. Pty
289-299 Swanston Street, Melbourne, Victoria 3000

Universal Motor Publications
c/o Automotive Motoring Bookshop
152-154 Clarence Street, Sydney 2000

NEW ZEALAND
David Bateman
'Golden Heights', 32-34 View Road, Glenfield, Auckland 10

SOUTH AFRICA
Motorbooks
341 Jan Smuts Avenue, Craighall Park, Johannesburg

PUBLISHER: Richard Poulter
EXECUTIVE PUBLISHER: Elizabeth Le Breton
EDITOR: Simon Arron
DESIGNER: Michèle Arron
PHOTOGRAPHER: John Townsend
PRODUCTION MANAGER: George Greenfield
GRAND PRIX STATISTICS: Maurice Hamilton
CIRCUIT DIAGRAMS: Steve Small
FRONT COVER PHOTOGRAPH: Gary Hawkins

CONTENTS

" Don't you just hate

 FOSTER'S. DO

when that happens."

YOU JUST LOVE IT.

1992 DRIVERS

Driver	Country	Team	No. GPs
Michele Alboreto	I	Footwork	169
Jean Alesi	F	Ferrari	55
Giovanna Amati	I	Brabham	—
Paul Belmondo	F	March	5
Gerhard Berger	A	McLaren	131
Enrico Bertaggia	I	Moda	—
Thierry Boutsen	B	Ligier	153
Martin Brundle	GB	Benetton	99
Alex Caffi	I	Moda	56
Ivan Capelli	I	Ferrari	92
Andrea de Cesaris	I	Tyrrell	181
Andrea Chiesa	CH	Fondmetal	3
Erik Comas	F	Ligier	28
Christian Fittipaldi	BR	Minardi	10
Bertrand Gachot	F	Venturi	31
Olivier Grouillard	F	Tyrrell	41
Mauricio Gugelmin	BR	Jordan	74
Mika Häkkinen	SF	Lotus	30
Johnny Herbert	GB	Lotus	31
Damon Hill	GB	Brabham	2
Ukyo Katayama	J	Venturi	16
Jan Lammers	NL	March	21
Nicola Larini	I	Ferrari	42
JJ Lehto	SF	Dallara	38
Perry McCarthy	GB	Moda	—
Nigel Mansell	GB	Williams	181
Pier-Luigi Martini	I	Dallara	86
Stefano Modena	I	Jordan	70
Gianni Morbidelli	I	Minardi	34
Roberto Moreno	BR	Moda	25
Emanuele Naspetti	I	March	5
Riccardo Patrese	I	Williams	240
Eric van de Poele	B	Brabham, Fondmetal	5
Michael Schumacher	D	Benetton	22
Ayrton Senna	BR	McLaren	142
Aguri Suzuki	J	Footwork	42
Gabriele Tarquini	I	Fondmetal	37
Karl Wendlinger	A	March	16
Alessandro Zanardi	I	Minardi	4

1992 WORLD CHAMPIONSHIP

	Drivers	Pts		Drivers	Pts
1.	Nigel Mansell	108	17.	Christian Fittipaldi	1
2.	Riccardo Patrese	56		Stefano Modena	1
3.	Michael Schumacher	53			
4.	AyrtonSenna	50		Teams	Pts
5.	Gerhard Berger	49	1.	Williams-Renault	164
6.	Martin Brundle	38	2.	McLaren-Honda	99
7.	Jean Alesi	18	3.	Benetton-Ford	91
8.	Mika Häkkinen	11	4.	Ferrari	21
9.	Andrea de Cesaris	8	5.	Lotus-Ford	13
10.	Michele Alboreto	6	6.	Tyrrell-Ilmor	8
11	Erik Comas	4	7.	Footwork-Mugen	6
12.	Karl Wendlinger	3		Ligier-Renault	6
	Ivan Capelli	3	9.	March-Ilmor	3
14.	Pier-Luigi Martini	2	10.	Dallara-Ferrari	2
	Johnny Herbert	2	11.	Venturi-Lamborghini	1
	Thierry Boutsen	2		Minardi-Lamborghini	1
17.	Bertrand Gachot	1		Jordan-Yamaha	1

1992 GRANDS PRIX

Race	Winner	Pole Position	Fastest Lap
South Africa	N Mansell	N Mansell	N Mansell
Mexico	N Mansell	N Mansell	G Berger
Brazil	N Mansell	N Mansell	R Patrese
Spain	N Mansell	N Mansell	N Mansell
San Marino	N Mansell	N Mansell	R Patrese
Monaco	A Senna	N Mansell	N Mansell
Canada	G Berger	A Senna	G Berger
France	N Mansell	N Mansell	N Mansell
Great Britain	N Mansell	N Mansell	N Mansell
Germany	N Mansell	N Mansell	R Patrese
Hungary	A Senna	R Patrese	N Mansell
Belgium	M S'macher	N Mansell	M S'macher
Italy	A Senna	N Mansell	N Mansell
Portugal	N Mansell	N Mansell	A Senna
Japan	R Patrese	N Mansell	N Mansell
Australia	G Berger	N Mansell	M S'macher

1992 DRIVERS

Who have won a GP, been on pole or set fastest lap

Grand Prix Wins	Races Contested	Pole Positions	Fastest Laps
36 Ayrton Senna	142	61	18
30 Nigel Mansell	181	31	30
8 Gerhard Berger	131	8	16
6 Riccardo Patrese	240	8	13
5 Michele Alboreto	169	2	5
3 Thierry Boutsen	153	1	1
1 Michael Schumacher	22	0	2
0 Jean Alesi	55	0	1
0 Andrea de Cesaris	181	1	1
0 Bertrand Gachot	31	0	1
0 Mauricio Gugelmin	74	0	1
0 Roberto Moreno	25	0	1

DURING 1992 ...

* In Hungary Nigel Mansell at last became world champion, having finished runner-up three times in 13 years of Formula One, only to announce his retirement two meetings later, disillusioned by his inability to agree 1993 terms with Williams. During the season he created new records by winning the first five Grands Prix, winning nine races and taking 14 pole positions in one season. He also beat Jackie Stewart's record to become the most victorious British driver, became the most experienced British GP driver, scored a record number of World Championship points in one season and moved up to third in the list of all-time winners.
* Honda announced its withdrawal from Formula One after 10 glorious years in which it won six constructors' and five drivers' World Championships with Williams and McLaren.
* Formula One returned to South Africa at the expense of the American GP.
* Three-times world champion Nelson Piquet retired from Grand Prix racing but was, sadly, badly injured practising for the Indy 500.
* Giovanna Amati became the first woman Formula One team member since Desiré Wilson in 1980, but she failed to qualify before being dropped by Brabham after Brazil.
* Grand Prix racing's most successful driver, Alain Prost, failed to be nominated by any team after being fired by Ferrari in 1991. Following a season's sabbatical, however, he announced a 1993 return to Formula One with Williams.
* Goodyear tyres were used by all the teams following the withdrawal of Pirelli.
* In Mexico, McLaren failed to get on to the front two rows of the grid for the first time in 67 races.
* The 50th Monaco Grand Prix was held.
* Ayrton Senna became only the second driver in Grand Prix history to score over 500 World Championship points. (The first was Alain Prost.)
* At the Canadian GP, Erik Comas's sixth place gave Ligier its first point for 48 races.
* John Barnard rejoined Ferrari as the team's design chief after acrimoniously parting from the team in 1990.
* FISA announced new construction and tyre regulations for 1993.
* Ferrari competed in its 500th Grand Prix (Belgium).
* In Belgium, 23 year-old Michael Schumacher's brilliant first win made him the third-youngest driver to achieve a GP victory and the first German to win a full-distance championship race since Wolfgang von Trips in 1961.
* Renault powered the constructors' championship winning team for the first time.
* McLaren became the highest points-scoring constructor in the history of the championship.
* Andrea Moda was the first team to be excluded from the World Championship since its inception in 1950.

PREFACE

Nigel Mansell's early-season run of five straight victories put him in a relaxed and confident frame of mind. His reward was to have first pick of the chicken drumsticks.

For the Grand Prix fraternity, the winter had been hectic and demanding. The worldwide economic downturn had made money scarcer than ever. And if there's one thing that Formula One needs more than anything else, it's money! But when the deals had been done, and the dust had settled, only two of the previous season's teams had dropped out — AGS and Lamborghini. Sadly, in spite of their efforts, they weren't going to be missed much. In 1991 they had only managed nine race starts between them out of a possible 64.

It was satisfying to record that 16 teams and 32 drivers were nominated for 1992's 16 races. As ever, there were a lot of changes and a lot of surprises. McLaren and Williams, who had dominated 1991 and looked certain to continue in that vein, were the only teams to field the same drivers and engines. With the immeasurable plus of continuity allied to the might of Honda and Renault, Senna and Berger for McLaren and Mansell and Patrese for Williams seemed more than likely to be the season's top men.

Every other team was different in at least one major respect. Tyrrell had lost its Braun sponsorship and its Honda V10 engines. Powered by the Ilmor V10, Olivier Grouillard and Andrea de Cesaris replaced Stefano Modena and the retired Satoru Nakajima. Nothing controversial about that, but the signing of Italy's Giovanna Amati to drive for Brabham raised a lot of eyebrows. For Giovanna was a woman and, moreover, one whose best placing was seventh in an F3000 race. To many her position in the team seemed to be the result of money rather than ability and was thus regrettable. Giovanna's team-mate was to be Belgium's Eric van de Poele, whose talent was yet to be proven after a season with the lumbering Lamborghini. The team's outgoing Yamaha V12 engines were to be replaced by the Judd V10.

It had been upheaval time for the Footwork team too. Thanks to its Japanese ownership, it had been able to replace the disastrous Porsche V12 engine with the Mugen (Honda) V10, and its new Alan Jenkins-designed car was to be driven by Michele Alboreto and Lola refugee Aguri Suzuki. And, joy of joys, major changes at Lotus were very much for the good, too. Team director Peter Collins had pulled a master stroke to get the Ford HB V8 engine, as used by Benetton and Jordan in 1991, and had retained his two young, and very impressive, drivers — Mika Häkkinen and Johnny Herbert. With a healthier budget it looked as though Lotus was back on the long haul to the top. Hurrah for that.

Giovanna Amati became the first woman to have attempted GP qualification for a decade when she signed for Brabham a few days before the start of the season.

Generation gap: Grand Prix racing's newest Fittipaldi. Christian of that ilk, just 21, graduated to F1 with Minardi, having won the 1991 European F3000 Championship. His father Wilson raced for Brabham in the early '70s; uncle Emerson was twice world champion and, more recently, in 1989, won the Indianapolis 500.

The Italian-owned Fondmetal team had also worked the oracle with Ford by getting the very impressive HB engine. Gabriele Tarquini, who had driven for the team at the end of 1991, would make the most of it, but his team-mate Andrea Chiesa, new to F1 after a long stint in F3000, seemed to be another who owed his place to a fat wallet.

Leyton House was no more. As someone who always felt uneasy with its bizarre name, I wasn't unhappy especially as, with its Japanese boss Akira Akagi having sold out, it had happily reverted to its well-known and much respected title of March. Still using the Ilmor V10, its drivers were to be Austrian Karl Wendlinger and Frenchman Paul Belmondo, another well-heeled driver who had failed to distinguish himself in F3000 and who had got a massive hill to climb in F1. For Benetton, on the other hand, prospects looked very good indeed. Not only did it have a very strong driver pairing, in Martin Brundle (in a top car for the first time in his Grand Prix career) and the brilliant young German Michael Schumacher, but this year the team, like Tyrrell, Brabham and Dallara, would be using Goodyear tyres instead of Pirellis. The Italian concern had pulled out of F1 at the end of 1991, having again failed to prove that it could do the job, and the switch to Goodyear was going to benefit its four new teams. In fact, with Goodyear, the improved Ford HB V8 engine and the ability to switch to the newer V12 if it developed well, Tom Walkinshaw's team was in especially good shape.

It looked as though better times lay ahead for the Scuderia Italia team too. Partly because of its switch to Goodyear, but also because its Dallara chassis were now to be powered by the Ferrari V12. And, in Pier-Luigi Martini and JJ Lehto, it had two excellent drivers. But the Italian team's good fortune was at the expense of its hard-trying compatriot Minardi, for whom Martini had driven in 1991 and which had also had the Ferrari engine. Now, with Italian Gianni Morbidelli and new-boy Christian Fittipaldi (the 1991 European F3000 champion and nephew of the great Emerson Fittipaldi) as its drivers, Minardi was to use a much revised Lamborghini V12.

There were a lot of questions to be answered in 1992, but none more intriguing than whether Ligier was going to make a comeback. The once-great French team had last scored a championship point as long ago as the 1989 French Grand Prix, and had performed pathetically ever since, in spite of a massive budget. But now it had the superb Renault V10 which had won seven races with the Williams team in 1991, plus a brand new Frank Dernie-designed car for Thierry Boutsen and Erik Comas to drive. And Alain Prost too? The world's most successful Grand Prix driver, fired by Ferrari in 1991, had negotiated with Ligier all winter and had tested the new car impressively — but he had not signed a contract. Would he substitute for Comas once the season had begun. And, if he did, could he win? Only time would tell, but it was going to be a very sad situation if the popular little Frenchman had to sit on the sidelines until 1993.

That McLaren and Williams would win races seemed a foregone conclusion. Would Ferrari? The world's most charismatic team had been a politics-ridden shambles in 1991, and had failed to win a race for the first time since 1986. Over the winter, though, its owner Fiat had

Time for reflection: Ron Dennis has often been cynical about certain teams' winter testing times. Those posted by the Williams-Renaults gave the McLaren supremo plenty to think about.

A new dawn? Max Mosley spearheaded FISA at the start of the new F1 campaign, the Englishman having ousted Jean-Marie Balestre during the previous autumn's presidential elections.

Ivan Capelli signed for Ferrari, the first Italian to have held a full-time position with the Maranello legend since Michele Alboreto.

taken what seemed to be the right action, hiring a new boss in Luca di Montezemolo who, with Niki Lauda, had helped the team back to the top in 1975 after a similarly bad patch. Niki had been appointed to act as a consultant and Harvey Postlethwaite had been persuaded to return as design chief after Mercedes-Benz had regrettably decided not to return to Grand Prix racing. With the charging Jean Alesi and the very impressive Ivan Capelli, whose talent had been unfulfilled in the Leyton House team, to drive the exciting-looking new F92A, the good times seemed to be about to roll again for Maranello.

As they might too for Gérard Larrousse. For years the ex-Le Mans winner had tried in vain to get his Lola-chassised team off the ground, only for misfortune after misfortune to drag him down. But now it seemed his luck might be turning. Backed by the small French car manufacturer Venturi and with a Robin Herd-inspired new chassis, powered by the Lamborghini V12 engine, Gérard's drivers were to be Japanese F3000 champion Ukyo Katayama and Belgium's Bertrand Gachot — the latter trying to rebuild his career after his traumatic 1991. A promising package.

Out of the uninspiring and totally unsuccessful Coloni organisation had emerged the new, and bizarrely named, Andrea Moda team, which was expected to be no more successful than its predecessor in spite of having the Judd V10. Its lead driver Alex Caffi had never lived up to his original expectations and his team-mate Enrico Bertaggia, who had repeatedly failed to pre-qualify the Coloni in 1989, seemed unworthy of a return to motor racing's top category. But the prospects for Eddie Jordan's team (after its brilliant debut in 1991, when it finished a staggering fifth in the constructors' championship) were really exciting. For now it had the Yamaha V12 (and Yamaha had demonstrated time and time again that it could beat Honda in motorcycle Grands Prix), lavish sponsorship from the South African Sasol organisation (another Eddie Jordan first!) and two competent drivers in Stefano Modena and Mauricio Gugelmin.

When 1991 ended it seemed almost certain that we had seen the last of the great three-times world champion Nelson Piquet and, sadly, 1992 confirmed that this was indeed the case. Unable to get a drive that would give him the chance to win, Nelson had decided to call it a day — although he planned to contest the Indianapolis 500, during qualifying for which he sadly suffered serious leg injuries, which brought his driving career to an untimely end. His volatile presence and forceful driving would be greatly missed. 1991 points-scorers Mark Blundell, Roberto Moreno, Emanuele Pirro, and Eric Bernard had been displaced too, as had Alessandro Zanardi. It is tough at the top, and nowhere is life tougher than Formula One.

But, as ever, the prospects for the new season were exciting. It was to start with a very welcome return to South Africa, last visited in 1985 and now replacing the USA Grand Prix at Phoenix. Despite endless efforts to popularise Formula One in the States, including locating the race at Long Beach, Watkins Glen, Dallas, Detroit, Las Vegas, Riverside, Sebring and Phoenix, America has never taken to Grand Prix racing, preferring its own categories. For the *world* championship its loss is a pity. In its absence the return of South Africa is truly welcome. The South Africans are knowledgeable and enormously enthusiastic and the totally rebuilt Kyalami circuit is an excellent venue. Welcome back!

So what had 1992 got in store? The promise of a resumption of the superb McLaren/Williams battles of 1991 and, for Nigel Mansell's fans, the Englishman's best chance

Road to nowhere: Enrico Bertaggia, who had unsuccessfully tried to qualify a Coloni in 1989, signed for Andrea Moda... and would be dropped before he completed a single lap in anger.

ever of winning the World Championship that had eluded him for so long. But, with every point to count, the need for reliability of paramount importance, the intense and dedicated Senna to overcome (not to mention Berger and Patrese), plus real opposition from, in particular, the Benetton, Ferrari and Jordan drivers, it wasn't going to be easy!

Jordan, the revelation of 1991, splashed into 1992 with a bright new colour scheme, backing from South African oil giant Sasol, Yamaha V12 engines and two new drivers. Mauricio Gugelmin (pictured) was a lot more sympathetic in his treatment of the team's gearboxes than partner Stefano Modena.

Kyalami had been completely rebuilt since F1's last visit in 1985. It didn't make much difference; Nigel Mansell won on that occasion, too.

What a joy to be in South Africa for the first Grand Prix of the new season! For the past two years the championship opener had been in Phoenix, Arizona. Although that city itself is most impressive, its Grand Prix atmosphere most certainly wasn't. America as a whole doesn't know about Formula One, doesn't want to know and is, at best, apathetic towards it (and that's a comment, not a criticism. Europe doesn't exactly go mad about Indycar racing. To each its own). But South Africa *does* know about it, wants it and is more than anxious to host the Grand Prix circus. Starved of it for political reasons since 1985, it welcomed the return of its World Championship event with enormous enthusiasm and made its visitors feel more than welcome.

But we returned to a very different Kyalami to the one at which Nigel Mansell had won his second Grand Prix for Williams. At enormous, government-supported cost the high altitude (5,000 feet) circuit near Johannesburg had been completely rebuilt to the very highest standards, with superb facilities. The garages equalled the best elsewhere, as did the press centre, the hospitality ''Bomas'' (luxury houses in most people's eyes!), the medical centre and the viewing areas.

Criticisms? Yes there was one major moan. The sinuous, anti-clockwise, 2.65-mile track held very few overtaking opportunities. Said Riccardo Patrese: "There are too many corners, no real straights and nowhere to overtake." Rather like Hungary — a fact that was to contribute to a processional race. The old-timers yearned for the previous Kyalami, with its long, blindingly fast, 200mph straight ending at Crowthorne Corner, which made for spectacular passing. They hadn't got it. But never mind. Everything else was good, the hot sunshine was a cheering change, the atmosphere was invigorating and the locals were friendly. The new season was starting on a high note.

The winter testing in Europe had been dominated by the Williams-Renault team using its 1991 FW14 equipped with a much-developed version of its 'active' hydraulic suspension. But its expected main rival, McLaren, had confined its activities to Silverstone, so no direct comparison had been possible. Of the four top teams, McLaren,

Williams and Benetton were all using updated 1991 cars. With three long-haul races (South Africa, Mexico and Brazil) starting the season, the devil they knew was better than trying to overcome teething problems with new designs thousands of miles away from base. Ferrari, though, had brought its dramatic, but little-tested, new 'twin-floored' F92A in the belief that anything would be better than last year's car. Now we would find out who had got their calculations right.

It didn't take long for it to become very clear indeed. From the moment Nigel Mansell let out the clutch of his Williams to start his first lap in Thursday's familiarisation session, no one could live with him. He was fastest on Thursday, fastest in all four Friday and Saturday sessions and again on Sunday morning. To a demoralising extent. His 18th career pole position was a stupefying 0.8s faster than Ayrton Senna's best. If the car was reliable and Nigel kept it on the island, there didn't seem much doubt about who was going to win the race. "There is no way we can catch the Williams here," said the resigned Ayrton.

Jean Alesi managed to hold Michael Schumacher and Gerhard Berger at bay until the new Ferrari F92A had a tantrum.

Nigel Mansell manages a smile, despite the fact that his growing trophy collection might force him to find a bigger family home in Florida. It was a feeling with which he'd become increasingly familiar as the season got into its stride.

TEAM ANALYSIS

McLAREN

All-new "fly-by-wire" MP4/7A not ready and so team uses three MP4/6Bs, exactly as at Japan and Australia 1991 except that Honda RA122 V12 had been optimised for 5,000 feet Kyalami altitude. "There's no way we can catch the Williams here," says dissatisfied Senna, "there's been zero development." As usual he is right. Ayrton second fastest qualifier a daunting 0.8s slower than Mansell. Berger third on grid 1.2s behind Nigel. With rocket start from fourth, Patrese (Williams) immediately passes both McLarens. Senna down to third where he stays for whole race, despite best efforts. Berger further demoted to sixth by Alesi and Schumacher at first corner. Slowed by excessive fuel consumption, Gerhard finishes lacklustre fifth, running out as he crosses line. What a turnabout! "We're not quick enough," says Ron Dennis, but much-needed new car not expected at earliest until race three, Brazil.

TYRRELL

Ilmor V10 engine, a staggering 40kg lighter than team's 1991 Honda V10, gives 020B superb balance and handling. With the added plus of Goodyear tyres, team very happy. Andrea de Cesaris, now driving for his ninth Grand Prix team ("the most professional in my long career"), qualifies well (10th), but is forced into sand trap by Brundle/Wendlinger collision on lap one. Rejoins 20th for stirring drive to ninth by lap 41 but retires, next lap, with misfire. Olivier Grouillard starts from encouraging 12th place but has clutch problem. Down to 17th lap one. Advances to ninth, lap 52, but retires, lap 63, also with misfire. Team nevertheless delighted with promising car.

WILLIAMS

Intensive development by team, Renault and Elf over winter, combined with decision to use 1991 FW14 car with developed active suspension, pays massive dividends. Leaner Nigel Mansell (at 76kg, now 2kg lighter than Patrese) uncatchable during whole meeting. Fastest in every practice session and takes 18th pole position a crushing 0.8s faster than Senna. Then runs away with race (in spare car), leading from start to finish, with 14 fastest laps, to take his 22nd win and set the lap record (1m 17.578s, 122.865mph). Patrese qualifies fourth after gearbox and set-up problems in practice but, with sensational start, passes Berger and Senna to second before first corner. Stays there, matching Senna's every effort, for first Williams one-two since Germany 1991. Team leads constructors' championship by 10 points after first race.

BRABHAM

Virtually all-new team arrives at Kyalami with no mileage on hastily built cars, now with Judd V10 engines. With minimal Formula One experience (one Benetton test), Giovanna Amati unsurprisingly fails to qualify. Eric van de Poele just does so — 26th — before going on to drive

determined race despite heavy steering. Finishes 13th (four laps down) for only second-ever finish. "Now we can start to develop car!"

FOOTWORK

Reassuring start after disastrous 1991. Team, now using Mugen (Honda) V10 engine, avoids pre-qualifying for one driver after Andrea Moda team exclusion. New boy Suzuki starts 16th, one place ahead of team-mate Alboreto. Aguri races to reliable eighth whilst Michele finishes 10th after losing third and fourth gears (both men two laps down). Team, aiming for reliability, well pleased with double finish.

LOTUS

Tremendously heartening race for much-strengthened team. Ford HB V8 and revised suspension featuring Penske dampers transform what is basically a 1990 car. Both Herbert and Häkkinen delighted with speed and handling improvements. Johnny starts excellent 11th and has superb race. Holds eighth place behind Williams, McLarens, Ferraris and Schumacher, but up to sixth after Alesi and Capelli retirements. Finishes there (one lap down) to score point for self and team. Mika also drives excellent race, in spare car set up for Herbert after race car develops oil leak on warm-up lap, to finish ninth (two laps down). A great start for rejuvenated Team Lotus, which fully vindicates Peter Collins' touching faith in his two young drivers.

FONDMETAL

Now a two-car team, Fondmetal avoids need to pre-qualify one driver when Andrea Moda team excluded. Andrea Chiesa fails to qualify for first GP but Gabriele Tarquini does so in 15th, despite fluttering butterfly in helmet! Races midfield until lap 24 retirement with failing oil pressure.

MARCH

Decimated and massively under-financed ex-Leyton House team does well to get to Kyalami in spite of everything. Lanky Austrian Karl Wendlinger, with only two GPs to his credit but now in car that fits him, staggers everyone by qualifying superb seventh in "as '91" car after looking good all through practice. Then sadly has radiator punctured by charging Martin Brundle's Benetton on first lap. Gamely struggles on but has to retire from excellent 11th, lap 14, with grossly overheated engine. But he'd made his point. Only 27th, Paul Belmondo fails to qualify for his first GP.

BENETTON

Sensational success for Schumacher. Misery for Brundle. Now very happy on Goodyear tyres, Michael qualifies magnificent sixth with Martin eighth for his first Benetton race. But Brundle out on lap one after collision with Wendlinger. Schumacher charges on behind fourth-placed, oil-spewing Alesi until Ferrari engine blows on lap 39. Now fourth, Schumacher impressively stays there for his highest-yet finish — well pleased, as is team.

Sensation of qualifying was Karl Wendlinger, who did wonders for the morale of the financially straitened March team.

DALLARA

Evil handling of new B192 chassis, allied to electrical, gearbox, fuel, clutch and Ferrari engine problems result in Lehto and Martini starting unexpectedly far down grid (24th and 25th). JJ battles up to 11th by lap 42 but retires, lap 47, when driveshaft fails. Pier-Luigi, after being rammed by BBC car on way into track, collides with Gugelmin and spins on lap one. Rejoins and races last until lap 57 retirement (clutch).

MINARDI

Christian Fittipaldi qualifies excellent 20th for first GP, only one place and 0.01s behind team-mate Gianni Morbidelli. Both retire from race, Fittipaldi from 13th, lap 44 (electrics), Morbidelli from 14th, lap 56 (engine failure).

LIGIER

Alain Prost "will he, won't he drive for Ligier?" mystery resolved in the negative when Erik Comas weighs-in (at 73kg) to join Boutsen in new and unimpressive JS37. But despite Renault V10 power they only qualify 13th (Comas) and 14th. Erik and Thierry race behind Johnny Herbert and advance to seventh/eighth on lap 41. Boutsen retires, lap 61 (electrics) but Comas finishes excellent seventh, exhausted after having not even sat in car before practice due to Prost having tested throughout off-season negotiations.

FERRARI

Stunning-looking new F92A with unique "twin-floor" aerodynamics goes well in practice with Alesi qualifying fifth and nervous Capelli ninth for first Ferrari race. Watched by 'new' consultant Niki Lauda, Alesi charges to fourth past Berger at start and holds position, challenging Senna and resisting Schumacher, until lap 39 retirement. Capelli fights for sixth with Berger until stopping on lap 29. Both out because of incorrectly-designed oil tank which causes starvation in high-G corners. This is easily correctable, so team content with first showing of exciting new design.

VENTURI-LARROUSSE

Using own Robin Herd-inspired chassis (with V12 Lamborghini power) for first time, both cars qualify, having avoided pre-qualification thanks to Andrea Moda team exclusion. Japan's Ukyo Katayama 18th for first GP and Bertrand Gachot 22nd after a multitude of problems. Bert passes five cars on first lap but, after being thumped by passing Grouillard, retires on lap nine with bent track-rod. Katayama delighted to finish 12th (four laps down), despite lap 38 spin, tyre change and dodgy clutch.

JORDAN

Disheartening start to season after 1991 promise. Succession of Yamaha V12 engines blow in practice due to unexpectedly high temperatures. Modena fails to qualify and Gugelmin only 23rd. With heavily revised cooling system and extra radiators fitted after Sunday morning warm-up, Mauricio more than relieved to finish 11th (two laps down) in front of South African Sasol sponsors. "A lot to do!"

ANDREA MODA

New (ex-Coloni) team excluded at scrutineering following failure to pay $100,000 registration fee — thus cancelling pre-qualification. So no drive for Alex Caffi and Enrico Bertaggia. Appeal lodged.

Eric van de Poele hauled his Brabham into the race — just. Here he leads the Ligiers of Comas and Boutsen (which benefited from Renault V10 power, though it didn't show) and Grouillard's Tyrrell.

"There has been zero development." But there's many a slip twixt cup and lip and, with Senna and Gerhard Berger in the super-reliable McLaren-Hondas immediately behind him on the grid, Nigel wasn't exactly without a care. And nor was his team-mate, Riccardo Patrese. Gear selection difficulties on Friday and suspension set-up problems on Saturday resulted in him being fourth, on row two. "I am still very competitive. It is a long race so we will have to see what happens," reflected Riccardo.

Next up were Jean Alesi's new Ferrari, the dazzling Michael Schumacher's Benetton-Ford, Karl Wendlinger's March-Ilmor and Martin Brundle's Benetton. Wendlinger's achievement was quite outstanding. The decimated, impoverished, renamed March team (formerly Leyton House) had literally had to cobble up a car from an early-1991 tub and Karl, with only two Grands Prix behind him, had had minimal testing time. But cockpit changes had made all the difference, enabling the lanky Austrian to be comfortable for the first time in his short Formula One career.

Sunday was much cooler than the practice days, when it had been over 35 deg C, and in the warm-up Schumacher and Patrese were second and third to Mansell, with Senna only fourth fastest. Interesting! But when South Africa's first Grand Prix for seven years began, the sensation was Riccardo Patrese. Like a rocket from its launcher he blasted between Berger and Senna and was tight up behind Mansell by the first corner. "Aha, he's using the new traction control device," said the cognoscenti. "Maximum revs, no wheelspin, super start." But he wasn't. It was pure, unadulterated Riccardo. "I knew I had to be in front of Ayrton on the first lap because on this track it is so difficult to overtake. I have to say I made a good start!" Indeed he did and it was to stand him in very good stead, for second he stayed. All the way. Behind Mansell. There were 15 fastest laps in the race. Nigel set 14 of them and Riccardo the other. That's how superior the two team-mates were in their Williams-Renaults, which went faster and handled better than anything else that day.

And, unlike the opening races of 1991, they stayed the distance.

With first and second places Mansell and Patrese scored 16 points for their team in the constructors' championship to start the new season in stark contract to their 1991 débâcle at Phoenix. Nigel's drive was a copybook demonstration of how to do it. After a winter in his new Florida home he was more relaxed, more cheerful and more confident than I'd ever seen him, and he didn't put a wheel wrong, building a lead of over 20 seconds, controlling the race from the front and dismissively making his final record lap on the 70th out of 72 (1m 17.578s, 123.576mph). He won by a commanding 24.4s, with Patrese over 10 seconds ahead of Senna — who had driven his heart out in a car which simply wasn't quick enough. But for most of the race the gap between second and third had been much closer. On lap 38 Ayrton had been within two seconds of the Williams, but every time the world champion got within striking distance of him Patrese found the extra speed to draw away. Try as he might — and he had no problems — Senna could do nothing really to challenge Grand Prix racing's most experienced driver (it was Riccardo's 225th World Championship race). "Williams deserves to be first and second right now. . .third was as good as we could get

under the circumstances."

A boring race then? Not for me! Because behind the front three there was a battle royal for lap after lap. Poor Karl Wendlinger's hopes were dashed half way round the first lap when he and Brundle collided. Martin retired immediately, Karl nine laps later, but Brundle's German team-mate Michael Schumacher, still in only his seventh Grand-Prix, was in scintillating form. Both he and Alesi passed Berger to lie fourth and fifth before the first corner and then, close behind Senna, fought each other just ahead of Berger and Capelli (nervously driving his first race for Ferrari). It was a great sight. McLaren/Ferrari/Benetton/McLaren and Ferrari all making a race of it. It may have been a by-product of the fact that passing was so difficult, but it looked and sounded marvellous! Seventh-placed Capelli fell off the end of the high speed snake on lap 29 when his engine gave up and, 12 laps later, having been passed for fourth by the persistent and very impressive Schumacher, out went Alesi with the same problem, caused by an oil tank design problem which starved the Ferrari V12 of lubricant in the high-G corners.

So, on lap 41, up to sixth place came — Johnny Herbert! His many admirers knew that he was good but in 1991, in the old, underpowered Lotus-Judd (when Japanese F3000 commitments permitted), he had little

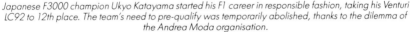

Japanese F3000 champion Ukyo Katayama started his F1 career in responsible fashion, taking his Venturi LC92 to 12th place. The team's need to pre-qualify was temporarily abolished, thanks to the dilemma of the Andrea Moda organisation.

Although the Lotus 102 is almost as old as he is, Johnny Herbert hauled it into the top six in one of the finest drives of his GP career. The Englishman eventually picked up a point.

chance to show it. But now he was a full-season member of the rejuvenated team and driving an updated car with vastly improved suspension (Penske dampers), powered by the very impressive Ford HB V8. Johnny started a fine 11th and by lap 12 he was eighth. With the Ferraris out he was sixth, storming along ahead of Comas and Boutsen in the new Renault-engined Ligiers. And there he stayed. A point for Herbert. A point for Lotus. Well deserved glory for both. Another fine drive was that of the much-maligned Andrea de Cesaris. At the last moment, his bulky wallet had secured him the drive in the second Tyrrell-Ilmor (his ninth GP team). And now he showed that his 1991 Jordan successes had been well deserved. He

qualified 10th, went off into a sand trap on the first lap avoiding the Wendlinger/Brundle coming-together but was back in the top 10 by lap 29 — having passed more people than anyone else in the whole race. Sadly for him, his outstanding drive ended with a misfire on lap 42, but he had shown that not only was he a man to watch in 1992 but that the Tyrrell 020B, 40kg lighter and better balanced after swapping the Honda V10 for the Ilmor engine, was now an excellent car.

But why, amidst all this action was McLaren's Gerhard Berger so unimpressive? Because his Honda V12, using too much fuel, obliged him to drive according to the gauge. Even then he ran out as he crossed the line to finish fifth. Not a happy man.

Nigel Mansell, first in 1985 had now, seven years later, won a magnificent and commanding victory. With a perfect blend of performance and reliability the two Williams-Renault men had driven their McLaren-Honda rivals into the ground. "But it is really early days yet," said Mansell. One race gone, 15 to come. "I am looking forward to the new car, new engine and new transmission to see if we can jump forward and catch them," said Ayrton Senna. But the earliest he was expecting it was for the Brazilian Grand Prix, two races later — and Williams intended to debut its new car in Spain. By that time, Mansell and Williams could be well on their way to the 1992 World Championship. But then again, remembering how McLaren had fought back in '91, maybe they couldn't!

Collectors' item: a shot of Alex Caffi exceeding urban traffic speeds in the Andrea Moda, a rebadged version of the hopeless 1991 Coloni chassis. A championship registration mix-up led to the team's expulsion from this meeting.

Been nice knowing you: the Williams duo thunder away into the lead at the start, leaving the rest to scrap for crumbs. In the background, Ivan Capelli's Ferrari is already in the fence... and out of the running.

Just 18 minutes into Friday afternoon's qualifying session for the Mexican Grand Prix, Ayrton Senna lost his McLaren in a big way. Only fifth fastest in the morning's free practice, and conscious of the Williams team's superiority in South Africa, he was trying very hard indeed over the track's notorious ripples. As he exited the 150mph Turn 13 in his stiffly suspended car, a major bump threw him off line. On the dirty surface, even Ayrton's skill couldn't prevent him from spinning off and slamming into the unprotected wall. The world champion was stretchered away with whiplash, concussion and a badly bruised left leg, his chances of driving in the race in doubt.

If it could happen to Senna, it could happen to anyone. The Autodromo Hermanos Rodriguez in Mexico City's Magdalena Mixhuca Park is a fine circuit marred by a rumpled surface — a consequence of the fact that it is built on a dried-up lake bed in an area unsettled by earthquakes. At 7,000 feet its altitude, even higher than Kyalami, creates breathing difficulties for drivers and engines alike. Doesn't sound attractive? There's more! The enormous city has one of the world's worst pollution problems and this year it was worse than ever — an official four times worse. With stinging eyes and burning throats, the Grand Prix visitors were liking it even less than usual — particularly as the corruption, deprivation and the lottery to avoid the stomach-churning 'Mexican Trots' seemed unchanged. And the fact that the race was being held three months earlier than usual hadn't reduced the heat problem. Temperatures of over 85 degrees, combined with everything else, made for a gruelling atmosphere.

But for viewers and spectators, the Mexican track has two great compensatory plusses. Firstly, the daunting 180 degree Peraltada corner, which the best drivers take without lifting at over 160mph. Secondly, the long main straight which leads into the 'slow' 85mph Turn One, the classic recipe for that regrettably rare Formula One occurrence — overtaking. After Senna's (and many others before him) spectacular departure from the track there in 1991, the Peraltada had been modified by reducing its banking, but it was still mighty spectacular, mighty demanding and mighty unpopular with the drivers. ''It's 10 times worse than it was before,'' reckoned Senna.

Ayrton's McLaren team was in even more trouble in Mexico than it had been at Kyalami. Its previously dominant Honda V12-powered MP4/6B was clearly past its sell-by date, Senna had his major off and Gerhard Berger had three spins, with the last one taking him into the wall at the same place as his team-mate. Gerhard was lucky to get away with it. With the

Gerhard Berger comes to a dusty end during qualifying . The Austrian pulled his socks up in the race, taking the sole surviving McLaren to fourth place and setting fastest lap in the process.

Despite its impending eligibility for the London-Brighton run, the Lotus 102 continued to yield results. It was Mika Häkkinen's turn to score a point for the resurgent Hethel team. (right)

Williams hydraulic 'active' suspension giving Mansell and Patrese a much easier time over the bumps and with the Benettons also handling better, 'Team Perfect' was up against it. The determined and dedicated Senna, who'd failed to qualify on Friday, did so (sixth) on Saturday, but with Berger ahead of him on the third row of the grid, McLaren was out of the top four for the first time in 67 races. There was a tense atmosphere in the Woking team's garages at the head of the pit lane.

This time, both the Williams-Renault drivers were on the front row, with Nigel Mansell in his 19th pole position — but only 0.02s faster than Riccardo Patrese. And, unlike Kyalami, they were both to use the team's new traction control device which prevents wheelspin. Was anyone going to see which way they'd gone? Well the Benetton men might, for they'd given the team its best-ever qualifying effort. Michael

Schumacher had qualified for only his eighth Grand Prix in a personal-best third place (at one time on Friday, he'd held provisional pole position ahead of Mansell), and Martin Brundle, increasingly at home in his new team, had equalled his best-ever grid position with fourth. A superb double achievement.

So it was all neat and tidy. Row one: Williams. Row two: Benetton: Row three: McLaren. The two Dallara-Ferraris of Lehto and Martini were well up in seventh and ninth thanks to aerodynamic changes following South Africa, sandwiching Gugelmin's improved Jordan-Yamaha. And Ferrari? Nowhere! After the team's massive restructuring and the production of its seemingly promising new F92A, Italy's pride was in greater disarray than ever with Jean Alesi starting a dispirited 10th (''No power. No grip. No handling. No straightline speed!'') and Ivan Capelli 20th.

TEAM ANALYSIS

McLAREN

Appalling meeting for team. Senna has very high speed spin into wall during Friday qualifying, suffering whiplash, concussion and heavily bruised left leg. Initially a non-qualifier (27th), he bravely returns to do so (sixth) on Saturday — his birthday. Berger spins off three times, once into wall, and only qualifies fifth. First time since Mexico 1987 (67 races!) that no McLaren in first two rows of grid. After superb start, Senna up to third by first corner but unable to close on Mansell and Patrese. Retires, lap 12 (transmission). Now 16 points behind Mansell in championship. Berger battles with Martin Brundle (Benetton) until, lap 43, squeezes through to fourth. Finishes there with fastest lap (1m 17.711s, 127.260mph, one second slower than Mansell's 1991 lap record). Both Senna and Berger, driving very twitchy cars, fiercely critical of "bumpy and dangerous" circuit. McLaren, 23 points behind Williams in championship and also outclassed by Benetton, now in race against time to ready new MP4/7A for Brazil in two weeks.

TYRRELL

Andrea de Cesaris very happy with sixth fastest time during Friday qualifying, but slips to 11th on Saturday due to engine problems. Similarly afflicted Olivier Grouillard starts 16th. Andrea takes to grass at first corner to avoid spinning Herbert but, from 17th, charges to fifth by lap 48 and remains there after fine drive to give team its first 1992 points. Grouillard retires from 15th, lap 13 (engine).

WILLIAMS

Second successive demonstration of devastating superiority. Using special Elf fuel and traction control device, Mansell and Patrese dominate qualifying to take pole and second positions on grid. Benefiting from 'active' hydraulic suspension over Mexico's awful bumps, they then drive away from opposition. After fierce duel with Riccardo during opening laps, Nigel wins his 23rd GP by over 13 seconds and, now with maximum 20 points, extends his championship lead. Patrese, slowed by blistered front tyre, takes second successive lead place to increase team's championship lead over McLaren to 23 points. "But we're not complacent," says Mansell. "With their new car in Brazil, we know they'll be throwing everything they've got at us!"

BRABHAM

Amidst financial crisis team fails to qualify either driver for first time in its great 31-year history. A very sad occasion. Van de Poele slowed by yellow flags on his hot lap whilst out-of-depth Amati, four seconds off pace, blows engine. Will they be in Brazil?

FOOTWORK

In cars badly affected by bumpy track, Alboreto qualifies 25th and Suzuki fails to do so after spinning off and bogging down in sand trap. Michele finishes 13th, four laps down, with slow puncture. Engine change to Mugen so far of little benefit to unimpressive, long established, team.

LOTUS

Well done Lotus! In continued fightback from near extinction, team again performs brilliantly. Despite car being some 43kg overweight, Johnny Herbert qualifies excellent 12th with Mika Häkkinen 18th after over-revving engine. Mika sensationally up to ninth on first lap but Johnny spins down to 21st at first corner. Häkkinen chases sixth-placed Alesi's oil-gushing Ferrari from lap 12 until passed by de Cesaris, lap 27. After Alesi and Brundle retirements, Mika finishes magnificent sixth despite having to drive with open visor, having used all tear-offs due to Ferrari oil. Herbert equally inspired. Charges from 21st to seventh by lap 48 and finishes there, like Häkkinen one lap down. With a point from both '92 races, team delighted. "Just wait until we've got the new car!"

FONDMETAL

Gabriele Tarquini well pleased with 14th place on grid. Andrea Chiesa qualifies 23rd for first GP but spins out from 15th, lap 38. Despite dodgy clutch Tarquini up to 11th, lap 42, but retires, lap 46, when clutch finally expires altogether.

MARCH

Wendlinger qualifies 19th, but out at start when goes for gap and rams Capelli's Ferrari. Belmondo again fails to make cut.

BENETTON

Great Mexico for Benetton. Best-ever grid with Schumacher superb third and Brundle fourth (Michael's best yet and delighted Martin's best since Monaco '89). What is more Schumacher, in only his eighth GP, briefly

Foot in the door. Fondmetal's new recruit Andrea Chiesa qualified for his first F1 start, only to spin into retirement.

takes pole from Mansell on Friday. Brundle surges past team-mate to fourth behind rocket-start Senna, but is demoted to fifth by Michael, lap two. Schumacher harries Senna for third until Ayrton retires, lap 12, and then drives to unflurried personal-best third place, setting fourth fastest lap of race. A great drive. Fourth-placed Martin resists non-stop pressure from Berger until lap 43 when passed by Gerhard. Then sadly has to retire when engine overheats due to Thierry Boutsen's discarded visor blocking oil cooler. Nevertheless a tremendously heartening meeting for whole team.

DALLARA
Car much improved by new front suspension and strengthened front wing. With its Ferrari V12 engine, Dallara B192 puts similarly powered Ferrari F92A to shame with excellent seventh on grid for JJ Lehto and ninth for Pier-Luigi Martini. Both have to stop for tyres (Martini three times after start-line collision) due to heavy steering. Martini gives best to tyre wear and retires from 17th and last, lap 37. Less troubled Lehto soldiers on to finish satisfied eighth, one lap down.

MINARDI
After electronic problems with Lamborghini V12 engine, promising Christian Fittipaldi 17th on grid (10th on Friday afternoon), out-performing more experienced team-mate Gianni Morbidelli, who starts 21st. Christian misses gear, goes off and retires at dreaded Peraltada, lap three, when 12th. Gianni exits at same place, lap 30, when 10th.

LIGIER
Alain Prost announces decision not to drive for Ligier in 1992. Very relieved Erik Comas qualifies 26th, four places behind team-mate Thierry Boutsen. Both complain of "total lack of grip" from new Renault-powered car, which seems little better than 1991 failure. Boutsen, delayed at start by Wendlinger/Capelli collision, finishes reliable but slow 10th, one place behind brake-troubled Comas (both two laps down).

FERRARI
Can this proud, great, but much-troubled team sink much lower? "No grip. No power. No handling. No straight line speed," moans Jean Alesi — again — after going off at Peraltada and qualifying only 10th. Capelli even worse — 20th on grid after clutch and lubrication problems. Ivan put out of misery immediately when taken out by Wendlinger at start. Hard-trying Alesi fights up to sixth after Senna retirement, lap 12, but South African oil system problem continues, despite new tank design, and Jean retires from eighth, lap 32. Embarrassed and ashamed team vilified by hysterical Italian media. All at sea, with no points after two races, urgent action needed to improve or replace failed new F92A. Who'd be in Luca di Montezemolo's shoes?

VENTURI-LARROUSSE
Bertrand Gachot qualifies excellent 13th. Katayama 24th on grid. Bert races strongly to finish 13th, three laps down, despite misfire. Ukyo finishes 12th in second GP, also three

Weekend to forget. After a heavy practice crash, Ayrton Senna was an unexpectedly early retirement.

laps down. A great relief for the hard-pressed Gérard Larrousse, who at last seems to have things going for him.

JORDAN
After South African overheating problems, Yamaha V12 cooling system much revised (aerodynamics, radiators and water pump). Gugelmin qualifies eighth (Yamaha's best yet) and Modena 15th. But Stefano has to start from pit lane in spare car after warm-up lap misfire. Gugelmin retires, lap one, with major power loss. Modena out from last-but-one (18th), lap 18, when gearbox packs up. Not a happy 1992 so far for Eddie's friendly team.

ANDREA MODA
After massive, highly commendable, effort, team arrives with new Simtek-designed cars after South African exclusion. But too late for pre-qualifying, which is therefore cancelled. So once again Caffi and Bertaggia fail to get a drive and, once again, team's future in doubt, dependent on FISA deliberations. Rough justice, but rules are rules...

Riccardo Patrese, the winner in 1991 and smarting from much-publicised criticism of his race performance in South Africa, was determined to make it two in a row in Mexico. How he tried! Mansell's getaway was superb but so was Riccardo's, and for lap after lap they fought for supremacy, Nigel leading the way. Both of them were driving flat-out and swapping fastest laps but Nigel, never in danger of being passed, had built a 3.5s lead by lap 11. Behind them, after a superb start, it was Senna, showing no sign of discomfort from his battered leg but unable to close on, let alone pass, the flying Williams-Renaults. On lap 11 he was nearly five seconds behind Patrese and on

lap 12 he was out. As he pulled off the circuit and rolled to a standstill on the grass, everyone naturally assumed that, physically, he'd had enough. And who could blame him? But no. It was transmission failure that had ended the Brazilian's disastrous weekend. As he sat and watched his championship rival dominating the race, Ayrton had plenty of time to reflect how vital it was that McLaren got the new MP4/7A ready for Brazil in two weeks' time. For now it looked like being 16 championship points behind Mansell at the end of the race.

Gerhard Berger wasn't doing well either, in fifth place behind the Williams duo and the multi-coloured Benettons. Schumacher, who'd

Three's company. Michael Schumacher (right) adjusts to the giddy heights of rostrum life, alongside old hands Patrese (left) and Mansell.

Häkkinen. Their modified 1990 cars were some 43kg overweight, but the Ford HB V8 had transformed their performance and Johnny and Mika were making the most of it. Herbert had started an excellent 12th on the grid with Häkkinen 18th but their progress thereafter had been meteoric. Mika was up to an incredible ninth place on the first lap after a sensational start and, although Johnny had spun down to 21st at the first corner, he was eighth by lap 32 of 69 with *both* Lotus drivers hotly pursuing Andrea de Cesaris. Over the years, Andrea had taken some richly deserved stick. In the Tyrrell-Ilmor, so much better than its Honda V10-powered predecessor, he was going as well as he had in 1991 in the Jordan-Ford. He'd qualified one place ahead of Herbert and had had to take to the grass at the first corner to avoid the spinning Lotus but, like Johnny, he'd made a great recovery to storm through the field from 17th. On lap 30 he passed sixth-placed Alesi's Ferrari and set about catching Berger's McLaren. So now it was Mika's turn to challenge Alesi — and it *was* a challenge with the Ferrari's V12 spewing oil over his helmet. Mika's misery ended when Alesi retired, to finish a dreadful race for Ferrari (team-mate Ivan Capelli had been rammed into the wall at the start by Karl Wendlinger's March).

On lap 48 Brundle's great drive came to an end bizarrely. Now fifth, after Berger had spectacularly passed him at the Peraltada on his way to posting the fastest lap of the race (1m 17.711s, 127.260mph), Martin had one of Thierry Boutsen's visor tear-offs blow into his sidepod and block the oil cooler. With a grossly overheating engine he had to retire, but he'd made his mark. So now de Cesaris was fifth, Häkkinen a superb sixth, to give Team Lotus its second point in two races, and Herbert seventh. And that's the way it stayed, with JJ Lehto an excellent eight in his Dallara-Ferrari despite a tyre stop, putting the Maranello works cars to shame.

Nigel Mansell's 23rd Grand Prix victory had been almost as dominant as his win in South Africa. Fastest in both qualifying sessions and fastest in the Sunday morning warm-up, he'd controlled the race from start to finish to win by 13 seconds. But it was no walkover. ''Riccardo

been impressively harrying Senna every inch of the way until Ayrton's retirement, was third and Brundle, revelling in a top-team car for the first time in his Grand Prix career, was a magnificent fourth. And try as he might, Gerhard just couldn't get by him. In another interesting but largely processional race, the high spot of the afternoon was when Berger pulled out of Martin's slipstream at turn one on lap 43 and dived past the Benetton. For just a few seconds! Because as he did so he ran wide on the exit to the corner and, quick as a flash, Brundle retook the place. Stirring stuff.

Just as exciting, though, were the two Lotus lions, Johnny Herbert and young Mika

Andrea de Cesaris drove superbly to give Tyrrell its first points of the year, recovering from a grassy moment at the first corner as he strove to avoid Herbert's errant Lotus.

lap 30 when Patrese had to nurse a blistered front tyre, but his excellent second place in his 226th Grand Prix not only showed that the 37 year-old Italian had lost none of his skill or will to win, but that the Williams-Renault (for which Elf had produced a very effective 'high altitude' fuel) was very much the car to beat. Mexico had also confirmed that young Schumacher was a superstar. On his way to his first podium finish he hadn't put a wheel wrong, had set the fourth fastest lap of the race and had now been in the points for every one of his five race finishes. Tom Walkinshaw must have been feeling very happy with his opportunistic signing of the young German after the 1991 Belgian Grand Prix!

Two races down, 14 to go. Williams now led the constructors' contest by a massive 23 points, with its two drivers first and second in the main championship. At the same point in 1991 the gap between Williams and McLaren, to the latter's advantage, had been 18 points. How times change! Would the new McLaren-Honda MP4/7A be in Brazil? And if it was, would it be good enough, and reliable enough, for Senna to win on his home ground? It was an intriguing prospect!

knows how much he was pushing and I know how hard I was having to push to stay in front. There are no team orders at Williams and, for the first 20 or 30 laps, we had a fantastic race, pushing one another with virtually nothing between us.'' The battle effectively stopped on

Michael Schumacher served further notice of his potential — as if anyone needed it — with his first podium finish in F1.

Mansell trailing shock! Riccardo Patrese held the upper hand until the scheduled tyre stops, the first time that Mansell had been headed all season. Ayrton Senna hangs onto third place, before an electronic malfunction sidelined him.

Not since 1982 had the World Championship series started with three successive 'long-haul' races, and the Grand Prix scene didn't like it. Particularly as two of them were Mexico and Brazil.

Their gloom wasn't just caused by the enormous transport and logistical problems involved in getting the teams and their equipment to three such far-flung venues in a five-week period. It was the fact that not many members of the Formula One world wanted to go to a Grand Prix in either country. Both Mexico and Brazil are blessed with superb circuits, but their deprived, poverty-stricken surroundings make them embarrassing and inappropriate settings for the money-laden, hi-tech atmosphere of Formula One. Sao Paulo is a scene of squalor, chaos, corruption and pollution every bit as bad as Mexico City. Not a pleasant place. Of course, it was great to be part of the championship scene wherever it was — though most of its members would have preferred it to be somewhere else. But it wasn't.

"These new fuels. Not by any chance toxic, are they?" Benetton's refuelling togs offer a none too subtle hint about the perils of F1 chemistry in the '90s.

So enjoy the vibrancy and excitement of South America and the passion of its inhabitants for Grand Prix racing. And savour the fact that the next round was in Europe.

Sao Paulo is the home town of world champion Ayrton Senna. In the previous eight years he had won his own Grand Prix only once, in 1991, and he was naturally more than anxious to do so again — especially as the championship gap between himself and Nigel Mansell was a worrying 16 points after only two races. But both Ayrton and his team-mate Gerhard Berger had a major problem. Amazingly, their team was in disarray. In South Africa and Mexico the 1991 McLaren MP4/6 had been inferior to the dominant Williams-Renaults of Mansell and Patrese and only *just* competitive with the Benetton-Fords. Development of its advanced MP4/7A successor had therefore been accelerated and the decision was taken to mount an all-out onslaught on the opposition in Brazil. And what an onslaught it was! Six cars, three each of the two types, nine tons of parts, 45 people from Woking, 23 Honda technicians to attend to their old and new V12 engines, plus various other people from suppliers. An enormous effort. For nothing . . .

Martin Brundle describes the 2.7-mile Interlagos circuit as the greatest in the world, and few would disagree with him. Rebuilt over the winter of 1990/91 it is fast, demanding, spectacular, has gradients, a grippy surface and just about every kind of corner. Perfect for the Williams-Renaults, with their 'active' hydraulic suspension and their semi-automatic gearboxes as Mansell and Patrese demonstrated to crushing effect.

They were not only demoralisingly quicker in both the qualifying sessions but, in Sunday morning's half-hour warm-up in race trim, they were *two* seconds faster than anyone else. In Formula One, two seconds per lap is light years. If they did that in the 71-lap race, they'd finish nearly two and a half minutes ahead of the opposition. But what about the all-singing, all-dancing, semi-automatic gearbox, new Honda V12-powered, electronic throttle, high-nose, advanced-aerodynamics McLarens? Disaster! The new engines produced less power than the old ones — and blew up. Once for Senna. Twice for Berger. Leaping in and out of the old and new cars, Ayrton and Gerhard did very well indeed to qualify third and fourth, coping as they did so with gearbox problems, a fuel fire and reduced downforce to compensate for the lack of power. All this from McLaren! It was an eye-opener for the dumbfounded media corps, who had been further fired up when the dominant Mansell, having already clinched his 20th pole position by over a second from his team-mate Patrese, spun into the wall trying to pass and demoralise Senna in the closing stages of Saturday's qualifying session. Unlike Senna in Mexico, he was unharmed by a hefty sideways thump into the wall — but he was very lucky to get away with it.

With the rising star Michael Schumacher (Benetton) and Jean Alesi (Ferrari) occupying the third row of the grid, followed by Brundle, Martini, the excellent Karl Wendlinger, Boutsen (in a much-improved Ligier), Capelli and Modena, the speculation was about who'd finish third behind the seemingly unbeatable Williams-Renaults and whether the McLarens would last the distance. They didn't. Indeed, Berger was almost out of the race before it began. Having blown an engine in the warm-up he just joined the grid in time with a new Honda V12 in his MP4/7A — only for an electrical gremlin to cause him to be pushed off to join the race, last, from the pit lane.

Riccardo Patrese's start in Brazil was even better than it had been in South Africa. This time he shot past Mansell into the lead and stayed there for 31 laps, with Nigel calmly sitting just behind him, matching his every move. Pulling away from the opposition as though they only had 2.5-litre engines, the battling twosome were over 22s ahead of third-placed Senna by lap 10. Over two seconds a lap faster! But it was Senna who was creating such a gap, for the off-the-pace Brazilian was a mobile chicane, obdurately blocking the frustrated efforts of Schumacher to force his Benetton past the slower McLaren. And it wasn't just the German who was being held up, because Senna was leading a nose-to-tail, snake-like, traffic jam comprising himself, Schumacher, Alesi, Brundle, Martini, Wendlinger (well done

Jean Alesi received the plaudits of the Ferrari team for launching Martin Brundle into a gravel trap without leaving a mark on his own car. The predictably adventurous Frenchman finished fourth.

TEAM ANALYSIS

McLAREN

Absolutely disastrous meeting for McLaren, Honda and both drivers. Rattled by double defeat by Williams in South Africa and Mexico, team takes three 1991 MP4/6 chassis, three new MP4/7As, 45 Woking personnel, 23 Honda technicians and nine tons of parts to Sao Paulo in dismally unsuccessful attempt to beat Didcot. Old car too slow and new car insufficiently developed. After blowing three new Honda V12s on Saturday morning Senna and Berger start third and fourth — both over two seconds off Mansell's pole time. Even worse in Sunday warm-up — ninth and 16th. Senna runs tardy third for 12 laps, creating nine-car traffic jam. Retires, lap 17, with engine electronics problem after being passed by Schumacher and Alesi. Berger just gets on to grid after engine change following morning warm-up but then has electronic failure. Starts from pit lane but retires from rear of field, lap four, with overheated engine. Team's worst race since Canada '91. Down to third in constructors' championship — 39 points behind Williams. Berger (five points) and Senna (four) lowly fourth and fifth in drivers' contest. Massive — and much-needed — testing programme planned during four weeks preceding Spanish GP.

TYRRELL

De Cesaris and Grouillard start disappointing 13th and 17th after variety of practice problems, including major engine fire for Olivier. Andrea forcefully zaps up to impressive eighth, lap 21, only to retire next lap (electrics). Grouillard also does well to reach eighth, lap 51, but retires, lap 53 (engine and suspension).

WILLIAMS

Third successive overwhelming one-two. Mansell again totally dominates meeting, despite thumping wall trying to pass and demoralise Senna at end of Saturday qualifying session. Takes third successive pole, with Patrese again second fastest. Williams duo then crush opposition with Riccardo just heading Mansell until positions reversed after tyre stops. Mansell wins third successive GP by 30 seconds to equal the great Fangio's 24 victories. Patrese sets fastest lap (1m 19.490s, 121.710 mph) and both lap entire field. Williams now leads constructors' championship by 37 points and Mansell drivers' contest by 12.

BRABHAM

Plagued by gear selection problems, both van de Poele and Amati fail to qualify.

FOOTWORK

At last some success. Michele Alboreto pre-qualifies second and then qualifies 14th, eight places ahead of team-mate Suzuki (22nd). Aguri retires from tail of field, lap three with oil system failure but Alboreto drives strong and persistent race to finish sixth (one lap down), giving

Giovanna Amati loses her place on the Interlagos A-Z. The Roman lady failed to qualify, despite the short-cut.

team its first point since Monaco 1990. A real stimulus after an awful 1991.

LOTUS

A third very impressive, but disappointing, 1992 GP for Team Lotus. With "no grip" both drivers qualify well down — Häkkinen 24th and Herbert 26th, but both then drive fine races after improving set-up on Sunday. Herbert a superb seventh on lap 33 after lap 25 tyre stop. Pushed off track into retirement by spinning Boutsen on lap 37. Häkkinen charges up to eighth, lap 53, but then loses all gears except third and finishes 10th (four laps down). But team's fine '92 record unsullied.

FONDMETAL

Both Tarquini and Chiesa delayed by spinners on their hot qualifying laps. Andrea fails to get in, Gabriele does so (19th). Delayed for three laps fitting new tie-rod after hitting Gachot at start. Races at tail of field until retiring from 11th, lap 63, with punctured radiator. But Tarquini impressively sets third fastest lap of race (two seconds slower than both Williams drivers!).

MARCH

Another impressive effort by Wendlinger. Another unimpressive effort by Belmondo. Karl qualifies excellent ninth. Paul fails to do so. Wendlinger races magnificent seventh before and after tyre stops but obliged to retire from ninth, lap 56, with clutch problems. Financially-strapped team deserves better than this.

BENETTON

Excellent performances by both drivers produce mixed results. Wunderkind Schumacher qualifies excellent fifth, two places ahead of team-mate Brundle. Frustrated Michael held up by third-placed Senna for 12 laps despite forceful efforts to pass. Does so, lap 13, and finishes third, lapped by Mansell and Patrese, to consolidate championship third place. Brundle equally frustrated as he tries to take fifth from Alesi. Punted off by Jean's Ferrari, lap 31, and retires with broken right front wheel. Both Benetton drivers fiercely critical of their rivals' tactics. Team moves past McLaren to take second in constructors' championship (37 points behind Williams!).

DALLARA

Unhappy with continuing handling problems, Martini qualifies eighth and Lehto 16th. Pier-Luigi up to excellent sixth after Senna retirement, lap 17, but retires, lap 24, when clutch fails. Lehto has two tyre stops due to puncture but finishes eighth (two laps down).

MINARDI

Team uses new Lamborghini V12 (lower, lighter, more powerful), which proves to be great improvement. Local hero Christian Fittipaldi (20th) again outqualifies team-mate Gianni Morbidelli (23rd), who crashes heavily on Friday. Christian runs well for only four laps before being delayed by fractious gearbox. Retires from 10th (of 13), lap 55. Gianni drives creditable race to finish seventh (first '92 team finish), two laps down. Team much-heartened by new engine's performance and reliability.

LIGIER

Car's performance much improved by new front wings and undertray, but team atmosphere fraught as everyone falls out with everyone else, notably Boutsen and Comas with each other. Thierry qualifies encouraging 10th. Erik 15th after traffic and comfort problems. Both race well — in points before tyre stops. Then, challenging seventh-placed Herbert, lap 37, Comas rammed by Boutsen who also removes Johnny and retires. Comas carries on but withdraws from seventh, lap 43 (engine). Harsh words follow! But team, now in much better shape, has four weeks to improve further before Spanish GP.

FERRARI

Using a variety of 91/92 engine specifications, Alesi and Capelli qualify sixth and 11th. Jean fifth in Senna-led traffic jam until lap 14, then fourth after Ayrton's retirement, constantly resisting Brundle's determined efforts to pass. Fifth after lap 25 tyre stop, collides with ever-present Martin, lap 31, but continues to first '92 finish in fourth place. Capelli has first Ferrari finish in fifth place, just beating Alboreto. Both a lap behind Mansell and Patrese. But in spite of major improvement — from abysmal to reasonable — and first two finishes of season, "We're a long way from being competitive," says team manager Claudio Lombardi.

VENTURI-LARROUSSE

Like Minardi, Larrousse team welcomes Lamborghini engine. After pre-qualifying fastest, Gachot starts 18th despite handling and engine mapping problems. Katayama 25th on grid. Bertrand collides with Tarquini at start and damages rear suspension which causes lap 24 retirement when 12th. Ukyo has steady drive to highest-yet finish, albeit three laps down.

JORDAN

Team's grisly 1992 continues. Stefano Modena qualifies encouraging 12th, despite heavy traffic, but retires on first lap with failed gearbox. Mauricio Gugelmin, suffering from flu after jet-ski holiday, starts 20th for home race. Charges to 15th on first lap and is impressive seventh on lap 28. Retires from 14th (gearbox), lap 37, after lap 32 tyre stop. In dramatic contrast to 1991 success, team now had only one finish from six starts following switch from Ford to Yamaha power.

ANDREA MODA

Yet-to-start team fires critical drivers Alex Caffi and Enrico Bertaggia and replaces them with experienced Roberto Moreno and new-to-Formula One Perry McCarthy. After administrative cock-up, FISA withdraws Perry's issued-and-paid-for superlicence, thus preventing him from trying to pre-qualify new Simtek-designed car, which replaces previously rejected (by FISA) Coloni-based design. In hastily-built new car, Moreno unsurprisingly fails to pre-qualify but team says "despite all the aggro we fight on." Unlike FISA, they have the sympathy of the entire pit lane.

Michele Alboreto gave Footwork cause to buy new batteries for its pocket calculator, notching up the team's first point since Monaco 1990.

Karl!), Boutsen, Capelli and de Cesaris. How long could it go on?

Until lap 13 was the answer. Exiting the climbing left-hander which leads into the pit straight, Schumacher was finally able to slingshot past the McLaren to third place. Alesi and Brundle, driving as one, then passed Senna on lap 18 as he rolled up the pit lane, climbed out of his car and disappeared into the back of the garage without a word. With Berger having retired from the tail of the field on lap five, McLaren's Brazilian nightmare was over. Not since Canada '91 had they had such a terrible result.

Now Patrese and Mansell led Schumacher by over half a minute, with Alesi and Brundle still together fourth and fifth, leading Martini, Wendlinger, Boutsen and de Cesaris — while Johnny Herbert had scythed his way through the field behind them after starting 26th and last in his Lotus. Tyre stops hadn't been a factor in Mexico, but they certainly were in Brazil. In fact they decided the race. Schumacher stopped for his new Goodyear Cs first, on lap 24 (7.55s). In third, out 10th. Then Alesi and Brundle. Down to seventh and eighth. But it was the Williams men we were waiting for, because they were so close that their tyre stops could make all the

Eddie Jordan teaches one of the locals the finer points of the Dublin Samba.

Back in F1, Roberto Moreno joined never-say-die Englishman Perry McCarthy in the reshaped Andrea Moda team. When the latter's F1 licence was revoked, Moreno was left to fly the flag on his own... for a few laps (below).

third time in as many races, with a broken wheel and in a state of some fury as Alesi raced on.

Now Patrese got the hammer down. A new lap record on lap 34, the fastest of the race (1m 19.490s, 121.710 mph) on his new Goodyears took him to within 3.7s of Mansell, but from then on he was to watch his team-mate draw away and finally win by nearly 30s. Meantime there had been a lot going on behind them. Notably the talented Ivan Capelli taking Brundle's fifth place in his Ferrari which, like Alesi's, was proving to be reliable for the first time in three races. There wasn't a lot in it between Ivan and his fellow Italian Michele Alboreto, who was having his best race since Mexico 1989. At last his Footwork, now powered by a V10 Mugen, was performing — and so was the experienced Michele as he challenged the Ferrari ahead. Chasing Alboreto there was a closely matched trio fighting for seventh place. An inspired Johnny Herbert, brilliantly up from last on the grid, held it in his Lotus-Ford just in front of the battling Ligiers of Erik Comas and his team-mate, but no longer friend, Thierry Boutsen.

It wasn't all plain sailing for Mansell. He clattered into the wall on Friday afternoon, after getting into a knot while trying to pass Senna. Damage was limited to pride and chassis.

difference. They did. In came Mansell. Using new equipment, his tyre men got him out in 8.54s, still second but now 21s behind Patrese. As Nigel switched off the rev-limiter to maximise his new-rubber advantage and close the gap on Riccardo, we waited for the leader's stop. It came on lap 31 and it took 9.11 seconds — 0.6s longer than Nigel's. On lap 32, after his charge, Mansell led Patrese by 5.3s and from then on it was his race. Repeating the crushing form he'd shown in South Africa and Mexico, he just drove away to a brilliant third win in three races to achieve his 24th victory and thereby equal the achievement of the great Juan-Manuel Fangio.

But his fellow Englishman Martin Brundle failed to finish. Driving as well as he had in Mexico, and still trying to get by Jean Alesi, after their tyre stops, he dived inside the Ferrari at the Curva do Senna. Only for Jean to slam the door, Formula Ford style. Exit Martin, for the

With the new Ligier aerodynamics doing a good job, so were their drivers. Both were determined to finish in the points. At the end of the pit straight Thierry pulled to the left, tried to go through inside Comas, lost control, hit Erik's car and then punted Herbert into the gravel trap and out of the race. Exit Boutsen too.

On lap 52 Mansell and Patrese lapped the third-placed Schumacher — and there were still 19 laps to go. That's how good the Williams-Renaults were in Brazil. It was shades of 1988 when Senna and Prost in their McLaren-Hondas won 15 of the 16 races and made everyone else look incidental. Now Williams led Benetton in the constructors' championship by a massive 37 points (with McLaren down to third, 39 points

adrift) whilst, with his three successive victories, Mansell led Patrese by 12 points and Senna, in fifth place, by 26. First time out with the MP4/7A McLaren had flopped spectacularly. With four weeks' development time before the Spanish Grand Prix, they consoled themselves with the memory that they'd led Wiliams by 34 points after three races in 1991, only for the Didcot team to take the lead just six races later. ''Maybe we can do the same,'' said McLaren. Maybe they could, but Williams too had a new car waiting, together with a new, improved Renault V10. With a new Benetton due to appear in Spain, and Ferrari and Ligier showing signs of getting their act together, the prospects for Europe looked exciting!

''No. I want another new company car.'' Senna and Ron Dennis discuss the implications of the new McLaren MP4/7A's failure to stem the tide of Williams successes.

"Excuse me. Are you lost?" Tio Pepe's hospitality girls were a familiar, and predictable, fixture at Jerez, previous home of the Spanish GP, which is slap in the heart of the country's sherry region. They managed to find work in industrial Barcelona, too.

The inaugural Grand Prix at Barcelona's magnificent Circuit de Catalunya in 1991 was the stage for one of Nigel Mansell's greatest drives. In wet/dry conditions, knowing he had to win to keep his championship hopes alive, he did just that with a storming performance. This included a breathtaking passing manoeuvre, Nigel almost brushing wheels with Senna's McLaren at some 200 mph down the main straight. Undoubtedly, that was the visual highlight of the year.

Nigel returned to Barcelona for the 'Grand Prix of the Olympics'. It was five months earlier in the year, but the weather was the same — and so was the result. The circumstances were very different, though. This time, with three successive victories behind him, he led the championship by a commanding 12 points. His alleged chief rival Senna was a further 14 adrift and Nigel's Williams-Renault was very much

the class of the field. Could he match Senna's 1991 record of four successive wins at the start of the season and further extend his lead? He could — and he did — with a drive which was even more impressive than his 1991 victory.

It had been a full four weeks since the Brazilian Grand Prix and there had been non-stop development and testing by all the teams that could afford it — especially McLaren,

Benetton and Ferrari. The thrice-beaten McLaren team was especially aware that if its new MP4/7A wasn't on the pace in Spain after its unsuccessful debut in Brazil, it would be a job to get it there for the rest of the frenzied European season. Together with Honda, McLaren had spared nothing in its efforts to close the performance gap between itself and the Williams-Renault team. Testing times indicated that it hadn't succeeded, but only the Grand Prix would show for sure. Benetton had

Damon Hill made his F1 debut for Brabham, replacing the underfinanced, and thus far uncompetitive, Giovanna Amati. Hill made the BT60B go a fair bit quicker than had his predecessor, but it still wasn't enough to qualify.

raced its B191 for the last time and arrived in Barcelona with three of its striking new Ross Brawn/Rory Byrne-designed B192s, powered by the improved Series VI Ford V8. Ferrari, meanwhile, was optimistic that development of the so far unsuccessful F92A at Maranello would have made it more competitive. For its part Williams had brought two cars equipped with the new, even better, Renault RS4 V10. How were they all going to shape up?

Nobody had as long as they wanted to find out. Friday was cool and overcast with a light breeze for the qualifying session. ''It's going to rain tomorrow,'' said Mansell — and he was so right! His determination to be in pole position when Friday's qualifying hour ended was awesome and successful. With a time of 1m 20.190s (132.420 mph) he was over a second faster than the next man and that would do nicely, thank you! But this time the next man wasn't Mansell's team-mate Riccardo Patrese. It was the brilliant young German Michael Schumacher — on the front row of the grid in only his 10th Grand Prix. The new Benetton obviously worked very well! Senna was third and Patrese fourth with Capelli and Brundle fifth and sixth followed by Berger and Alesi. And that was the front of the grid for Sunday because Nigel's prophesy came true. In fact it didn't just rain on Saturday, it hosepiped down so hard and so unremittingly that there was absolutely no question of anyone improving on his Friday time. But, significantly, it was a very hard-trying Jean Alesi, liberated from the team dominance of Alain Prost, who was fastest in both the wet Saturday sessions in his Ferrari, beating the Williams for the first time in 1992.

The track was still wet for Sunday's warm-up four hours before the race (Berger fastest, Patrese next, Alesi third and Mansell — the only one to use both wet and dry-weather tyres — fourth). But when they rolled on to the grid for the two o'clock start everyone was on slicks.

Until it started to rain again just minutes before the off.

With the exceptions of Wendlinger, Belmondo and Chiesa, everyone selected Goodyear's new asymmetric wet-compound tyres for only their second race (Australia '91 was the first). When the lights turned to green

Mansell boiled away with a copybook start. Patrese shot up to second as Schumacher left too soon and then stopped, whilst third into the first corner was Alesi — from eighth on the grid! ''My place was sheltered from the rain by the bridge across the track. My rear wheels were starting in the dry!'' Straight between the two rows ahead went Jean, passing Berger, Brundle, Capelli, Senna and Schumacher before the first corner and banging wheels with Ayrton's McLaren as he did so. Incredible! Shades of Gilles Villeneuve, and Ferrari loved him for it.

Poor clutchless Martin Brundle spun on lap two and then, biffed by Erik Comas, did so again three laps later to retire, stranded on a kerb. But ahead of him the action was thrilling. In a daring move on lap seven Schumacher took third from Alesi as Berger and Senna fought for fifth ahead of Capelli and an on-form Comas. Then Senna, brilliant in the wet which masked his car's comparative lack of power, surged past the Ferrari to fourth and started to close on Schumacher. Behind him Alesi and Berger fought for fifth, nearly driving into each other. On lap 10 (of 65) Mansell led Patrese by three seconds having just set what was to be the fastest lap of the race (1m 42.503s, 103.594 mph). And now the rain really began to fall.

On lap 13 Berger and Alesi finally collided. Jean spun down behind his team-mate Ivan

Pier-Luigi Martini gave Dallara its first point of the season, and its first since the team became official recipient of 'customer' Ferrari engines.

Capelli to seventh and everyone was fighting for grip on wet-compound tyres which had been worn by drying tarmac (which was now nearly flooded in parts). So much so that on lap 20 the Williams team's chances of a fourth successive one-two disappeared in the increasing gloom as Patrese lost downforce trying to pass Mika Häkkinen's Lotus and spun into the wall at Nissan corner. Schumacher was

Nifty Footwork: Michele Alboreto brought his FA13 into the points yet again. The following Bertrand Gachot wasn't so lucky, retiring with engine failure.

TEAM ANALYSIS

McLAREN
Four weeks of work after Brazil improves new MP4/7A. "Better balance, better engine and track suits car," says Senna, third on grid, with Berger lowly seventh. Ayrton down to fifth on lap one. Past Alesi and Berger to third by lap 20 but unable to pass Schumacher, despite vigorous efforts. Spins on rain-soaked track, lap 56, Recovers without losing place only to spin again, out of race, lap 63. Classified ninth, three laps down, now 36 points behind Mansell. Gerhard fourth by lap 20, battling with Senna after colliding with Jean Alesi, lap 13. Finishes fourth after being caught and passed by charging Alesi, lap 63. Team faces fact that MP4/7A still off pace after being beaten by new Benetton B192 as well as dominant Williams.

TYRRELL
Not a happy birthday Sunday for 'Uncle' Ken Tyrrell. Engine and traffic problems during dry Friday qualifying ("They thought I was a Brabham and baulked me!" said de Cesaris) result in Andrea starting 11th and Olivier Grouillard 15th. With dragging clutch, de Cesaris muffs start. Retires from 25th, lap two, with failing oil pressure after nearly spinning off on lap one. Grouillard up to encouraging seventh, lap 30, but spins out, lap 31.

WILLIAMS
Fourth successive demonstration of total dominance by team and Mansell. Four cars at track, two with new Renault RS4 V10 which, used in qualifying only, is "already better than the RS3" according to both drivers. Mansell a full second faster than sensational Michael Schumacher in dry Friday qualifying to take his 21st pole position. Then repeats his 1991 success by driving one of his finest races, leading from start to finish without putting a wheel wrong in the rain-soaked conditions. In equalling Senna's 1991 record of four successive wins, Nigel joins Jim Clark and Niki Lauda on 25 victories — exceeded only by Prost, Senna and Stewart. Also posts fastest lap — 1m 42.503s, 103.594 mph. Patrese charges up to immediate second at start but spins out of race, lap 20, after losing downforce whilst trying to lap Häkkinen. Despite no points from Riccardo, Williams now leads Benetton by 47 points in constructors' championship.

BRABHAM
Hard-pressed team has cars impounded by creditor at French border. Two released, the other retained as surety. Damon Hill replaces impecunious Giovanna Amati, but neither he nor Eric van de Poele succeeds in qualifying.

FOOTWORK
Team continues encouraging progress. With now reliable car improved by weight reduction and better aerodynamics, Michele Alboreto pre-qualifies second

The availability of a friendly marshal with an umbrella was of little consolation to Senna. His second spin of the race proved to be terminal.

and qualifies 16th (excellent fifth in soaking Saturday session). Then races to fine fifth (one lap down), thanks to good wet set-up and his own skill and experience. Suzuki qualifies 19th and takes seventh place (two laps down) after "very hard race." Team well pleased with second successive points finish, but less enamoured with March-inspired $10,000 fine for changing Alboreto's slick tyres to wets on grid, after five-minute board…

LOTUS
Very impressive new Lotus 107 launched, but not raced, in Barcelona. With lack of grip, neither driver qualifies well — Häkkinen 21st and Herbert 26th. Both make superb starts — Mika to 14th and Johnny to 19th on lap one. Herbert spins out of race when 17th, lap 14. Häkkinen collides with Alesi, lap 40, but rejoins before spinning out of 12th, lap 57. Team aims to have two new 107s at Imola for next GP.

FONDMETAL
Tarquini 18th on grid. Races with Alboreto and the two Dallaras. Up to excellent seventh, lap 31, but spins out from 10th, lap 57, trying to regain lost position. Chiesa pre-qualifies fourth and qualifies 20th. Is one of only three drivers to start on slicks and immediately sinks to rear of field. Changes to wets, lap 10, but spins out from 20th, lap 23.

MARCH
Still on its chinstrap for money (although optimistic that some coming), team finds smooth track suits car. Wendlinger qualifies magnificent ninth with Belmondo 23rd for first GP start. With rain restarting after five-minute board, both start on slicks to comply with rules. Soon in for wets when rain intensifies — Karl lap eight, Paul lap 10. Wendlinger drives superb race to finish eighth (two laps down), with eighth fastest lap. Belmondo takes praiseworthy 12th place (four laps down). Team protests Footwork drivers for changing tyres after five-minute board, but this rejected though Footwork is fined. Hopefully, Karl's fine drive will generate sponsorship.

BENETTON
Magnificent debut for new B192. Despite heavy off on Friday, Schumacher takes stunning best-yet second place on grid for only his 10th GP. Brundle starts sixth, loses clutch, lap two and spins. Rejoins but hit by Comas, lap five, and disconsolately retires with car beached on kerb (yet to finish a GP for Benetton). Schumacher drives inspired race after starting and stopping before green light. Fourth, laps one-six. Past Alesi to third, lap seven. Second after Patrese retirement, lap 20. Keeping ahead of Senna, majestically closes to within four seconds of Mansell, lap 50, but finishes second, 24s behind, now only one point behind second-placed Patrese in championship. With more powerful Ford Series VII engine scheduled for Imola, team spirits high.

DALLARA
Lehto and Martini 12th and 13th on grid. Both spend most of race battling with Alboreto and Tarquini, until lap 58

as JJ spins out when eighth. Pier-Luigi benefits from late Senna/Capelli retirements to finish sixth (two laps down), giving team its first point since Monaco 1991.

MINARDI
After trying new M192, Morbidelli qualifies brake-troubled M191 25th — three places behind Christian Fittipaldi. Christian drives exemplary first wet GP to finish 11th (four laps down). Gianni races M191 without being able to set it up properly and retires from 18th, lap 27 (handling).

LIGIER
On Friday, Erik Comas (10th) out-qualifies clutch-troubled Boutsen (14th). Neither turns in saturated Saturday session. Thierry retires from 24th and last, lap 11 (engine). Comas hits Brundle, lap five, but up to seventh laps 26-29. spins down to 10th, lap 30. Changes tyres lap 32 but spins out from 13th, lap 56.

FERRARI
Best '92 GP yet for Ferrari, including inspired drive by Jean Alesi. In presence of boss Luca di Montezemolo and consultant Niki Lauda, Jean records fastest time in waterlogged Saturday qualifying but starts eighth after Friday's dry time. With rear wheels on dry patch, Jean makes stupefying start, passing Berger, Brundle, Capelli, Senna and Schumacher to take third by first corner (banging wheels with Senna on way). Down to fifth, lap five. Collides with Berger, lap 13, and spins down to seventh behind Capelli. Changes tyres (7.95s) lap 33, spins again passing Häkkinen, lap 41. Catches and passes Capelli, lap 46, despite bent front suspension. Then to fourth past Berger, lap 59. To third when Senna retires, lap 63 and finishes only 2.5s behind Schumacher. Ferrari overjoyed. Capelli also drives fine race from fifth on grid but aquaplanes off when sixth, lap 63. Classified 10th (three laps down).

VENTURI-LARROUSSE
Gachot pre-qualifies fastest and qualifies 24th. Races well to 11th, lap 31, but retires, lap 35 (engine). Ukyo Katayama fails to qualify for first time.

JORDAN
Team's troubled season, a sharp contrast to 1991, continues on dull note. Stefano Modena fails to qualify after engine, brake and visor (someone cleaned it with brake fluid!) problems on Friday and is unable to improve in wet Saturday session. Mauricio Gugelmin starts 17th, but spins into wall when 15th, lap 25.

ANDREA MODA
Almost unbelievably, team strikes new problems. Perry McCarthy, now with superlicence, stalls four yards over line dividing pit lane from track on first attempted lap, whilst Roberto Moreno's engine fails on circuit. After long debate, officials allow McCarthy car to be pulled back for Moreno to use. Final result is that neither driver pre-qualifies. "But we'll get there!" says the irrepressible Perry. They surely must, because now there is nothing else that can go wrong (is there?).

second! And, try as he may, Ayrton Senna behind him could do nothing about it.

Lap 30, nearly half-distance. Mansell had lapped everyone up to Alesi in sixth place and led Schumacher by 17 seconds as Senna and Berger fought for third, three seconds behind the amazing German. But from now on, with Nigel not even looking like putting a wheel out of place and Schumacher driving as though it was his 100th Grand Prix rather than his 10th, all eyes were on Alesi. He had devoted Saturday to perfecting the wet-weather set up of his Ferrari, which was blessed with a very effective traction control system. Now he was reaping the benefit. On lap 33, in a 7.95s stop, he changed his Goodyears, excessively worn by a power-burning spin-turn to recover from his earlier collision with Berger. He rejoined sixth, got his head down and charged! Reeling in fifth-placed Ivan Capelli he collided with Häkkinen on lap 41 and spun again. Both continued, but Jean had lost more time. Despite this he recovered some 30 seconds to pass Capelli on lap 46 and then set about catching Berger who, in turn, was still battling with Senna. Ayrton too was on a charge, closing up on Schumacher. Michael responded so well that on lap 50 he was within four seconds of race leader Mansell. Was Nigel in trouble or racing conservatively?

''I was driving as hard as I could and Michael was catching me by about two seconds a lap. The conditions were terrible but then I began to pull away again.'' Indeed he did, to reveal that he had been driving a mature, tactical race with

Berger finds himself in a Ferrari sandwich. Alesi, leading, was in irrepressible form, surviving a couple of collisions and a pit stop to bring his Ferrari home third. Team-mate Capelli narrowly failed to get into the points, spinning off shortly before the end of the race, thereby increasing media speculation in his homeland that he may not be a Ferrari driver for much longer...

In the moments leading up to the start, the rain had abated a little, persuading a fistful of cars to start on slicks. The technical term for this is 'error'.

plenty in hand for when he needed it — which was now. "I was watching the gap between Senna and I," said Schumacher, "and I didn't notice I was catching Mansell! But when he pulled away there was no way I could keep up." Maybe so, but brilliantly he kept ahead of three-times world champion and rainmaster Ayrton Senna. Indeed, on lap 58, the Brazilian spun in his efforts to catch the Benetton-Ford. He recovered superbly but, five laps later, he did it again. This time he was out. No points for the third successive race. And it wasn't the car's fault.

Such were the conditions that Senna was the 11th driver to spin out of the race. Now his team-mate Gerhard Berger was fourth, having been caught and passed by the incredible Alesi, the Frenchman gaining fast on Schumacher and, on fresher tyres, in with a chance of taking second. He only just missed it, finishing a mere 2.5 seconds behind the German after a superb drive which would surely put an extra 20,000 spectators on the gate for the San Marino Grand Prix at Imola two weeks hence! Sadly though, Ferrari's apparent guarantee of having both its drivers in the top five expired when Capelli aquaplaned off the circuit, the 12th man to be claimed by the rain. But, to the delight of the Italian *tifosi*, fifth and sixth places were claimed by ex-Ferrari veteran Michele Alboreto in his Footwork-Mugen and the vastly underrated, and enormously likeable, Pier-Luigi

Martini's Dallara-Ferrari.

But, for the second year in succession, Spain belonged to Nigel Mansell. His fourth consecutive victory was a *tour de force* which put him head and shoulders above the rest. Senna spun off. Patrese spun off. So did Alesi (twice!) and Capelli. Nigel not only stayed on the track but never looked like going off and he set the fastest lap to boot. Now he had won 25 Grands Prix, the same number as greats Jim Clark and Niki Lauda. His 40 points meant he led the World Championship by 22, with Senna now 36 adrift. But, despite McLaren's

awful start to the season, most people still regarded them and Senna as chief rivals to Williams and Mansell. They remembered how the Woking team, with a seemingly uncatchable lead, had been overhauled momentarily by Williams in 1991 and wondered if the positions could be reversed in 1992. The season still had 12 races to go.

The *tifosi* would be out in force for the San Marino Grand Prix. They like *Il Leone*, aka Nigel Mansell, almost as much as Ferrari. If he won a record fifth successive Grand Prix at Imola they'd go berserk!

Mansell was in imperious form once again in Spain. No other driver has yet won an F1 race at the relatively new Circuit de Catalunya, situated half an hour from Barcelona (frequent traffic jams permitting).

Johnny Herbert gave the new Lotus 107 a short race debut, but the car showed promise while it lasted.

Imola 1991 was miserable. Wet, overcast and dull. Five of the top contenders were out after only 17 laps. In their McLarens, Senna and Berger had lapped everyone else and only 10 cars were running at the end. But Imola 1992 was very different, a rewarding and enjoyable contrast.

As a circuit it is one of the best in the world, with excellent facilities for the teams, spectators and media and, most importantly, it is also immensely challenging and demanding for car and driver. No other nation is as knowledgeable or as enthusiastic about Grand Prix racing as Italy. Imola is close to Maranello, the home of Ferrari, and the fanatical *tifosi* generate a uniquely vibrant atmosphere. The food is great, the wines are better, the surrounding scenery is pleasant and the whole area is steeped in the traditions of the fabled, but long extinct, Mille Miglia sports car race. Add clear blue skies, blazing sunshine and 30-degree temperatures and you have the recipe for a great motor racing experience.

In Italy, Ferrari is, quite literally, a religion, even when its drivers can't differentiate between tarmac and gravel traps.

Situated in the Emilio Romagna region close to Bologna, Imola is actually some 50 miles from the tiny principality of San Marino. Calling the race the San Marino Grand Prix is a crafty dodge to ensure two Grands Prix in Italy. A bit like having a Welsh Grand Prix at Oulton Park! The anti-clockwise 3.1-mile lap includes the daunting Tamburello curve, which is taken at some 200 mph, the 155 mph drop down the Acque Minerali chicane and the stretch from the start line to the Tosa bend where the cars are at maximum revs for some 13 seconds. It is low in grip, hard on tyres when it is as hot as it was this year and makes heavy demands on fuel consumption.

One question was uppermost in everybody's minds. Could Nigel Mansell make it five wins in the first five GPs and thereby break Ayrton Senna's 1991 record? With the superiority of the Williams-Renaults so far, it seemed more than likely. Some time or other, however, the streak had to be broken, and it might be here. Ayrton Senna had been faster than Patrese and a mere 0.04s slower than Mansell at the pre-race Imola tests, and both Ferrari and Benetton had improved. "It looks as though we're going to have a motor race here," said Williams

designer-in-chief Patrick Head after Friday morning's free practice, because Senna was only 0.1s off Mansell's pace and Alesi's Ferrari was almost as close to Patrese. But that was the last their rivals saw of the Williams-Renaults for the rest of the weekend. Mansell's 22nd, and fifth successive, pole position was the fastest lap ever at Imola, faster than Senna's 1991 pole time on qualifying tyres, and an incredible full second quicker than his team-mate Patrese who, for the third time in five races, was second on the grid. "It was a perfect lap. The tyres came in at just the right time and, most importantly of all, I had no traffic. I am very happy!"

So, two Williamses on row one. Two McLarens on row two — Senna third, a depressing 1.2s slower than Mansell, and Berger fourth. Two Benettons, Schumacher and Brundle, on row three and two Ferraris, Alesi and Capelli, on row four. Perfect symmetry. And, notably, behind them in ninth and 11th places, sandwiching Boutsen's Ligier, were veteran Michele Alboreto and Aguri Suzuki in their Footwork-Mugens which, after ceaseless work by the Milton Keynes team, were now reliable, quick and on the Imola grid for the first time in three years. Not much for the *tifosi* to be ecstatic about, but that didn't stop them from packing the place out. If their beloved Ferraris didn't do well they could cheer another idol, *Il Leone* — Mansell, who was, of course, an ex-Ferrari driver!

The track temperature was 42 degrees at 14.00 hours on Sunday, and that is very hot indeed. "Tyre choice and reliability are going to be crucial," said Mansell. "I hope to get ahead at the start and to control the race in the early stages." Which is exactly what he did after an aborted start, precipitated by Karl Wendlinger, who stalled. Straight into the lead went Nigel with Patrese behind him, Senna third and Brundle audaciously charging past Berger and Schumacher to fourth. He didn't stay there for long though, because Gerhard immediately retook the place, but Martin kept ahead of his German team-mate.

Up front, Mansell's charge was awesome as he implemented his plan by reeling off a succession of fastest laps — six in the first nine.

Heading for a record fifth staight win at the start of a season, Mansell did his reputation no harm in front of a packed house. The Italians remember his Ferrari days fondly.

King Nigel the Fifth: Mansell savours his triumph (inset).

TEAM ANALYSIS

McLAREN

A very depressing Imola with the new MP4/7A still well off the pace despite improved Honda engine. Both drivers lapped everyone else in 1991, but neither shines in '92. Senna only 0.1s slower than Mansell on Friday morning but qualifies third, a massive 1.2s behind Nigel's Williams-Renault. Berger starts fourth. Ayrton races to reliable, but too slow, third, finishing 49s behind Mansell in great pain with shoulder cramp. Up to fourth in championship but now 42 points behind *Il Leone*. Gerhard fifth after lap 26 tyre stop. Closes with, and tries to pass, non-stop Alesi, lap 40, but tangles with the Ferrari and retires with wounded car.

TYRRELL

De Cesaris starts 14th and Grouillard 20th after having faster time disallowed for rear wing infringement. Andrea up to eighth, lap 47, after lap 25 tyre stop, but retires with no fuel pressure, lap 56. Classified 14th, five laps down. After cracking start Olivier up to 11th, laps 1-11. Stops for harder Goodyear Cs, lap 10. Down to 24th. Recovers well to finish eighth, two laps down, with failing oil pressure.

WILLIAMS

Team's overwhelming dominance continues. Mansell takes 22nd career pole with "perfect lap" track record and races to unchallenged 26th victory, creating new 'opening-five-in-a-row' record. On his home track, Riccardo Patrese starts second for third time in five races, after complete recovery from very high speed crash at notorious Tamburello during pre-race testing. Fails to threaten Nigel in race despite record fastest lap (1m 26.100s, 130.943 mph) and again finishes second, 9.5s behind. Mansell and team now lead respective driver's and constructor's championships by massive 26 and 54 points.

BRABHAM

Both Eric van de Poele and Damon Hill miss Friday free practice session due to team's financial problems and, with no testing, not enough practice and ·only two engines, sadly, but unsurprisingly, neither driver proved able to qualify.

FOOTWORK

Team's enormously encouraging revival continues. Thanks to reliability-based development and Mugen V10 suiting circuit, Alboreto pre-qualifies fastest and qualifies excellent ninth, two places ahead of delighted Suzuki (first time team on Imola grid in three years). Michele has non-stop battle with Dallaras of Martini and Lehto and finishes fifth (one lap down). In the points for third successive race. Suzuki spins, lap eight but finishes 10th, two laps down, despite gearbox problem and stop for radiators to be cleared. Footwork now fifth in constructors' championship. What a change!

LOTUS

Team brings one new 107, reserved for Herbert. Following gear selection and fuel pressure problems Johnny has to qualify in 102 (26th) but races 107 on "nothing to lose" basis. Excellent 10th fastest in Sunday warm-up. Pits for new track rod after being clipped by Wendlinger's March at start. Rejoins but retires, lap nine, stuck in third gear. Disappointed Häkkinen fails to qualify 102 after two engine failures. Team immensely encouraged by new car, which shows great potential.

FONDMETAL

Chiesa pre-qualifies fourth but crashes on Saturday and fails to make race. Tarquini qualifies 22nd after breaking one engine, over-revving another and being attacked by dog whilst traversing a garden on way back to pits! Races against Gachot and Wendlinger up to 16th, lap 13. Drops back before retiring from 22nd and last, lap 25 (engine).

MARCH

Still soldiering on with major financial problems. Wendlinger again qualifies impressively in 12th. Has massive off at Tosa during Sunday warm-up and races rebuilt car with T-car gearbox and new rear suspension. Causes aborted start when clutch problem stalls engine. Starts from rear of grid and clouts Herbert's Lotus but finishes 12th (three laps down) with transmission problems, after brisk battle with Tarquini during opening laps. Belmondo starts 24th and finishes second GP 13th, three laps down, after stopping twice (tyres and grass removal following off).

BENETTON

This time (at last) Martin Brundle takes the honours. Is furious with Alesi after Friday qualifying, having been "deliberately driven into" as alleged reprisal for slowing in front of Jean's Ferrari. They subsequently meet and shake hands. Martin starts sixth, immediately muscles up to fourth, loses the place to Berger and then closely chases Senna and Gerhard for 24 laps. Spins approaching pits, lap 24, changes tyres and resumes sixth. Up to fourth, lap 40, following Berger/Alesi collision and retirements and stays there for first Benetton finish, only four seconds behind Senna, having set fourth fastest lap of race. Well deserved success a great morale builder. Schumacher qualifies fifth but comes off worst in confrontation with Berger at start and drops to sixth. Spins off, lap 19, after umpteenth thrusting attempt to pass Brundle. Rejoins after pits check but retires, lap 21, with handling problems. Retains championship third place and team still second to Williams (albeit 54 points behind!).

DALLARA

Using 1992-specification Ferrari V12 engines, Martini and Lehto qualify 15th and 16th after suffering handling and broken driveshaft problems with all three team cars. Both then race nose-to-tail with Alboreto, laps 8-57, advancing to excellent sixth (Martini) and seventh. JJ heartbreakingly retires with overheated engine, lap 58, but classified 11th, three laps down. Pier-Luigi finishes sixth (one lap down) for second time in 1992.

MINARDI

Two new M192s and one M191 but disheartening Grand Prix. Morbidelli starts 21st and Fittipaldi 25th after handling, grip and transmission problems. Christian retires, lap eight (transmission) and Gianni lap 25 (same thing).

LIGIER

"Following a great deal of very hard work after Spain we have managed to make the car slightly worse than it was before," said Thierry Boutsen, before going on to qualify well (10th) as result of balance and grip improvements. Comas 13th. Boutsen racing strongly (seventh) when engine cuts out, causing spin. Rejoins but retires from 10th, lap 30, when motor again misbehaves. Erik loses four places at start through not being able to see green light. With "no grip", drives cautious race to finish ninth (two laps down).

FERRARI

Still off the pace, despite intense development. Alesi qualifies seventh after angry exchange of accusations with Brundle following collision with slowing Benetton on Friday. Starting on Goodyear's harder C compound, Jean races non-stop. Third by lap 27, benefiting from others' tyre stops. Slowly worn down by freshly-shod Senna and Berger. Ayrton passes, lap 40. Gerhard tries to follow but collides with Alesi. Both retire. Capelli starts eighth and stays there until spinning out, lap 12. "We progress," says team boss Claudio Lombardi. "It is slow, but it is steady."

VENTURI-LARROUSSE

Gachot and Katayama pre-qualify second and third. Ukyo qualifies an excellent 17th for his first Imola race — two places ahead of Bertrand. After dropping to 25th, lap one, Gachot recovers superbly to 13th, lap 30, but retires, lap 32, after driving over Katayama's dislodged engine cover. Ukyo spins out of race and 11th place, lap 40.

JORDAN

An absolutely disastrous Imola for Eddie's already depressed team — and not their fault. After breaking five Yamaha V12 engines in two days of practice, Gugelmin and Modena qualify 19th and 23rd (Modena also having several gearbox and differential failures — some allegedly his fault). Stefano has another engine let go on parade lap and runs back to start from pit lane in spare car. Retires from 20th and last, lap 25 (gearbox again!). Mauricio saves day by giving team best '92 result so far — non-stop seventh (two laps down), with engine detuned for reliability. Yamaha's seeming inability to get to grips with Formula One of grave concern to team.

ANDREA MODA

Things getting better at last. Car much improved following Imola pre-race testing by Roberto Moreno, who only fails to pre-qualify by 0.1s. Perry McCarthy also fails to get beyond nine o'clock on Friday, but at least manages to do seven laps this time — each one faster than the last.

Seldom lost for words, Perry McCarthy remained cheerful in the face of Andrea Moda's uphill battle to be taken seriously as a Grand Prix team. He finally completed his first F1 laps at Imola, though pre-qualifying was understandably beyond him.

On lap 10, one-sixth distance, he was five seconds ahead of Patrese and 18 ahead of Senna. So much for any hopes McLaren may have had. But there *was* a race behind Patrese with three seconds covering Senna, Berger, Brundle and Schumacher, Michael trying all the time, everywhere, to get past his team-mate. Martin wasn't having any of it though. Driving as well as he ever had, he calmly resisted Schumacher's every move, determined to finish this time, to do so well and thereby boost his reputation by beating his team-mate.

The Ferraris came next with Alesi seventh and Capelli eighth, both of them on Goodyear's harder C compound, intending to race through non-stop and hoping to benefit when the softer D compound users ahead of them had to stop for new rubber, as they surely would. But Capelli never got the chance. He slid off on lap 12 letting Thierry Boutsen take his place in the Ligier, hotly pursued by a three-car snake made up of Alboreto's Footwork and the Dallaras of Martini and Lehto.

Riccardo Patrese was the first of the leaders to stop for new tyres, on lap 19. Such was his lead over Senna that he rejoined without losing his second place, now some 23 seconds behind Mansell. Nigel's lead would go down when he stopped, of course, and there was no doubt that that would have to be soon because Schumacher showed how worn the tyres were getting by spinning into the tyre wall at the 125 mph Rivazza. Into the pits he came but, although he rejoined, his race ended a lap later — only the fourth time he had been out of the points in his 11 Grands Prix. Mansell's stop was a leisurely one by Grand Prix standards — nine seconds. Why risk things going wrong, as they had so disastrously in Portugal last year, when he had such a secure lead? A lead which he still held as he emerged from the pit lane four seconds ahead of Patrese, who'd just put up the fastest lap in a bid to pass the pit-bound Mansell. From then on, Nigel just speeded up and drew away, totally in command.

At half-distance, lap 30, Jean Alesi was the

Minardi wheeled out two of its new, Lamborghini-engined M192s for the occasion, though transmission failures accounted for both Fittipaldi (pictured) and Morbidelli before half-distance.

Niki Lauda contemplates the thrill-a-second experience of being part of Ferrari's management structure. Having rejoined the Prancing Horse in a consultancy role, the thrice world champion faced another grim weekend, both Ferraris crashing out on home soil.

man to watch. For now, with both Senna and Berger having stopped for tyres, the non-stop Frenchman's Ferrari was third. Slowly the gap between him and the freshly-shod McLarens, racing together, came down. On lap 40 they blasted across the line together with 20 laps still to go. Alesi was convinced he could keep his pursuers at bay, and so was his team manager Claudio Lombardi. "Our calculations showed that his tyre performance should have been the same or slightly better than those of the McLarens. I'm sure he could have finished fourth." But Jean didn't finish at all. As he rounded the second gear Tosa bend, Senna slipped inside him with Berger attempting to follow. "I tried to take the corner as wide as possible," said Jean, "but on the exit Gerhard hit my rear wheel and we spun." Indeed they did. Berger's McLaren was stranded in the middle of the track for the marshals to drag clear, Jean's Ferrari was beached in the sand trap.

Now Martin Brundle was fourth and going

well, the gallant Michele Alboreto was fifth and Pier-Luigi Martini, still just behind, sixth, a car's length ahead of his team-mate JJ Lehto. And that's the way it stayed as the broken-hearted *tifosi* deserted Imola en masse with their Ferrari flags drooping forlornly over their shoulders.

Thousands may have left but far, far more stayed to invade the pit lane amidst quite astonishing scenes of enthusiasm for Nigel Mansell's superb victory, a win that took his total to 26. More than Fangio. More than Jim Clark. More than Niki Lauda. Only three people had now scored more Grand Prix wins than he had. Jackie Stewart, Ayrton Senna and Alain Prost. Unlike them, he had yet to win a World Championship, a possibility he still refused to discuss. And the reigning world champion? Ayrton Senna was not on the podium when his greatest rival was joyously spraying the champagne. He was still in the cockpit of his McLaren, totally exhausted and racked with pain from shoulder cramp. It had been a tough and dispiriting race for Ayrton.

Matching pairs: Senna, Berger, Brundle and Schumacher head the vain pursuit of the Williams duo. Accidents accounted for one McLaren and one Benetton; Senna and Brundle went the distance, the latter finally notching up his first finish of the season.

Never looking like challenging the flying Williams-Renaults of Mansell and Patrese, he had finished a demoralising 49 seconds behind the winner — who was now 42 points ahead of him in the championship. After five races!

Imola had been a great disappointment for Patrese too. ''I am racing for the World Championship,'' he had declared before the start. ''This is my home circuit, I live near here, I feel the *tifosi* are with me, I won here in 1990 and I would like to do so again.'' It will have been of little consolation to him that his 60th lap was the fastest of the race and a new record (1m 26.100s, 139.943 mph) in a situation where his team-mate had been so crushingly superior. But Martin Brundle was well pleased with his fourth place. ''Above all I was determined to finish after my appalling luck in the first four races. I

had a good clean race. I spun but went straight into the pits to change my tyres which I was about to do anyway. I drove very carefully to the finish and I'm very happy!'' And so, of course, was Alboreto, with his second successive fifth place. Rightly so. It really looked as though his team's luck had changed.

But the *tifosi* knew the score. ''NI-GEL! NI-GEL! NI-GEL!'' they chanted ceaselessly in the pit lane. ''*Il Leone* — we love you!'' their banners declared. A bit over the top, some may have thought, but Mansell's fifth successive drive to an unchallenged victory had truly been something for them to savour. And Nigel? ''It was fantastic for me but I dedicate this win to all the team. To the designers, the engineers and all the sponsors. It feels like a dream. I've never been so happy in my life!''

In Monaco, it is vital that you have all the right gear for socialising. JJ Lehto packed a 1956 Chevrolet Corvette in his kit bag.

Monaco is called the 'jewel in the crown' of Grand Prix racing, but Formula One has a love-hate relationship with the championship's last real street race. The twisting, turning, rising and falling roads of the Principality are too narrow for passing; the teams have to work in primitive and overcrowded conditions; the pit lane is downright dangerous; the drivers regard the race as a lottery.

So why do they go there?

Because Monaco has a unique location, tradition and charisma which overcome its disadvantages and because it is *the* Grand Prix to the rest of the world. Nowhere else do you see, hear and *feel* the racing at such close quarters. Nowhere else makes it so clear that the drivers are supermen as they race their 750 bhp projectiles through the everyday streets, the famous tunnel and round the harbour,

Brabham felt that the undeveloped (ie not tested at all) BT60B stood more of a chance of making the race in the Monaco lottery. Neither car qualified, however, a particular source of disappointment to Damon Hill, whose father had made his F1 debut here in 1958, and had subsequently won the event five times, a record finally equalled this year by Senna.

making some 34 gearchanges per lap (over 2,500 during the 78-lap race), shaving the metal barriers at over 180 mph and braking down to a mere 30 mph to roll round Loews hairpin.

The sponsors love it as they entertain their big buyers on super-luxury yachts. The sun-soaked spectators, jet-setters and package-tourers alike, love it as they watch the action from their ludicrously-priced grandstand seats, the crowded slopes below the Royal Palace and windows and balconies overlooking the circuit. Monaco loves it because it can multiply its prices out of sight for a financial bonanza.

Like it or not Monaco is still *the* one to win, as Ayrton Senna and Nigel Mansell both knew well: Ayrton because he had already scored four of his most famous victories here (plus his most heartbreaking defeat when, in 1988, with a massive lead and only 12 laps to go, a lapse of concentration put him into the armco); Nigel because, in spite of being on the front row four times in 11 starts and leading twice, he had yet to win in Monte Carlo.

This was to be the 50th Grand Prix here. The first, held in 1929, had been won by an Englishman racing under the *nom de plume* of 'Williams'.

Surely this had to be a happy omen for the all-conquering Mansell and his Williams team, aiming for a sixth successive win?

Sadly for Nigel, it wasn't, but it certainly seemed to be until he'd raced even further than had Senna in 1988. The two days of practice were demoralising repeats of Mansell's 1992 supremacy. Fastest on Thursday morning (with an eye to extra income, the astute *Monégasques* start their meeting a day earlier), fastest in Thursday's qualifying and fastest on Saturday morning, Nigel's 23rd pole position seemed to be a foregone conclusion when the final session started at one o'clock on Saturday. But not to Riccardo Patrese. Second to Mansell in the championship, and second to him four times in the last five races, Riccardo meant to win this one. "This track has a special significance for me. I drove my first Grand Prix here in 1977 and won my first here in '82. The grid position is very important..." So Riccardo went for pole — and took it. Back came Mansell, 0.2s faster. Then it was Patrese's turn, a mere 0.001s quicker than Nigel but good enough for pole. And that seemed to be it, because Mansell had used both sets of new tyres. "Put the first set back on," he said, and shot out again. The result was a 1m 19.496s — nearly a full second faster than Senna's 1991 pole time, which had been set on qualifying tyres! It was the first ever lap of Monaco in under 1m 20s and the first at over 150 kmh. Stupefying. It was Nigel's 23rd pole position and one of the most important of his career, putting him, as it did, first on the grid at the place where it mattered most.

The master of Monaco, Ayrton Senna, tried so hard that he spun and knocked his rear wing off but the best he could do was third. "We can't live with the Williams here. I must just be patient during the race and hope for something to happen to Nigel." Prophetic words! Jean Alesi was fourth, highest yet for Ferrari in 1992, ahead of Gerhard Berger, Michael Schumacher (his first time at Monaco) and Martin Brundle, with Ivan Capelli eighth and

Not a million miles from the apartment which he uses as a summer home, Senna finally broke his 1992 duck in Monte Carlo, although McLaren's first win of the season owed more than a little to Mansell's ill-fortune.

TEAM ANALYSIS

McLAREN

A lucky but well deserved first win since Australia 1991, but no real progress against Williams. Despite lighter and more powerful Honda engine, master of Monaco Ayrton Senna only able to qualify third, 1.1s slower than Mansell. Audaciously passes Patrese to second before first corner and doggedly chases Mansell "trying to keep the gap as small as possible." Is 29 seconds behind, lap 70, but takes lead as Nigel pits with wheel problem. Caught by inspired Mansell, lap 75, but brilliantly copes with worn tyres and Nigel's aggression to win his fifth Monaco GP in six years (plus the coveted Graham Hill Trophy) and raise his F1 career points total to over 500. Berger qualifies fifth after major off at Massenet on Thursday and Saturday spin. Retires from fifth, lap 33, with gearbox hydraulic pressure failure.

TYRRELL

New front wing and Elf qualifying fuel help de Cesaris to 10th on grid. Only lasts nine laps on his 33rd birthday before retiring with gearbox failure. Olivier Grouillard, increasingly wound-up about his team-mate's superiority, cautioned for obstructing marshals during Saturday qualifying. Starts 24th and retires lap five (also broken transmission).

WILLIAMS

Team maintains superiority but fails to win for first time in '92. Nigel Mansell battles for grid supremacy with Patrese, taking sixth successive pole with stupefying lap (first-ever under 1m 20s at Monaco). Looking unbeatable for his first win in 12 attempts at Monaco, Nigel calmly builds lead of 29s over Senna on lap 70. Sensationally into pits, lap 71 out of 78, with presumed puncture. Resumes 5.1s behind Senna, lap 72. Catches Ayrton, lap 75, but despite heroic attempts and record lap 74 (1m 21.598s, 91.234 mph) is unable to get by and finishes second, 0.215s behind. 'Puncture' subsequently turns out to be wheel-wobble caused by vibration-loosened wheel nut. Patrese starts second after having held pole twice on Saturday. Is passed by Senna at start and finishes third after fighting from lap 35 to stave off ever-challenging Schumacher. After six races, team leads constructors' championship by staggering 58 points.

BRABHAM

Future prospects now looking very grim with team allegedly in receivership. With no development or testing, both Eric van de Poele and Damon Hill (whose father, Graham, won here five times) fail to qualify. Would they be in Canada for the next GP?

FOOTWORK

Rejuvenated and experienced Michele Alboreto (12th time at Monaco) again pre-qualifies fastest and goes on to qualify 11th. "The car is great, but still too heavy," (Mugen-Honda V10 engine). Drives another gritty race,

Up to sixth by lap 34 but spins down to ninth after colliding with Brundle's Benetton. Finishes seventh (one lap down). Suzuki slams into pre-Rascasse armco during Sunday warm-up but allowed to start, 19th, after hospital check. Despite severe leg pain has "great race with Erik Comas", finishing 11th, two laps down. No retirements for team so far in '92.

LOTUS

Disappointing results from encouraging race. Johnny Herbert superbly qualifies new, undeveloped, 107 ninth and is racing ninth right behind Berger and Capelli, lap 29, when unbalanced car spins into Rascasse armco. Mika Häkkinen, waiting for new car, uses 102 on Thursday but qualifies 107 excellent 14th in first-time drive on Saturday. Excellent eighth, challenging Alboreto, lap 29, but retires, lap 31, when gearbox fails. But team not discouraged as new car shows great potential.

FONDMETAL

Hoped-for new car not ready. Both drivers crash on Saturday morning after complaining of lack of cockpit room. Tarquini qualifies 25th but Chiesa fails (after pre-qualifying fourth). Gabriele retires from 20th, lap 10, with overheated engine.

MARCH

Belmondo does not qualify. Wendlinger, an excellent eighth on Thursday morning, starts 16th. Retires, lap two, with gearbox failure.

BENETTON

Team's excellent 1992 continues on high note. Michael Schumacher qualifies incredible sixth for his first Monaco GP with Martin Brundle seventh after losing two engines and overcoming handling problems and back discomfort. Schumacher has another superb race. Up to fifth past Berger at start. Aggressively challenges Alesi for fourth, including contact at Loews which bends Benetton's right front wing. Forces by, lap 21. Then dynamically obliterates eight-second gap to Patrese by lap 35 and harries Riccardo to the end, finishing magnificent fourth (with no first gear). Brundle damages nosecone, lap 19, trying to take sixth from Berger. Sets two fastest laps on new tyres, unlaps himself and finishes fine fifth. Team well pleased with its increased competitiveness.

DALLARA

Following repeated driveshaft failures, and major crash for Martini in tunnel on Saturday, Pier-Luigi and JJ Lehto start 18th and 20th. Martini punted into guardrail and retirement by Modena at Portier on first lap. JJ does well to progress steadily through field and finish ninth (two laps down).

MINARDI

After qualifying a reasonable 12th in new M192, Gianni Morbidelli has to start from pit lane due to starter motor breakage. Joins race two laps down but retires after only one lap with broken gearbox. Christian Fittipaldi continues impressive GP debut season by qualifying 17th for first Monaco and driving unflurried race to finish eighth, only one lap down.

Merde alors! What's one of these doing here on a Sunday? Roberto Moreno didn't only get his Andrea Moda through pre-qualifying. He made it into the race.

LIGIER

With no points since France '89 (47 races), will team ever come right? Both drivers fed up — especially with lack of grip at Monaco. Frequent set-up changes fail to effect improvement. Depressed Boutsen and Comas qualify 22nd and 23rd and race to 10th (Comas, two laps down) and 12th (Boutsen, three laps down) out of 12 finishers. With Renault power and massive budget, this is more than disheartening. Demeaning need to pre-qualify after France looks probable. Designer Frank Dernie recalled to Magny-Cours to explain things to irate Guy Ligier. Glad I'm not him!

FERRARI

Team's non-stop hard work improves cars, but no result at Monaco. Jean Alesi charges his socks off to qualify fourth (best yet for team in '92), with Ivan Capelli eighth — and rumoured to be on his way out. "Not bad. This is the first time that the F92A has been faster than last year's car," says Alesi. Never-say-die Jean runs fourth, challenging Patrese whilst resisting Schumacher, who savages the side of his Ferrari at Loews Corner, lap 13. Passed by Michael, lap 21, and ends race from increasingly distant fifth, lap 28, with car suffering from gearbox electronic control unit damage, a consequence of the collision at Loews. Capelli fifth, laps 33-60, but bends steering arm and ends race tilted up on Rascasse barrier, having done his future with Ferrari no good at all. "Our problems are still difficult to overcome, but the hard work is beginning to bear fruit," says team manager Claudio Lombardi.

VENTURI-LARROUSSE

Happy days are here again, after team's first point for 16 races. Revised Lamborghini V12 engine with wider power band proves to be just the job for twisty Monaco. New boy Ukyo Katayama, bemused by track and troubled by oil leak, clobbers barrier and fails to pre-qualify. Gachot does so — second to Alboreto — and then qualifies 15th, very happy with improvements to car over last few races. Drives intelligent and cautious race to finish sixth, giving team vital point and chance to avoid pre-qualifying after France — at the likely expense of its bitter Ligier rivals!

JORDAN

Misery continues. Amidst continued team gloom over Yamaha's apparent inability to get to grips with its engine problems, Gugelmin starts 13th and Modena, having been ninth on Saturday morning, a lowly 21st after breaking driveshaft. Modena loses control at Casino, lap seven, hits barrier and retires. Mauricio has gearbox problem right from start and retires when troubled 12th, lap 18. Only two team finishes from 11 starts so far.

ANDREA MODA

Perry McCarthy, permitted only usual token lap or so, does not pre-qualify. Roberto Moreno not only does so (third) for first time, but qualifies 26th, having been excellent 20th on Thursday. Runs last until lap 12 retirement (engine), but Monaco real encouragement for disorganised but hard-trying team.

As Mansell assumes command at Ste Devote on the first lap, Senna thrusts inside Patrese, the art of surprise giving him an early second place. Happily this year, there were no first-lap mishaps at the notoriously crowded right-hander, which is similar to the Kingston one-way system during the rush hour, albeit a lot narrower...

Johnny Herbert an excellent ninth in his very promising new Lotus 107.

It is a late start at Monaco and it was bright, sunny and warm, a stimulating contrast to 1991's miserable conditions. A perfect start saw Mansell first into the dreaded right-hander at Ste Devote as Senna audaciously thrust past Patrese into second place and Schumacher somehow slid his Benetton past Berger's McLaren into fifth. After 10 laps Mansell led Senna by a commanding eight seconds, calmly drawing away by nearly a second a lap, totally in control. But Ayrton was only one second in front of a non-stop blur of action, with Patrese third just ahead of a fierce battle between Alesi and Schumacher. Time after time, all round the circuit, Schumacher, driving as though he'd been racing at Monaco for years, tried to get by the scarlet Ferrari. And time after time he was rebuffed. On lap 13 he got inside Alesi at Loews hairpin and hit the Ferrari's left sidepod, pushing Alesi sideways. Jean recovered and held his place but, on lap 29, having been slowed by damaged electronics and passed by Schumacher, he had to retire from a fine, fighting drive. Up to fifth, albeit 14 seconds behind, came Berger's McLaren followed by

Capelli (Ferrari), the back-on-form Michele Alboreto (Footwork-Mugen) and Mika Häkkinen. Mika's achievement was outstanding, for he was in a Lotus 107 which he had only driven for the first time in Saturday's practice, when he'd qualified an excellent 14th. Sadly he wasn't to last very much longer, for he retired two laps later, but he'd made his point as he walked back home to his Monaco apartment.

Meantime Martin Brundle, his confidence restored by his impressive fourth place at Imola, had been trying ceaselessly to take sixth place from Berger. On lap 19, moving off line to get a run at the McLaren at the harbour chicane, he hit a bump, went sideways and smote the barrier. By the time he'd stopped for a new nosecone and tyres he was down to 15th and lapped but, nothing daunted, he got his head down and charged. On new tyres he flew, lapping fastest of all on lap 22 and moving up. As Berger retired on lap 33 (gearbox hydraulics), Martin put in another fastest lap and on lap 36 he passed the excellent Christian Fittipaldi's Minardi-Lamborghini to take seventh — albeit still one lap down. His team-mate Michael Schumacher in the other nimble Benetton-Ford, admirably suited to Monaco's twists and turns, was going even better though. For he had reduced to nothing the eight-second gap which had separated him from third-placed Riccardo Patrese, and he was giving the Italian no rest at all. Weaving and feinting he swarmed all over the back of the Williams-Renault, but Riccardo was unmoved. ''The car was a bit difficult to drive by then, so I just forgot about Ayrton and used my experience to stay in front of Michael.'' Which he did, and it was riveting to watch! Indeed, to be honest, their battle provided the real interest in the race for a long time, with Mansell drawing further and further ahead of Senna and Capelli, now fifth ahead of the rejuvenated Alboreto, a long way behind Schumacher. Ivan blotted his already spotted copybook at Ferrari on lap 61, by tipping his car sideways on to the barrier at the Rascasse. This let Brundle, who'd passed Alboreto, into a lapped fifth place, followed by a hard-charging Bertrand Gachot (Venturi-Lamborghini).

Now only 12 of the 26 starters were left and, seemingly, Mansell was unchallengeable. He was a massive 30 seconds ahead of Senna, who had briefly had to stop when Alboreto spun in front of him, but who was typically driving as hard as he could to minimise the gap and benefit from any misfortune which might affect his rival ahead. It was Ayrton's only hope, but it looked to be a slim one for Nigel's Williams-Renault hadn't missed a beat and Nigel hadn't put a wheel wrong. But it was a wheel that was to be his downfall. Leading by 29 seconds on lap 71, the race in his pocket with only seven laps to go, he exited the tunnel at reduced pace! ''I had a left rear puncture. The back end went down and I had to go slowly back to the pits on three wheels. I lost 10 to 15 seconds and then had a longer than usual pit stop. I could see Ayrton go by and I thought then that I had lost it.'' Sensation! Senna's patient game plan had been rewarded. Or had it? There were still seven laps to go.

On lap 72 he led by 5.1s... on worn tyres with his McLaren sliding when he put the power down. On lap 73 the gap was 4.3s as Mansell, fighting as hard as he had ever fought and benefiting from his new Goodyears, broke the lap record. On lap 74 he broke it again. An incredible 1m 21.598s, 91.234 mph. The first-ever 90 mph-plus race lap at Monaco, nearly

The Venturi team's hopes of escaping the pre-qualifying dungeon were raised by Bertrand Gachot's sixth place. All would be rosy if Ligier didn't score any points in the next two races...Despite Ligier's abysmal form to this point, however, there was glum news around the corner for Gérard Larrousse's squad.

Cocking a snook at French anti-tobacconists, Marlboro threw a party to celebrate 20 years in F1, on the 20th anniversary of Jean-Pierre Beltoise's Monaco victory for BRM. In attendance were world champions, past and present, (from left) James Hunt, Alain Prost, Keke Rosberg, Niki Lauda, Ayrton Senna and Denny Hulme (who sadly passed away in October).

three seconds faster than Alain Prost's 1991 Ferrari record! On lap 75, Nigel was with the McLaren. Catching is one thing, getting past is quite another. Especially Ayrton Senna — at Monaco! If Mansell had had a blade on his nose cone he would have sawed the Mclaren in half as he lunged from left to right and back again trying to find a gap. The experienced Senna, sensing his first win since Australia 1991, knew better than to leave one though. For four spellbinding laps he kept the door shut, resisting Nigel's every effort, to win his fifth Monaco Grand Prix in six years by 0.215s and equal the record of the great Graham Hill.

Ironically, Mansell hadn't had a puncture at all. A misaligned brake disc had caused a vibration which had loosened a wheel nut. What Nigel had thought was a flat tyre was wheel wobble. A dash into the pits for a burst with the wheel gun would have solved his problem long before Senna had arrived. ''But that's Monte Carlo,'' said a generous-in-defeat Nigel. ''Ayrton was fantastic. He did nothing wrong at all and I have no complaints.''

To most people, Nigel's charging second place had been even more praiseworthy than a sixth dominant win, and for Martin Brundle it was a bonus that enabled him to finish fifth unlapped! Monaco's 50th GP had been a cracker.

After an early pit stop to replace a damaged nose, Martin Brundle returned to set lap times that had previously been the exclusive preserve of the Williams-Renaults. Fifth place was his reward.

Canada marked Gerhard Berger's first 'real' win for McLaren, his success in the 1991 Japanese GP having been a last-corner hand-me-down from Senna. On this occasion, the Austrian looked to be the quicker McLaren driver even before Senna's retirement.

Thanks to Nigel Mansell's misfortune, McLaren's win at Monaco had been by default, for they had not closed the performance gap to Williams. But the Didcot team certainly wasn't complacent. Knowing that neither McLaren nor Honda would give up, Williams just regarded its massive 58-point championship lead as a spur to try even harder. More testing of the new Renault RS4 engine at Magny-Cours in France saw the team fastest of all in the tyre tests and reassured them prior to the trip to far-off Montreal, scene of Mansell's incredible retirement from a commanding lead the previous year, when he was almost within sight of the chequered flag. Once again, Williams was favourite to win.

In 1991 the Canadian Grand Prix had been part of a two-race, long-haul double-header, Montreal first and Mexico two weeks later. This year, it stood alone. It was a long way to go for the one event, but nobody minded because it offers a great location, close to a cosmopolitan city, and has a terrific atmosphere. The excellent 2.75-mile circuit runs around the perimeter of the Île de Notre Dame in the St Lawrence Seaway, and is a notorious car breaker. Long and thin with hairpin bends at either end, it is hard on transmissions, brakes and fuel, and Quebec's bitter winters rumple the surface to make it very bumpy indeed. In 1991 there were only nine finishers and, traditionally, Canada is where the lesser teams hope to pick up points thanks to retirements. They were to do so in 1992.

Like too many tracks these days, the Gilles Villeneuve circuit (named after Canada's greatest driver, who won his first Grand Prix here in 1978) is almost impossible to pass on. So, like Monaco, like Hungary, like Kyalami, like Magny-Cours and like Suzuka, getting pole position is all-important. Which is what Nigel Mansell failed to do for the first time in 1992. On Friday he had problems setting-up his Williams-

1978 world champion Mario Andretti was forced to spectate on crutches, after breaking a toe or three during the Indianapolis 500. One week later, the Italo-American grandfather would be back in the driving seat, finishing sixth at Portland...

Renault's active suspension, and a telemetry glitch meant that he was short of some 40 horsepower. Combine that with heavy traffic, and the result was a very unhappy Nigel on Friday evening. Fourth fastest was bad enough, but in provisional pole it was the dreaded Ayrton Senna, followed by Riccardo Patrese and Gerhard Berger. As usual, everyone said "I'm confident I can go faster tomorrow." Nigel did, but not fast enough. After heavy overnight rain the track was a second slower, and although Mansell was one of the few who improved their times he was still behind Senna and Patrese. Six successive poles, and now he was third at a place where a lightning start mattered so much.

A mere 0.17s covered the first three, and the first corner was going to be critical. "If I get there first, it will be a good race," said Senna, heading the grid for the 61st time, "but if Mansell does he'll be long gone." So the green light was going to be something to savour, especially as behind Berger and Schumacher, fourth and fifth, was Johnny Herbert in the new Lotus 107, ahead of Martin Brundle and the two Ferraris of Alesi and Capelli. A superb achievement.

Mansell's departure was just incredible. From third on the grid his Williams seemed to be directly geared to the ground as he exploded past Patrese to draw alongside Senna. But Ayrton had the inside line and eased ahead as they exited the corner. So it looked as though we were in for a good race! And indeed we were, as Brundle passed Herbert to take sixth and Senna led a nose-to-tail eight-car snake, which rocketed round the island for 15 spellbinding laps. Ayrton was holding up the thrusting superstars behind as they all jockeyed for a way past the man ahead. There wasn't room, though. The individual gaps between the eight front-runners varied from lap to lap as Senna, Mansell, Patrese, Berger, Schumacher, Brundle, Herbert and Häkkinen (past both the two Ferraris on lap one!) attacked and defended, but four seconds consistently covered the lot. Something had to give. On lap 15, it did.

As the 180mph train approached the right/left flick before the pits, Mansell jinked out from

Michael Schumacher's rostrum excesses make a refreshing change from dour custom. The German celebrates second place with a Moët & Chandon shower.

TEAM ANALYSIS

McLAREN

For the first time since Australia 1991 McLaren heads the grid, leads whole race and deservedly wins. With yet more power from Honda V12, Senna takes 61st pole position with Friday's time 0.1s faster than Patrese's 1991 pole on qualifying tyres). Berger starts fourth. Ayrton leads, with Mansell attached to gearbox and closely pursued by next six cars, until lap 15 when over-ambitious passing attempt by Nigel fails. Mansell spins out of race and is replaced by Berger, who passes Patrese in confusion. Back to the good old days as Senna and Berger race one-two for McLaren, until lap 38 when Ayrton retires with electrical failure. Despite gearchange problem from lap 37, Berger resists first Patrese, then Brundle, and finally Schumacher to win his seventh Grand Prix by 12.5s, with fastest (and record) lap (1m 22.325s, 120.372mph). Post-race scrutineering reveals excessive rear wing overhang, but this sensibly ignored as being so small that no performance benefit possible. But, despite second successive victory for team, Senna, Berger and McLaren still well behind in respective championships.

TYRRELL

Both drivers finish for only second time in 1992. With

revised front suspension de Cesaris starts 14th and Grouillard 26th. Andrea steadily drives up through field to fifth (one lap down), giving team second points finish of year. Olivier races to 12th and last (two laps down) after stopping for tyres on lap 41.

WILLIAMS

For first time in 1992 Mansell fails to take pole and neither driver finishes. Patrese second on grid with Friday time. Mansell fails to perfect set-up for faster Friday qualifying and, although faster (and fastest) on Saturday, starts 'only' third. After being quickest in Sunday warm-up, Nigel makes superb start, passing Patrese to second before first corner. Then races within half a second of Senna, constantly trying to pass, but chooses wrong place to do so on lap 15. Runs out of track, spins out of race and furiously protests that "Senna pushed me off" (which everyone ignores). Patrese, opportunistically passed by Berger during Mansell's rallycrossing departure, races third until lap 38 when increasingly gearless transmission causes retirement. But, thanks to Senna's failure to finish, Mansell and Williams still have massive championship leads.

BRABHAM

New Japanese sponsor enables team to continue. But although both Eric van de Poele and Damon Hill improve their Saturday qualifying times in worse conditions than Friday, neither makes the race. Seven races, only one start.

A convincing qualifier, Ukyo Katayama fared even better in the race, rising as high as fifth until his Lamborghini went pop with seven laps to go.

FOOTWORK

Heavy Mugen-Honda V10 causes handling problems in Canada. Alboreto pre-qualifies fastest but Suzuki fails to qualify after Saturday off and Michele only 16th on grid. Alboreto down to 17th, lap one, behind rapid-starting Erik Comas, after hitting Morbidelli. Stays with Erik for whole race to finish seventh (one lap down).

LOTUS

Under-funded team continues very impressive recovery, with new 107 greatly improved since Monaco. Johnny Herbert takes quite sensational best-ever sixth place on grid (ahead of both Ferraris), with Mika Häkkinen an excellent 10th. They then run superb seventh (Johnny) and eighth, closely tailing the McLarens, Williamses and Benettons, until Herbert retires from sixth on lap 35 (clutch) almost immediately followed by Häkkinen (gearbox). "Very disappointing but we're getting there!"

FONDMETAL

First appearance of new, and good-looking, HB Ford-powered GR02 designed by Sergio Rinland. Gabriele Tarquini starts 18th but out, lap one, with broken gearbox. Andrea Chiesa fails to qualify in GR01.

MARCH

At last, very well deserved success for struggling team, supported by numerous low-budget local sponsors — including free meals from Montreal restaurants! Both drivers qualify, Wendlinger 12th and Belmondo 20th. Karl drives magnificent race. Closely chasing Alesi's Ferrari, up to seventh, lap 36, and then, lap 38, into points. Finishes a superb fourth (one lap down) to score his first points and the team's first since Hungary '91. Real encouragement! Paul Belmondo races at tail of field to finish 14th in his third GP, five laps down.

BENETTON

Another great race for team, but depressingly disappointing result for Martin Brundle. On first appearance in Canada, using new Ford Series VII engine, young superstar Michael Schumacher qualifies fifth with Brundle seventh. Positions reversed in Sunday warm up — Brundle excellent second and Schumacher fourth. Delighted with race set-up, Brundle passes Herbert to sixth at start and tails Schumacher for 38 laps — moving up to fifth, lap 15, and fourth, lap 38. Audaciously passes Michael to third, lap 39, and then takes second, lap 44, when Patrese retires. Sadly, that's it. Martin retires, lap 46 (final drive breakage) after one of his best-ever Grand Prix drives. Schumacher moves up to finish brilliant second for second time in 1992 — now only two championship points behind second-placed Patrese.

DALLARA

Both Lehto and Martini almost speechless about Dallara's appalling handling. Pier-Luigi improves from 25th to 15th on Saturday but JJ only 23rd on grid after front wheel comes off at speed. Both benefit from car's reliability to finish eighth (Martini) and ninth, one lap down.

MINARDI

Morbidelli starts badly by crashing brand new M192 on Friday but recovers to qualify 13th. Collides with Alboreto on first lap and tyre-stops, lap 40, but finishes 11th, two laps down. Christian Fittipaldi starts 25th, unhappy with set-up. Retires from 13th, lap 65 (gearbox).

LIGIER

Still-floundering team gets break with first point for 48 races. As usual, both Boutsen and Comas complain about lack of grip and qualify 21st (Boutsen) and 22nd. Dramatic set-up improvement sees Thierry ninth and Erik 10th in Sunday warm-up. Comas up to 16th, lap one, pursued by Alboreto who battles with him for whole race. Benefiting from retirements and reliability Erik finishes sixth (one lap down) for first-ever point. Boutsen 10th (two laps down) after coping with race-long engine problem. Relief all round as single point looks likely to remove need to pre-qualify after France.

FERRARI

No real satisfaction in Montreal. Alesi and Capelli qualify eighth and ninth, hampered by insufficient straightline speed. Ivan lucky to escape unhurt after colossal crash into concrete barrier when 10th on lap 19 ("something broke at the back"). Jean gives his all, as usual, but cannot keep up with McLarens, Williamses, Benettons — nor Lotuses. Nevertheless, finishes third, thanks to retirements ahead.

VENTURI-LARROUSSE

Japan's little Ukyo Katayama brilliantly qualifies 11th for his first Canadian Grand Prix and does even better to race up to in-the-points sixth on lap 44 (especially after having been driven into by team-mate Gachot on lap three). Fifth on lap 46, after Brundle retirement, but drops out, lap 62 of 69, when over-revs engine. Bert stops for new nosecone after clobbering Ukyo. Runs at tail of field, hits wall and stalls, lap 15. Is then disqualified for receiving push-start. Ligier's point means team will now almost certainly have to pre-qualify post-France (after its Monaco point seemed to have offered a reprieve). If only Katayama had finished...

JORDAN

Still underpowered by Yamaha, Modena and Gugelmin qualify 17th and 24th. Stefano's fraught season continues. He has to go to back of grid after engine fails to start. Retires from 17th (last but two), lap 37 (transmission). Mauricio battles with Boutsen, Lehto and Grouillard but retires from 22nd, lap 15 (gearbox). With only two finishes from 13 starts, team desperately needs some sponsor-impressing success.

ANDREA MODA

Almost unbelievably, a new misfortune strikes team when its Judd engines fail to arrive. Team boss Andrea Sassetti borrows one from Brabham (as if they hadn't got enough problems), but Moreno fails to pre-qualify and poor Perry McCarthy doesn't even get to drive.

''I had £200 on you at 14/1...'' Bernie Ecclestone attempts to throttle the unlucky Brundle, who was running second, and closing on Berger, when his transmission packed up.

under Senna's rear wing, drew alongside the McLaren and nosed ahead. Ayrton had no need to move over, as Nigel later furiously protested he had. By just staying on the racing line he left Mansell with nowhere to go but straight on. That took him over the kerbing, shot him over the infield, removed both his front wings, by-passed the left turn and brought him back on to the track ahead of the McLaren as he spun to a standstill. Nigel was out! For a whole lap he sat in his cockpit before being helped out of the car and into the pit lane to stump off to the stewards and grizzle about Senna's driving — a point of view they ignored completely. Apparently the world champion, now ahead of his team-mate Gerhard Berger, who had passed Patrese during the Mansell fracas, was going to lop 10 points off the gap between Nigel and himself.

Two seconds now covered the first four, Senna, Berger, Patrese and Schumacher, with Brundle only a second behind Michael and Herbert a fine sixth. And in ninth place, right on the tail of Jean Alesi's Ferrari, was Karl Wendlinger's March-Ilmor. The March suited Montreal and Karl was making the most of it. The lanky Austrian is a fine driver whose ability had repeatedly been masked by the problems of his under-funded team, but already there was talk of him being approached by major teams, one of them rumoured to be Ferrari. On lap 19, Karl's prospects improved when the unfortunate Ivan Capelli, already under a cloud and a place behind the March, thumped the wall at colossal speed and retired, unhurt but even more downcast.

On lap 32 out of 69, the struggle at the front was undiminished. Only 2.1 seconds covered the first five, with Martin Brundle right on the tail of Schumacher's Benetton after the Englishman had posted the fastest lap of the race so far. But then the rot set in, as Montreal started to live up to its destructive reputation. Johnny Herbert lost a fine sixth place (clutch, lap 35), having stuck brilliantly to the leaders from the start. All too briefly, his team-mate Mika Häkkinen inherited sixth, only to retire a lap later (gearbox). Great disappointment for Lotus, but encouragement, too, because the car was obviously a potential winner.

And, on lap 38, out went Senna!

Now this was sensational. From his first pole position since Australia 1991, Ayrton had held the lead, driving only as fast as he needed to, knowing that if he preserved his car and his tyres he couldn't be passed. But his engine's electrical system decided otherwise, and for the fourth time in seven races he had to retire.

Big changes at the front then. Berger led a Grand Prix for the first time since his 'donated' win in Japan the previous year, with Patrese snapping at this gearbox. Schumacher was third, half a second ahead of the press-on Brundle, and Alesi was up to a fighting, but poor, fifth, just in front of Wendlinger. Great for

Karl, his first time in the points, and it was to get better. We hadn't known it at the time, but Gerhard had felt he could go a lot faster than Senna. ''It was impossible to overtake, so I waited behind, but when Ayrton went out I got gearchange problems and had to change my way to drive — like I used to at Ferrari. It took me 10 laps to learn how, but after that everything was fine.'' It may have been fine for Gerhard, but on lap 44 the Montreal malaise struck Patrese. First sixth gear went, then fifth, then fourth — and that was it. Both FW14Bs were out and, with both his main rivals on the sidelines, there was a sigh of relief from Mansell, for whom another race had passed without his enormous championship lead being eroded.

The drama was a long way from being over in Montreal, though. While Berger and Patrese had been grappling with their semi-automatic gearchange problems, Brundle had been making his do-it-yourself shifts with great effect. As Schumacher lapped Gianni Morbidelli's Minardi, Martin had seen his chance and taken

Katayama's misfortune promoted a Ligier — that of Erik Comas — into the points for the first time this decade, thus alleviating the possible embarrassment of pre-qualifying for the lavishly funded, Renault V10-powered team.

Karl Wendlinger finished an excellent fourth, giving March a big boost as it sought to find further funds to ensure its F1 survival.

it, audaciously diving between the two cars ahead to take third. When Patrese dropped out, he was second, the first time he had been so far up since his superb drive for Tyrrell at Detroit in 1984. And that was a terrific fillip for Martin, who had been immensely depressed by his consistent

Gabriele Tarquini gave the new Fondmetal GR02 its debut, but couldn't deduce much from the 100 yards it lasted on raceday.

failure to beat his brilliant young team-mate. But his elation lasted only two laps as, on lap 46, Montreal claimed him too — another transmission failure and rotten luck, as he was catching Berger at the time.

Now, only 15 of the 26 starters were left. Berger first, Schumacher second, Alesi third and a long way back, Wendlinger a well-deserved fourth, little Ukyo Katayama fifth in his Venturi and Grand Prix veteran Andrea de Cesaris sixth. But the circuit hadn't finished yet. Katayama, who had qualified a magnificent 11th for his first Canadian GP and had done superbly to drive his way up into the points, retired on lap 62, with only seven to go. That was ironic and disastrous for the hard-trying Venturi-Larrousse team. For it let a Ligier — that of Erik Comas — into sixth place, and into the points, for the first time in 48 races. Ironic, because now Ligier might not have to pre-qualify in the second half of the season — in which case Venturi would.

With 14 finishers, it was victory in Canada for McLaren and Gerhard Berger, who also claimed the fastest lap after mastering his revised gearchange technique (1m 22.325s, 120.372mph — 0.06s faster than Mansell's 1991 record). McLaren had now won two successive races, but somehow you felt that they were by no means on top. And for the first time in a long while there were six different constructors in the top six, with Berger first, Schumacher second, Alesi third, Wendlinger fourth, de Cesaris fifth and Comas sixth. Montreal had done it again!

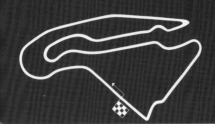

As the heart of the midfield streams through the Adelaide hairpin, Senna and Schumacher contemplate life from the comfort of the escape road. The Brazilian went no further; the German crashed there again at the restart.

In 1991 the historic French Grand Prix was moved from its popular home at the Paul Ricard circuit near Marseilles to the rebuilt, state-of-the-art track at Magny-Cours, about 150 miles south of Paris. It was a contentious decision, though it turned out pretty well. True, the hotel situation was diabolical and, likewise, it was a nightmare to get in and out on race day, but the facilities were superb and the GP was a good one. Thus it was no hardship to be going back there in 1992. Until French truckers decided they were going to blockade roads to protest against new traffic laws, that is.

They're very good at this sort of thing in France, where aggressive confrontation has been developed into an art form. The *autoroutes* were blocked and urban roundabouts were partly or completely sealed, making movement difficult and, sometimes, impossible. But Formula One has overcome worse problems than that. The resourceful transporter and motorhome drivers found their way to the track by minor country roads and, by

"What should I ask for at Christmas this year? A Williams-Renault or a Williams-Renault?" Senna contemplates the best way back to Victory Lane.

Thursday, nearly everyone was there. Come Friday morning it was almost business as usual, but the Andrea Moda team never appeared (to no one's great surprise). The BP, Mobil and Agip fuel supplies were missing and the Yamaha truck, carrying engines and vital equipment for Jordan, was trapped for the whole meeting. *Vive la France!*

The Magny-Cours circuit, like all too many these days, offers few overtaking possibilities. A major change had been made, following removal of the ess-bend after the Adelaide hairpin. This improved things, but the man who occupied pole position was still going to have a big advantage over his rivals when the race started.

Surprise, surprise, the man who got it was Nigel Mansell. Nigel's form had been awesome all year, and France was no exception. For the seventh time in eight races, he was at the top of the list at two o'clock on Saturday afternoon. He was fastest in every one of the four practice sessions. His time of 1m 13.684s (128.71 mph), on race tyres, was not only a course record but nearly a second faster than Riccardo Patrese's 1991 pole time, which had been set on sticky qualifiers. Nigel was clearly determined to get back into the victory groove by making France his sixth win of the year. But, as ever, he'd have to deal with his team-mate first. Riccardo Patrese still felt he could win the championship; there were no team orders and he needed to get cracking if he was to qualify for race number 'one' for 1993. His second place grid time (Williams's fifth one-two of the season) was a disheartening 0.6s slower than Mansell's, but he was a lot quicker than anyone else. The two McLarens of Senna and Berger, third and fourth, were over one and a half seconds off Mansell's pace and the Benettons and Ferraris were even slower (Schumacher fifth, Alesi sixth, Brundle seventh and Capelli eighth). It looked like another Williams whitewash — which is what it turned out to be, but not in the way that everyone expected.

There had been rain before the Sunday morning warm-up and the track was wet when they went out. Mansell was fastest again with Alesi second, Patrese third and the two Lotus

Judge Tread: tyre choice posed a tricky dilemma for much of the afternoon. The eventual torrents brought everyone in for wets, although Mansell took both starts on slicks, as did everybody else.

107s of Mika Häkkinen and Johnny Herbert fourth and fifth ahead of Senna. Very interesting! Four hours later, there were black clouds overhead when the race began, but the track was dry. Everyone started on slick tyres, which meant that it was automatically a 'dry' race that could be stopped if heavy rain fell.

Patrese's start was a blinder and he took the lead from Mansell as, behind them, Berger passed Senna to take third and Schumacher closed on the Brazilian. So much so that, at the Adelaide hairpin, he T-boned Ayrton's McLaren and removed the world champion from the race before driving to his pit for a new nosecone. Wow! It was mayhem further back too as, unsettled by the collision ahead, Gachot, Gugelmin and Chiesa were involved in separate accidents and retired. Only 22 cars left after half a lap.

TEAM ANALYSIS

McLAREN

A weekend to forget. Revised underbody aerodynamics designed to overcome MP4/7A's balance problem fail to do so. Both Ron Dennis and Ayrton Senna gloomy about prospects after Senna and Berger qualify third and fourth, well off Williams-Renault pace. Senna makes bad start, is passed by Berger and rammed into retirement by Schumacher's Benetton on lap one. ''My fault,'' says Michael. Berger runs third for 10 laps, eight seconds behind Patrese/Mansell, before retiring, lap 11 when engine blows. ''At least we can get away early and try to dodge the truckers' blockade!''

TYRRELL

Olivier Grouillard, already in bad odour for previous obstructive tactics, very much the Man in the Black Hat at Magny-Cours. After damaging spare car on Saturday prior to qualifying 22nd, hits Wendlinger at first start, jumps second start and incurs 10s stop/go penalty. Collides with Lehto at Adelaide hairpin on lap one and is blamed by Aguri Suzuki for his lap 21 gravel-trap retirement. After spinning three times Olivier finishes 11th (three laps down) and is subsequently strongly criticised by Peter Collins of Team Lotus for his ''arrogant driving attitude and behaviour when being lapped.'' Andrea de Cesaris fails to qualify on Friday (''no grip'') but does so, 19th, on Saturday. Stays out on slicks in wet second half, expecting race to be stopped again, and spins out of 10th place, lap 52.

WILLIAMS

Another dream meeting for the team — especially for its engine supplier, on home soil. For their fifth front row monopoly of 1992, race-tyred Mansell and Patrese both beat Riccardo's 1991 qualifying rubber pole time. After superb start, Patrese takes lead and resists repeated attacks by Mansell until race stopped because of rain. After being cautioned by Patrick Head not to defend his position too vigorously, Patrese waves thrusting Nigel by after restart. Riccardo finishes second, 46s behind the victorious Mansell — whose sixth win of the year raises his total to 27, equalling Jackie Stewart's score. Nigel also sets fastest lap in a record 1m 17.070s (123.355 mph) and now leads drivers' championship by 32 points. Williams leads constructors' contest by demoralising 64.

BRABHAM

New sponsorship, revised underbody and new livery make no competitive difference. Damon Hill and Eric van de Poele fail to qualify.

FOOTWORK

Michele Alboreto clobbers pit wall on Friday but qualifies 14th on Saturday. Drives usual reliable race to seventh (one lap down), becoming driver with most racing mileage in first half of season. Suzuki qualifies 15th but runs out of road and retires on lap 21 whilst trying to pass Grouillard. Joy bells ring as team says goodbye to pre-qualifying.

LOTUS

Team continues its great recovery. In spite of BP fuel supply being blocked by striking French truck drivers, Häkkinen and Herbert qualify 11th and 12th in new 107 (Mika using passive suspension after problems with active). Stimulating fourth (Häkkinen) and fifth in warm-up prior to race. Häkkinen rockets up to sixth, lap one, and then to fourth, lap 11, after passing Alesi's Ferrari. Mika and Johnny fifth and eighth on reformed grid for second start. After stirring battle with Brundle, Mika finishes highest-yet fourth with fourth fastest lap of race. Johnny sixth (both one lap down). Both thus in points for team's best 1992 result so far. Major sponsorship deal with Castrol announced after race. At long last, Lotus really is on its way back to the top!

FONDMETAL

Tarquini and Chiesa (no pre-qualifying) qualify 23rd and 26th, both using new GR02. Chiesa out first lap after colliding with Gugelmin's Jordan. Gabriele up to strong 14th, lap one, but retires, lap seven, when throttle cable breaks. Both drivers have to pre-qualify from British GP onwards.

MARCH

After damaging car floor on Friday, Karl Wendlinger qualifies 21st on Saturday but crashes heavily. Helicoptered to Nevers hospital for check and declared fit to race. Is hit by dreaded Grouillard on first lap of first part and by Schumacher on first lap of second. Races 15th until lap 34, when retires with broken gearbox. Belmondo fails to qualify.

BENETTON

Like Lotus, team inconvenienced as fuel was blockaded by striking French truck drivers. Nevertheless Schumacher qualifies fifth and Brundle seventh. Michael makes complete porridge of race day. Challenging Senna for fourth on lap one, drives into the world champion, removing him from race. Continues after stopping for new nosecone. Starts part two 20th (and last) on grid and drives into Modena on first lap, breaking front wishbone and retiring. Brundle compensates with fine drive. Up to fourth lap one and to third following Berger retirement. Starts part two third. Has misfire and is caught and passed by Alesi and Häkkinen on aggregate. Wet weather corrects misfire by reducing g-forces. Despite spin on dropped Alesi oil, Martin regains third for first official GP podium place. Camel announces renewal of sponsorship. Cheers all round.

DALLARA

After taking original start 17th (Lehto) and 25th, Martini restarts 14th and JJ 16th (having had new nosecone fitted after breakage). Pier-Luigi given 10s penalty for jumping start when car jerks forward on being put into gear. Races to demoralised 10th (two laps down), unhappy with poor-handling and lack of power. Lehto collides with Grouillard following second start but finishes ninth (two laps down).

MINARDI

Christian Fittipaldi crashes during Friday morning practice and is forbidden to race after hospital check reveals cracked fifth vertebra. Morbidelli qualifies 16th and starts part two 12th. Drives sensible race, benefiting from retirements, to finish eighth (one lap down). Team will nominate replacement driver until Fittipaldi is fit again.

LIGIER

At team's home base Thierry Boutsen predicts: ''We should be less uncompetitive here!'' With improved grip following suspension changes, he qualifies ninth, his best-yet for Ligier. Erik Comas starts 10th. Both race strongly in part one to finish sixth and seventh. In part two, Thierry's clutch packs up when he's sixth, lap 47. Spins and stalls, cannot restart and retires. Comas takes his place, battling with Lotuses of Häkkinen and Herbert, but improves to fifth between them (one lap down) after Alesi retires. A good end to the first half-season.

FERRARI

Alesi/Capelli qualify sixth/eighth and finish part one fourth and ninth. Jean superb in part two, staying out in wet on slick tyres, lapping as fast as those ahead on wets. Passes misfiring Brundle to lie third, laps 43-56. Survives high speed spin but retires with blown engine, lap 62, after having stopped for tyres at team's insistence and stalled

engine after change. Heroically sets third fastest lap of race. Capelli retires from eighth, lap 38 (ECU).

VENTURI-LARROUSSE

No need to pre-qualify as Andrea Moda fails to arrive. After a torrid Saturday, damaging both race and spare cars, Gachot starts 13th with Katayama 18th for first Magny-Cours race. Bert out on first lap after being hit by Suzuki and breaking rear suspension. Ukyo starts part two 13th and improves to 10th, lap 50, when engine gives up. Sadly the hard-trying team must now pre-qualify from British GP onwards. It doesn't deserve that.

JORDAN

Team very badly hit by striking French truck drivers, who block Yamaha artic containing spare engines and other essential equipment. Team borrows and flies in replacements but is severely inconvenienced. Sunday not Stefano Modena's day. After starting 20th is hit by Wendlinger when 14th and restarts 18th. On first lap of part two is hit by Schumacher's Benetton but continues. Retires (oil pressure), lap 26, after running 12th. Gugelmin fares even worse, being taken out by Chiesa at first corner.

ANDREA MODA

Team fails to arrive and now seems likely to be drummed out of the Brownies.

''Great news! Our engines are stuck in the French lorry drivers' blockade.'' Eddie Jordan (left) and Herbie Blash discuss the pleasures of Yamaha V12 custodianship.

Jean Alesi's lap times at the height of the downpour were enough to convince most folk that the Ferrari F92A would make a good class one powerboat. Still running on slicks, he was barely slower than the wet-shod Williams-Renaults. A blown V12 was poor reward.

Past the pits they blasted, with Patrese just ahead of Mansell, Berger third, Brundle up three places to fourth, Alesi fifth and the impressive Häkkinen sixth, having gained five places! And that's the way it stayed until Gerhard Berger retired in a cloud of smoke on lap 11. What a day for McLaren! The team had been gloomy about its prospects, but it hadn't expected both their drivers to be out so soon. And then, in a day that was to be full of incident, down came the rain. All the time, the aggressive Mansell had been looking for a way past Patrese. And Riccardo had refused to yield. Several times things looked extremely fraught; there seemed a geniune prospect that the two warring team-mates might take each other out. With Brundle now a fine third, a similar battle was raging behind him between Alesi and Häkkinen for fourth. Alesi had it until lap 16. Then it was Mika's. Then Jean's again. But on lap 20, with the rain belting down on the slick-shod cars, the race was stopped. It would be restarted according to the complex rules and run as a two-parter, comprising the first 18 laps . . . and another 51 to make a 69-lap race (three less than originally intended). The results would be decided on the aggregate times of the two parts. A simple and clear situation for television commentators to communicate!

The grid reformed according to positions held after 18 laps. Patrese in pole position, Mansell second, Brundle third, Alesi fourth, Häkkinen fifth and Thierry Boutsen sixth in his Ligier (by far his best showing since he joined the team in 1991). Enter Patrick Head of Williams to talk to Patrese on the grid. ''Riccardo, if you can stay ahead of Nigel, it's your race. But *please* be mindful of the fact that both cars must finish.'' It wasn't an order to yield, but to an agitated Riccardo it might have seemed like one. Agitated because he, like everyone else, was deciding what tyres to fit. It had stopped raining but it looked very likely to start again. So wets or slicks? In the event the *officials* (as opposed to the teams' tyre selections) decided that the second part would officially be 'wet', which meant that it wouldn't be stopped if it rained again. That decision was to be controversial as, later, teams said they had not known about it.

The 20 survivors all set off on slicks and, again, Patrese led into the first corner as an over-eager Olivier Grouillard jumped the gun, for which he incurred a 10s stop/go penalty. Mansell attacked right away, passed Patrese at the hairpin and was repassed before the end of the lap. But that was it for Riccardo. As he passed the pits he raised his arm and waved Nigel through. After the race, tight-lipped and obviously unhappy, he said: "Nigel was pressing me very hard and I thought it would be best to let him go." And go Nigel did, pulling steadily away from the Italian. But again Michael Schumacher had overcooked it. Starting from last on the grid after his earlier débâcle he hit Modena's Jordan at the hairpin, and this time he didn't get away with it. Out he went with a broken front wishbone as an irate Modena drove on, with Michael later saying, cheerfully, "that's motor racing!"

Now the race became very difficult to follow, as track positions in the second part had to be reconciled with time gaps at the end of the first. But you didn't need a calculator to work out that Brundle and Alesi were having a terrific scrap for third place behind the increasingly distant Williams leaders. Fourth-placed Jean was charging and Martin was being slowed by a misfire caused by a loose wire. Alesi caught and passed the Benetton on the track and, on lap 43, his Ferrari was third on aggregate time. Then Häkkinen passed Brundle — a superb

performance by the young Finn which demoted the stricken Benetton to fifth. But Brundle was later reprieved by violent rain, which cured his misfire by reducing the g-forces and thus steadying the wire.

There was plenty of other excitement too. Thierry Boutsen, without a clutch, had spun, stalled his engine and retired from his well-deserved sixth place. His team-mate Erik Comas took Thierry's place and Johnny Herbert followed him to seventh. With no sign of the race being stopped, despite the foul conditions, the first to change tyres was Nigel Mansell. With a 27s lead he had a brilliant 5.1s stop and left the pit lane still in front of Patrese. Then it was Brundle (7.11s) and Patrese (8.51s), but Alesi stayed out on his slicks! Demonstrating quite incredible car control he kept charging round only a few tenths slower than Patrese in front of him, and Riccardo was on wets! Of course it had to end, and it did when Jean had a gigantic 170 mph spin which he got away with thanks to the enormously wide run-off area

Martin Brundle was on superb form on raceday, finishing on the podium for the first time since Dallas in 1984. And this time it really counted…

''Two Lotuses in the points? You'll be telling me a Ligier was in the top six next.'' Mika Häkkinen was a superb fourth for the resurgent Hethel team, two places ahead of team-mate Herbert.

''What d'you mean? There was a Ligier in the top six?'' Comas, heading for fifth, leads the continually unfortunate Capelli.

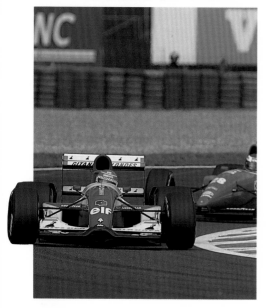

at Magny-Cours. Finally, obeying team orders, he came in, changed tyres, stalled his motor, and rejoined only to have his engine expire in a burst of flame and smoke. Poor reward for a brilliant, fighting drive.

So now Brundle was back in third place, which is where he finished in spite of spinning on Alesi's oil, the only man other than Mansell and Patrese to go the full distance. Lapped but charging, the two Lotus men, Häkkinen and Herbert fought with Comas for the three remaining points places. For five glorious laps Erik was fourth, Ligier's best place for years, but two laps from the end Häkkinen got past him to take the place for Lotus, its best position for years too — and Mika's best yet.

It had been a confusing race, but a great one for Britain. Nigel Mansell's majestic 27th victory equalled the score of the great Jackie Stewart, Britain's most successful Grand Prix driver, and his fastest lap (1m 17.070s, 123.355 mph) was another record for his CV. With Martin Brundle at last back where he deserved to be, on the podium in third place, and Johnny Herbert sixth it meant there were three Britons in the top six. It was a very long time since that had happened. With the British Grand Prix the following Sunday, they must have been rubbing their hands at Silverstone!

The only time Mansell was beaten all weekend was at the pre-race Camel Quiz, when Martin Brundle's team outanswered the world champion elect and his accomplices. Here, Mansell considers introducing a substitute as the gentleman on his right struggles to recollect the surname of the only man called Nigel to have won the first five races in a GP season...

Two words summarise the 1992 British Grand Prix. Nigel Mansell. For, in front of the largest crowd ever seen at Silverstone, Nigel was fastest in every one of the five practice sessions, took his 25th pole position, two seconds faster than anyone else with the fastest lap ever at the revised Northamptonshire circuit, led every one of the 59 laps, set 11 fastest laps, created a new lap record and won his fourth British and 28th Grand Prix by nearly 40s, to become the British driver with the most victories in the history of Grand Prix racing. In devastating form, driving the best car, he was in a class of his own for the whole meeting.

Mansell loves Silverstone. "I think it is the finest circuit in the world. It's a tough circuit. You have to commit yourself and attack everywhere and the g-force you get on the switchback corners at Becketts, Stowe and Club is unreal. There is no other circuit like it and I am able to do something special here." In no small measure this is due to the fanatical support he

Short change: Alessandro Zanardi stepped into erstwhile F3000 rival Christian Fittipaldi's shoes at Minardi, but only until the Brazilian recovered from his French GP injuries. Race-rustiness didn't help; the Italian failed to qualify.

gets from his fans, who make the notorious Monza *tifosi* look apathetic. In years past, those fans had gone to Silverstone in their tens of thousands to cheer their idol who, feeding on their adulation, had responded with some of his finest and most spectacular drives. This year, supercharged by Nigel's championship lead and the fact that two British drivers had been on the podium in the previous French GP, they poured into Silverstone in unprecedented numbers. On Friday there were 45,000 spectators, with the main grandstand full for pre-qualifying at 08.00. On Sunday, a record crowd of some 150,000 jingoistic Union Jack-wavers, lusting for British success, filled the circuit almost to bursting point — with what turned out to be potentially disastrous consequences.

Their expectations had been fuelled by Friday's qualifying. Only two minutes into the hour Mansell beat his 1991 pole time of 1m 20.939s. And 23 minutes later he fulfilled his prophesy that, with everything going for him, he could get into the 1m 19s bracket. Again he reduced his time — to 1m 19.161s, leaving everyone gasping. But then, right at the end of

the session, he went out once more "to please the fans". He certainly did so with a blistering 1m 18.965s (148.04 mph), two seconds faster than both his '91 pole time and his Williams-Renault team-mate Riccardo Patrese, who was second. "That was a perfect lap and I can't imagine going any quicker!" With a provisional sixth front row monopoly of the season, Williams seemed certain to stay there because no one was likely to beat its times on Saturday. Nor did they, as driving rain made everyone content themselves with finding set-ups for a possible wet race.

Third on the grid, saying "I did the best I could with the available equipment" was world champion Ayrton Senna in his McLaren-Honda (2.8s slower than Mansell), followed by Michael Schumacher in his Benetton, Gerhard Berger's McLaren and the Benetton of a disappointed Martin Brundle, who had expected to do better. In magnificent seventh and ninth places were the improving-by-the-race Lotuses of Johnny Herbert and Mika Häkkinen, sandwiching the lacklustre Ferrari of Jean Alesi, with Erik Comas's Ligier a very respectable 10th. Erik destroyed his car and that of Riccardo Patrese when he took the Italian off at some 150 mph on Saturday morning, for which he was found guilty by FISA and fined $5,000. Amazingly both drivers, although sore, were fit for Sunday's race, using new cars.

To everyone's relief, especially the vast crowd, Sunday not only started dry but stayed that way for an enthralling 59-lap race. In fact for two enthralling 59 lap races: Nigel Mansell's and the others'. Nigel's was easy to follow. After spinning his wheels at the start and losing the lead to Patrese he passed the aching Italian between Copse and Maggotts, the first and second corners. "After that I just forgot about him," said Riccardo. It was a cracking first lap. Brundle made a sensational getaway, shooting along the pit wall from the third row of the grid, to pass Berger, Schumacher and Senna into third place at the start of what was to be one of his finest races ever. Schumacher took Senna too and momentarily passed Brundle, only to take to the grass at Becketts and drop back to fifth, but Johnny Herbert's opening lap was more successful. In his under-developed Lotus, from seventh on the grid, he calmly passed Berger's McLaren to take sixth — and proceeded to stay there for over half the race until he retired.

At the end of lap one Mansell led by a stupefying 3.2s. On lap two it was 5.9s, on lap three 7.9s and on lap four, after breaking the lap record on full tanks, it was 10.1s. By lap 10, after five fastest laps, he was 20 seconds ahead of everyone else. Seldom had Formula One seen such a crushing demonstration of overwhelming superiority. Boring? Not a bit of it! The crowd loved it, waving their flags, cheering their hero and revelling in his dominant progress. But they'd got plenty more to delight them. Not just the Williams-Renault of Riccardo Patrese, holding a secure second place, but a terrific struggle for third between Martin Brundle, Ayrton Senna and Michael Schumacher, who were circulating virtually nose-to-tail. "I was pushing like hell the whole race," said Senna. "On some corners I could catch him, on some he was going away. I tried many times." But he couldn't get past Martin, whose Benetton, running reduced downforce

to maximise its straightline speed, was "perfect for the whole race."

The best way to beat Silverstone traffic. Unfortunately, Mika Häkkinen didn't have it with him on Sunday morning. Driving on the wrong side of the road in a bid to beat the massive traffic jams, he was nicked by vigilant traffic police and carted off to the station, forcing him to miss the warm-up he was desperately trying to reach. Sixth place offered some consolation for impending acquisition of driving licence points.

TEAM ANALYSIS

McLAREN

Still no joy. After being slower in practice than at the Silverstone tyre tests, Senna and Berger qualify third and fifth (Senna slower than 1991). Ayrton down to fourth at first corner and Gerhard to seventh on lap one. Senna shadows and harries superb Martin Brundle's Benetton for 52 laps, getting by on lap 53 only to retire, three corners later, with broken gearbox. Berger stops for tyres, lap 29 (6.71s). In seventh: out ninth. Up to fourth, lap 53, but finishes fifth after being passed by Schumacher at last corner when engine blows. Gerhard up to fourth in championship. Ayrton down to fifth. Team down to third behind Benetton in constructors' contest. Senna criticises team for not keeping up technically and talks of retiring in 1993 "if I cannot get a competitive drive."

TYRRELL

After "trying every conceivable set-up" de Cesaris and Grouillard qualify 18th and 20th. Andrea's rear tyre ripped by Modena wing endplate when 17th, lap 21. Loses lap getting back to pits. Rejoins last. Retires, lap 46, after spinning due to damaged suspension. Grouillard drives steady race to finish 11th, two laps down, 0.1s behind Boutsen and 0.5s ahead of Suzuki.

WILLIAMS

Another whitewash. After being fastest at tyre tests by incredible two seconds, Mansell is again fastest in every practice session and takes 25th successive pole position with fastest-ever lap of revised Silverstone (1m 18.965s, 148.04 mph). Then totally destroys race opposition. Takes lead from faster-starting Patrese out of Copse on lap one and leads by stupefying 20 seconds on lap 10, having broken lap record on full tanks as early as lap four. Tyre-stops with 39s lead on lap 30, rejoining still 10s ahead. Sets 11 fastest laps, including final record, lap 57 (1m 22.539s 141.633 mph) and wins by 39s. Nigel's 28th victory beats Jackie Stewart's record of most wins for British driver. Riccardo Patrese has major 150 mph accident on Friday morning (his fourth in four years at Silverstone), when taken off by Comas at 120 mph. Still qualifies second and races to sixth second place of 1992, in car built up overnight, to score his first-ever points at Silverstone. Team and Mansell now lead respective championships by 74 and 36 points.

BRABHAM

At last a glimmer of success. At circuit where father Graham announced retirement in 1975, Damon Hill qualifies 26th for his first GP and only the team's second of 1992. Drives sensible race to 16th (four laps down). Eric van de Poele does not qualify after only being able to do two laps due to Hill having prior use of only available car in Friday's dry session.

FOOTWORK

Alboreto and Suzuki start 12th and 17th (no pre-qualifying for Michele now) and both have another reliable race. Alboreto takes his fourth successive seventh place (one lap down) and ninth successive 1992 finish, beating Erik Comas by 0.5s. Aguri finishes 12th (two laps down) after battling with Boutsen, Grouillard and Lehto. Team announces that it is working on active suspension, power shift gearbox and traction control for 1993 with David Brabham as test driver.

LOTUS

Team marks Castrol sponsorship by arriving with three new 107s. Excellent qualifying sees Herbert seventh on grid (ahead of both Ferraris) and Häkkinen ninth. Mika misses Sunday morning warm-up after being arrested for driving misdemeanours on way to track. As usual both drive superb races. Johnny passes Berger to take sixth, lap one, and stays there for 30 laps before retiring, lap 32, when gearbox jams. Mika passes Alesi to eighth, lap 21. Fifth, laps 34-42, after Schumacher tyre stop, but caught and passed by both Michael and Berger. Finishes sixth for team's fourth points finish of season, consolidating its fifth place in constructors' championship.

FONDMETAL

At first pre-qualifying for both drivers, Tarquini is second and Chiesa fourth. "Too-tall-for-car" Andrea again over-revs engine and fails to qualify, but Gabriele in (15th). Tarquini has good race in new GR02, posting eighth fastest lap and finishing 14th (two laps down) for his first finish in 10 races, despite no clutch, terrible pit stop and last lap crowd invasion which forces him angrily to abandon car.

MARCH

After no Silverstone testing, Karl Wendlinger qualifies 21st. Up to 18th, laps 3-14, but retires from 20th, lap 28 (gearbox). Belmondo fails to qualify, also due to gearbox problem in only dry qualifying session.

BENETTON

Another magnificent result for the team. Schumacher fourth and Brundle disappointed sixth on grid. Both faster than Senna and Berger in Sunday warm-up. Superb race for Martin. Up to third at start, passing Berger, Schumacher and Senna. Calmly stays ahead of hard-trying Senna, resisting non-stop pressure for 52 laps. Finally passed by Ayrton who retires three corners later ("I had a wry smile when I saw that..!"). After great drive, Martin takes second successive third place and moves up to sixth in championship. Schumacher shadows fourth-placed Senna until lap 34 tyre stop. Down to seventh but passes Häkkinen, lap 53, and then, after second fastest lap of race, takes Berger on last lap when McLaren engine fails. So team takes seven points from third and fourth places which, after best-yet '92 race, again moves it ahead of McLaren in championship.

DALLARA

Car reliable but handling poor. Using new double front shock absorber system JJ Lehto qualifies 19th. Martini 22nd on grid with single unit system. Both have hard race but finish 13th (JJ, two laps down) and 15th (Pier-Luigi, three laps down).

MINARDI
Hard going continues for financially-troubled team. Gianni Morbidelli qualifies 25th. Classified 17th and last (six laps down) after stopping with fading oil pressure. Alessandro Zanardi substitutes for injured Christian Fittipaldi but, with no racing since 1991, is rusty and fails to qualify.

LIGIER
At-odds-with-itself team slips back after improvement at French GP. Comas qualifies 10th on Friday but has gigantic collision with Patrese on Saturday morning for which he is blamed and fined $5,000 by FISA. Boutsen, having had no set-up mileage from tyre tests, starts 13th. Erik races to eighth (one lap down), after lap 24 tyre stop, beating Capelli by 0.6s. Angry Thierry persistently blocked by de Cesaris until lap 20. Decides not to tyre-stop and finishes 10th (two laps down), 0.1s ahead of Grouillard.

FERRARI
"We knew we wouldn't be competitive here," says team manager Claudio Lombardi. He was right. Despite his considerable best efforts Jean Alesi starts eighth with Ivan Capelli a demoralised 14th. Jean loses eighth to Häkkinen, lap 20, tyre stops lap 34 and retires from eighth, lap 44, when fire extinguisher bottle ruptures and freezes his backside (literally!). Capelli stops for tyres, lap 35, rejoins behind Comas and finishes ninth (one lap down), just 0.6s behind the Ligier but apparently now for the chop.

VENTURI-LARROUSSE
Both drivers pre-qualify — Gachot first and Katayama third. Bertrand qualifies 11th and is an excellent eighth on Sunday morning ("I tell you, this car is good!"). Retires from 12th, lap 32, when wheel bearing breaks up. After qualifying 16th for first Silverstone GP, Katayama slips back with transmission problem. Retires from 22nd, lap 28 (gearbox).

JORDAN
At its Silverstone home base the Jordan team has another humiliating and intensely depressing meeting. With its Yamaha engines again not up to snuff and with repeated fuel pump problems, Modena and Gugelmin qualify only 23rd and 24th. Both race with minimum downforce to

1983 revisited: former F3 sparring partners Brundle and Senna fought a spirited tussle. Seconds after the Brazilian got through, his gearbox packed up.

compensate for lack of power. Stefano climbs to 14th, lap 33, but is rammed by Schumacher and drops a place. Ignores oil light and retires, lap 44, when engine unsurprisingly blows up. Gugelmin also sees oil light from lap five and similarly retires from 17th when V12 seizes, lap 38. "The problem was oil pressure," says Takaaki Kimura of Yamaha. "We will thoroughly investigate this." And a lot else, hopes Jordan.

ANDREA MODA
Unlike France, team arrives, but needn't have bothered. Moreno 1.5s slower than the fourth pre-qualifier and poor Perry McCarthy only goes two laps before clutch expires. Team must have highest-ever cost per mile in F1.

At the circuit where his late father had announced his retirement 17 years previously, Damon Hill finally made his debut in the underdeveloped Brabham BT60B, which had more spent on its paint job than it did on its test programme.

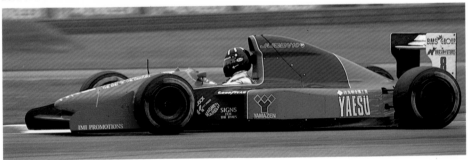

On lap 29 Gerhard Berger (still behind Johnny Herbert!) went in for tyres, letting Häkkinen, who had passed Alesi's Ferrari, move up to seventh. As in France the Lotuses were superb but, sadly, it didn't last. Out went Johnny with a jammed gearbox on lap 30. And in came Mansell for a pre-planned tyre stop. With 39s lead (yes, 39!) he could afford it to be a careful, deliberate stop; remembering the disasters they'd had in the past, his tyre men took their time — 11.7s in fact. But Nigel was still leading as he left the pit lane on his new Goodyears, some 10s ahead of Patrese.

With Mansell and Berger's tyres to study, Williams and McLaren were able to tell Patrese, second, and Senna, fourth, to stay out, as did Brundle. But Michael Schumacher, his tyres affected by his minor lap one excursion, stopped on lap 34, promoting Häkkinen to fifth. So now Senna had literally got Michael's Benetton off his back as, up front, Mansell remorselessly rebuilt his lead over Patrese. On lap 40, with 19 to go, Nigel was 20 seconds ahead of Riccardo, who led Brundle by seven seconds. "I knew my car would improve as the fuel load went down," said Senna, in fourth

The moment 150,000 people came to see. The bloke with the chequered flag got as close to Mansell as anyone else had managed all weekend.

How to win friends, influence people...and in all probability get flattened by a Dallara-Ferrari. The post-race track invasion, a British GP tradition, was worryingly premature. Only one fan was hit, though he wasn't injured. The consequences of such stupidity could have been far worse. The crowd's actions brought the sport into the headlines for the wrong reasons, and detracted from Mansell's 28th GP success.

place, and he never gave up. "It seemed like old times, scrapping round Silverstone with Senna," said Brundle, who'd beaten the Brazilian nine times in their stirring 1983 battles for the British Formula Three championship, "and I really enjoyed it!" So did everyone else — as they did the battle for fifth which had developed between Häkkinen, Berger and Schumacher (Jean Alesi having retired with a frozen bum after his fire extinguisher bottle had ruptured!). On his original Goodyears, Mika was trying to stave off the two freshly tyred chargers, but it just wasn't on. Slipping and sliding on his worn rubber he had to give way on lap 49, but his resistance had been great to watch and further increased the young Finn's considerable reputation.

Lap 53. Senna out! For the sixth time in nine races the world champion failed to finish. This time it was a gearbox failure, just three corners after he'd finally managed to force his way past Brundle when they were both inadvertently baulked by Damon Hill's Brabham (on his way to finishing his first ever Grand Prix). And, to rub salt into the wound, it happened at Club, where Ayrton had retired in 1991 prior to being given a lift home by the victorious Mansell. This time he walked back!

So, with a final crowd-pleasing record lap (1m 22.539s, 141.663mph) which did not endear him to his concerned team, Nigel Mansell extended his championship lead over Patrese to a massive 36 points with seven races to go. Brundle duly took a magnificent second successive third place but, to fill McLaren's cup of misery to overflowing, it was Schumacher who finished fourth after passing Berger on the last lap when the Austrian's Honda V12 broke in a cloud of oil smoke, Gerhard just making it across the line to take fifth ahead of Häkkinen's Lotus. Welcome reward for Mika, who'd ended up in the slammer and missed the morning warm-up after being arrested for driving on the wrong side of the road on his way to the track!

The end of a perfect day for Nigel Mansell, Williams, Renault, Martin Brundle, Benetton

"They're always complaining about repeats on the BBC." For the second consecutive Sunday, Messrs Patrese, Mansell and Brundle shared a few pints of Moët & Chandon in front of the TV cameras.

and, above all, for the crowd, who'd got exactly what they'd come to see: Mansell brilliantly winning one of the finest races of his outstanding career to become the British driver with the most GP wins in the history of the sport. "I dedicate this historic win to all the fans," said Nigel. "I have never experienced a crowd like this anywhere in the world. They are just incredible and fantastic."

Some of them too "incredible and fantastic" though. For, even as Nigel crossed the line, one headbanger ran across the course, immediately to be followed by hundreds more, particularly at Copse and Club. All this while others were still racing...

Indeed, Mansell never completed his victory lap, being stopped by the surging crowd at Club and having to be rescued by the incident vehicle. True, they did no harm (if you except damage to Patrese's halted Williams and the theft of its steering wheel) and, true, it was nothing more than uninhibited enthusiasm that caused the traditional Silverstone course invasion to happen earlier than usual. But what could have happened if, for instance, Berger had spun on his own oil as he finished, surrounded by over-the-top spectators, doesn't bear thinking about. Silverstone had got a major problem to solve before 1993, and it wasn't going to be easy.

The bumpy surface of the revised Ostkurve attracted widespread criticism from drivers. Michael Schumacher passes through en route to a third place which delighted the locals.

From the excitement and euphoria of Silverstone to the imposing, but characterless, Hockenheim, where Nigel Mansell had completed a run of three victories in 1991, to close within eight points of Senna in the World Championship. This time, with seven victories already, he led the series by a massive 36 points. Only his team-mate Riccardo Patrese seemed to have a chance of denying the Englishman his first title — especially as the Williams-Renault had already proved to be just as superior in Germany as it had been everywhere else.

To win at the 4.2-mile track near Heidelberg you need bags of grunt to power down two long, mildly curving 210 mph 'straights' and perfect chassis balance to cope with three chicanes and the twisty stadium section. The Williams-Renault had both. Mansell and Patrese had comfortably topped the times at the pre-race tyre tests, so it looked as though they were going to have a relatively easy time. McLaren, their main rival, had forecast that it would be more competitive after Silverstone. However, in spite of a new evolution of the Honda V12, new diffusors and better Brembo brakes, there was a gloomy atmosphere in the Woking team amidst the realisation that its cars still weren't quick enough. And there were persistent rumours that Honda was to pull out of Formula One at the end of the season.

The four practice sessions proved that Mclaren's gloom was well founded. Once again, Mansell was fastest every time. On Friday afternoon he was a full two seconds clear of Ayrton Senna, on Saturday just under a second ahead of Riccardo Patrese. It hadn't been easy for Riccardo though. On Friday morning he had active suspension problems which decimated his track time and on Saturday his engine had gone off, necessitating a change. So his grid time was set in Mansell's spare car before Nigel took it over to take his ninth pole position of the year, 48 minutes into the hour-long session. It was an excellent example of how well the top teams react to pressure.

So another all Williams-Renault front row — the seventh of the season. And again it was the two McLarens next, Senna third and Berger fourth, followed by Jean Alesi's Ferrari, Michael Schumacher's Benetton (using the new Series VII Ford V8 engine for the first time), the Ligiers of Erik Comas and Thierry Boutsen — their best practice of the season so far — Martin Brundle's Benetton and the very impressive Karl Wendlinger's March.

Four hours before Sunday's race there is half an hour of practice for teams to fine-tune the set-up of their cars on race tyres with full fuel tanks. This is the only time during the three-day meeting that all of them practise in race trim and it is usually uneventful. Not this time, though. Michael Schumacher, under enormous pressure to do well in his first German Grand Prix, came running in after having gone off into a sand trap when a tyre deflated (due to a missing valve cap). Then, right at the end of the session, Senna spun off, rumpling his McLaren chassis along the top of the concrete kerbing and writing it off. With no time to go out in the back-up chassis, Ayrton would be starting in Gerhard Berger's untried spare car.

With most of the cars set up with minimum downforce to maximise speed on the long straights, grip and tyre wear were going to be major problems. Many had spun off during qualifying while trying to find the best balance, and the problem was whether to fit Goodyear's softer C compound, and lose time with a stop for replacements, or go through non-stop on the harder, but less grippy, Bs. Most went for Cs, as a result of which we were to see inspired top-four drives from Ayrton Senna and Martin Brundle.

As he had been in 1991, Nigel Mansell was utterly dominant at Hockenheim. His eighth victory of the season took him ever closer to that elusive title.

Johnny Herbert faces the wrong way down a one-way street after a practice mishap. JJ Lehto would be contemplating evasive action if he had the slightest clue about what lay beyond that sandstorm curtain.

Hockenheim may not be the most atmospheric track in the world, but the race was a cracker. As Mansell squeezed the lever under his Williams steering wheel to change from first to second, his semi-automatic gearbox gave him third. Rather than risk another mis-selection he left it there as Patrese surged into the lead — as he had at Silverstone. But not for long. Before the first (115 mph) chicane Mansell was in the lead, with Senna and Berger jostling behind Patrese for third place — into which Senna forced his way. Two Williams led two McLarens and then it was the two Benettons with Schumacher ahead of Brundle — who had thrust past both the Ferraris and Boutsen's Ligier! Then it was Alesi, Comas, Capelli and Boutsen — Ferrari, Ligier, Ferrari, Ligier — the Ligiers benefiting from their Renault horses at power-happy Hockenheim. Capelli moved past Comas to take eighth, and for 13 laps the order stayed the same. Mansell was drawing away from Patrese after his usual opposition-crushing opening burst, including a new record as early as lap 12. By lap 10 he was over five seconds ahead of Patrese, who was a massive 13s ahead of Senna. Not too exciting at the front, but behind the Williams stars there was no more than 2.5s from Senna to Schumacher, who were third and fifth, sandwiching Berger. Then came the tyre changes.

Mansell was the first of the leaders to come in, unexpectedly early on lap 15. "I thought I had a puncture. The warning light came on and, as I'd picked up some debris and the handling was terrible, I thought it best to come in." After an 8.11s stop he rejoined, now fourth behind Patrese, Senna and Schumacher. Berger stopped and rejoined, too, but was in again next time round to retire with a misfire.

Mansell quickly passed Schumacher and then caught Senna. Ayrton is seriously difficult to pass but, no problem, Nigel would do so

TEAM ANALYSIS

McLAREN

Tense atmosphere amidst escalating rumours that team will lose Honda engines in 1993 and that Senna will not renew contract. Ron Dennis's statement that "we should be more competitive after Silverstone" not fulfilled, despite further Honda V12 evolution and aerodynamic changes. After engine failure on Saturday morning and "driving over the limit everywhere", Senna qualifies third, 1.2s slower than Mansell. Spins at end of Sunday warm-up and destroys race car monocoque. Races Berger's spare car. Up to second after Mansell tyre stop, lap 15. Waves Nigel by, lap 19, and then back to second when Patrese tyre-stops, lap 20. Thereafter drives superb non-stop race on soft-compound C tyres to finish second, resisting determined Patrese's efforts to get by in closing stages. Also sets second fastest lap of race. "This was a good result for me, making the best of our equipment" (which he regards as inadequate). Berger starts fourth for another unsatisfactory race. Has over-long tyre stop (14.65s) from fourth, lap 14, and rejoins 11th. Back again with misfire and retires (for the sixth time in 10 races) on the very next lap.

TYRRELL

Using new semi-active front ride height control system, Grouillard and de Cesaris qualify unhappy 14th and 20th after being eighth and ninth in earlier sessions. Olivier called in on lap nine for 10 second stop/go penalty (with which he bitterly disagrees) for jumping start. Retires from 16th, lap nine (engine), and is later angrily condemned by Gabriele Tarquini for "crazy and very dangerous driving". Andrea has enormous spin on lap 13 and drops to 19th. Stops for new tyres but retires from 16th, lap 26 (engine).

WILLIAMS

Another great race, but in uneasy atmosphere due to rumours of 1993 driver changes. Mansell's ninth 1992 pole with Patrese second in team's seventh front row monopoly, despite car problems on both days. Riccardo again out-drags Nigel at start when Mansell's gearbox misses second, but Mansell back in lead by first chicane. Nigel in for tyres, lap 15, suspecting puncture. Rejoins fourth, passes Schumacher, catches Senna and short-cuts chicane on way past Brazilian, lap 19. Lucky not to be protested. Retakes lead when Patrese tyre-stops, lap 20. Wins again but by only 4.5s after slowing with tyre vibration. Nigel's eighth win of season (career 29) equals Senna record. Riccardo drives magnificent race after rejoining fourth, lap 20. Eventually forces past inspired Schumacher to lie third, lap 33. Eliminates 7s gap to Senna and repeatedly tries to pass to maintain championship hopes. Makes final effort entering stadium on last lap but spins and retires with stalled engine. Sets fastest lap during chase (1m 41.591s, 150.060 mph — a record). Mansell now within sight of first World Championship.

BRABHAM

Only 28th and 30th, van de Poele and Hill fail to qualify.

FOOTWORK

Using new sequential-change gearbox, Alboreto qualifies disappointed 17th after being eighth on Friday. Maintains 100 per cent finishing record by racing to non-stop ninth on B tyres (one lap down). Suzuki starts 15th but traps foot under steering column (!) on lap two, spins and retires.

LOTUS

Still experimenting with active/passive suspension, Herbert qualifies 11th and Häkkinen 13th (both using passive mode). After tyre stops both suffer from engine problems, Mika retiring from impressive ninth, lap 22, and Johnny from similarly impressive 10th, lap 24.

FONDMETAL

Two new GR02s for Tarquini. Chiesa, increasingly out-of-favour, has to make do with old GR01 — which he pre-qualifies fourth but fails to qualify. Gabriele 19th on grid after pre-qualifying fastest. Passes five cars before first corner and tyre-stops from strong 11th, lap 21. Out of race from attacking 14th, lap 34, when engine blows. Strongly condemns Grouillard for "crazy and very dangerous driving."

MARCH

Both Wendlinger and Belmondo qualify, Karl an excellent 10th in car which does not really suit circuit and Paul 22nd. Following lap three spin, Wendlinger has three pit stops for tyres, new nose and to fix loose ballast. Finishes 16th (three laps down). Despite gearbox problems, Belmondo maintains 100 per cent finishing record with 13th place (one lap down).

BENETTON

Another great result. Both Schumacher and Brundle have major spins during practice but qualify sixth (Michael) and ninth using same spare car. Schumacher goes into gravel trap on Sunday morning when tyre deflates due to missing valve cap. Both he and Brundle pass Alesi on first lap to run fifth/sixth for 13 laps. Michael to third after Patrese tyre stop, lap 20. Running non-stop on B tyres, magnificently stays there, despite fluid from damaged radiator spraying left rear tyre and ceaseless pressure from Riccardo, who finally forces by on lap 33. But the two Benettons, using new Ford V8 Series VII engine for first time, finish excellent third and fourth, 2.5s apart, when Patrese goes off on last lap. Schumacher overjoyed to be third in his first home GP. Despite back pain that affects braking, Martin posts fourth fastest lap on way to fourth place (his fifth '92 points finish). Team consolidates second position in constructors' championship.

DALLARA

New double-shock front suspension improves handling, but Martini and Lehto still only qualify 18th and 21st. Both run reliable races to finish 10th (JJ) and 11th (one lap down), separated by 1.5s.

Christian Fittipaldi turned up to lend Minardi a supporting hand. Still stifled by a neckbrace, the Brazilian expressed his intention to be back in F1 by Spa.

MINARDI

Alessandro Zanardi again substitutes for the injured Christian Fittipaldi and qualifies 24th — two places ahead of Morbidelli. Both complain that, on Hockenheim power circuit, car is too slow. Both have multiple spins in practice after reducing downforce to increase straightline speed. Zanardi retires, lap two, when gearbox gives up. Gianni finishes 12th (one lap down), 0.8s ahead of Thierry Boutsen after sliding out of 10th at the Sachskurve on lap 42.

LIGIER

Things are improving. Thanks to Renault power, team has best-yet 1992 qualifying with Comas seventh and Boutsen eighth. Both race reliably to finish team's best '92 GP so far. Comas sixth, in points for third time, and Boutsen seventh, both having gone full distance and with Thierry having set sixth fastest lap.

FERRARI

"We have more power and an improved set-up, but are still too far away," says design chief Harvey Postlethwaite. Alesi and Capelli prove him right. Jean starts excellent fifth, but loses it on lap one as Schumacher and Brundle go by. Races non-stop on B tyres to finish out-of-touch fifth, 36 seconds behind fourth-placed Brundle. Poor Ivan Capelli again fails to finish (eighth time in 10 races) when engine expires on lap 22. Much revised F92A chassis promised for Belgian Grand Prix, at Spa-Francorchamps in two weeks' time . . . where Alesi led the race in 1991.

VENTURI-LARROUSSE

Fraught time in practice for Gachot and Katayama. Bertrand blows engine as does Ukyo, who also destroys monocoque with impactful spin. But both get in, Katayama an excellent 16th for his first German GP and Gachot 25th (after Bertrand pre-qualified second, Ukyo third). Gachot drives steady, non-stop race on B tyres to finish 14th (one lap down). After having oil pump failure on first lap of morning warm-up, Katayama misses gearchange when 19th on lap nine and spins out of race.

JORDAN

No let-up in team's season of misery, although there is hope of future improvement as John Judd's organisation is now advising Yamaha on development of its off-the-pace V12. Team does not expect to qualify well on Hockenheim's power circuit, and doesn't. Gugelmin only gets in 23rd thanks to a hefty tow from his friend Ayrton Senna's McLaren, and Stefano Modena fails to qualify. Mauricio relieved to finish 15th (two laps down) in car which "performed well without any problems", but was just not quick enough.

ANDREA MODA

Team gets Elf qualifying fuel, but Moreno's Judd V10 massively expires and he fails to pre-qualify by 0.3s. Perry McCarthy's season of woe continues when he fails to see red light at pit lane entrance and does not stop for weight check. With time disallowed, he does not pre-qualify (he was too slow anyway, but the penalty was an extra blow).

Alessandro Zanardi's first race start for Minardi was fruitless. Victim of several qualifying misdemeanours, the Italian (left) notched up the first retirement of the afternoon.

when he stopped for tyres. But Ayrton never did stop! Mansell attacked and was severely rebuffed. At the reprofiled, and much-criticised, Ostkurve chicane he tried again and went off! Fortunately for him, he was able to dive straight across the apex on hard tarmac and avoid the gravel trap. It could so easily have been the end of his race. No one protested his excursion, which had technically caused him to miss part of the course. Then, seeing Nigel swarming about aggressively in his mirrors, Senna waved him past, tacit but surprising admission that he was aware he wasn't going to beat the Mansell/Williams combination here at Hockenheim. On lap 20, race leader Patrese stopped for new tyres and Mansell retook a lead that he was never to lose, although retaining it was going to be a close run thing at the finish.

When Patrese shot out of the pit lane on his new Goodyears he was fourth, behind Mansell, Senna and the quite brilliant

Senna (above) leads Patrese in the closing stages of their dice for second place, which went the Brazilian's way after Patrese's last-minute bid for glory earned him no more than a mouthful of sand. Senna drove magnificently to finish within five seconds of Mansell, given their respective levels of chassis performance.

Schumacher, who was more than satisfying his compatriots' expectations, 3.5s behind Senna and gaining! But the man to watch was Patrese. In his 234th GP he had never driven better. After closing on the non-stop Schumacher (using B tyres), Riccardo tried time and time again to get by the Benetton. But every time, fairly and cleanly, driving in his 16th Grand Prix as though it was his 160th, Schumacher resisted the determined Italian. Until lap 32 when, after another *banzai* move at the third chicane, Riccardo managed to scramble past when Schumacher, with a rear tyre lubricated by coolant from a cracked radiator pipe, locked up, slid violently and lost momentum. From then on Michael dropped back, almost to be caught by his equally inspired team-mate Brundle, who was also driving a non-stop race . . . but on the softer C tyres.

Now Patrese was charging even harder, intent on finishing second to keep his championship hopes alive. His 35th lap was a record and his 36th, fastest of the race, beat that — 1m 41.591s (150.060 mph). Two laps later, he had caught Senna. Seven to go — Ayrton on his original tyres and Riccardo on new ones. Surely Patrese, with his superior grip, would find a way past the McLaren? But Senna was a tougher proposition than Schumacher, quite apart from the fact that he hadn't got Michael's lubricated-tyre problem. Riccardo gave him no peace, but somehow Senna kept his place. "The last 10 laps were very worrying as I had bad vibrations from my tyres, but the only way I could get on to the podium was to go through without stopping and take a chance." Which is what he did. At the entrance to the stadium on the last lap, Patrese made a final super-determined effort, only to spin off on the dusty edge of the track, stall his engine and retire. Thus he got no reward for a magnificent, fighting drive.

Mansell also had severe tyre problems after his enforced early stop, and his lead was

While the Williams-Renaults were running at well over 200 mph down the straights, the Jordan-Yamahas were only mildly faster than the quickest F3000 cars on the support programme. "I had enough time to read the Sunday Times between chicanes," reflected Mauricio Gugelmin later.

With FISA stipulating narrower tyres for 1993, the topic of rubber was on everyone's lips in Germany. Ayrton Senna contemplates the likely effects of running 15in tyres, some three inches narrower than the 1992 article.

dramatically cut in the closing laps. His eighth win of the year, which equalled Senna's 1988 record, was his closest of the season so far, for only 4.5s separated him from Senna's McLaren as he crossed the line. "I had big holes in my tyres and blisters all over them. The vibration at the end was so bad that I had to slow down on the straights to see where I was going for the next corner. The first person I'm going to see after this is a dentist!"

Patrese's unfortunate departure elevated an overjoyed Schumacher to third place in his first German Grand Prix — joy all round in his homeland! Another fine race by Brundle, too. He finished fourth, only 2.4s behind Schumacher, despite having had to nurse his tyres and cope with back pain so severe that his left leg eventually went numb and affected his braking.

So Hockenheim 1992 turned out to be a race that was full of incident and excitement. Berger out (again). Great drives by Senna, Patrese, Schumacher and Brundle and another magnificent performance by Mansell, who would be world champion if he won the next race in Hungary. A prospect to savour, even if Nigel understandably refused to talk about it!

In a final bid to keep the World Championship contest alive, Riccardo Patrese was several months ahead of his rivals when he spun off. The Italian eventually dropped out when Renault suffered its first engine failure for two seasons.

Could he get the job done in Hungary? With eight wins and a second from the 10 races so far, Nigel Mansell led the World Championship by a staggering 46 points. With 60 still up for grabs, Riccardo Patrese and Michael Schumacher had mathematical chances of beating him, but if he scored just four more points than Patrese he would be one of the earliest-ever champions in the 42-year history of the series. The BBC had its 50-minute TV special ready for transmission on Monday; the magazines and newspapers had prepared their features. But there's many a slip 'twixt cup and lip — and if there's one place where the cup can slip, it is Hungary.

For one major reason. When the superb 2.5-mile circuit was built in 1986, a magnificent site was chosen in a natural amphitheatre on the outskirts of the glorious city of Budapest. The facilities were the best that could be provided and the track layout was exciting, but it is almost impossible to overtake. In 1990, Thierry Boutsen had led all the way from pole position and in 1991 Ayrton Senna had done the same. So if Mansell didn't get into the first corner first, he looked unlikely to be celebrating his first World Championship at the end of the 1992 Hungarian GP, after 13 seasons in Formula One.

Well he didn't start the race where he ideally needed to be — in pole position. Nigel had problems in qualifying, a fire and an ECU failure on Friday and an off on Saturday. His team-mate and main rival Riccardo Patrese had none and was fastest in all four sessions to take his eighth pole position, with Mansell one place behind him on the staggered grid. The start was going to be something to see! Especially as Ayrton Senna, the reigning champion, was in third place, followed by the aggressive Michael Schumacher, Gerhard Berger and Martin Brundle. The two McLaren drivers had a new rear wing, traction control for the first time, and seemed to have benefited marginally from the revised fuel regulations. They were faster than the two Williams-Renaults in the Sunday morning warm-up and had made tyre choices that might (or might not) help them. Senna would be on Goodyear's soft D compound all round whilst Berger had opted for the harder C on the left and Ds on the right. More cautiously, Mansell and Patrese were to use Cs. Senna's

tyres would grip better, but would they go the distance? The Hungarian race is one of the longer ones; nearly two hours would be a severe test. In fact, it turned out to be a real cliff-hanger.

Patrese made a perfect start, straight into the lead with Mansell trying to get by on the inside — which was his mistake. It was dirty there and the grip was less. So both Senna and Berger passed him on the outside. Down to fourth he went, with three of the fastest men in the world in front of him. Bad news, for at the Hungaroring nose-to-tail snakes build up and writhe round, places remaining static for lap after lap as the drivers try to pressure the man ahead into making a mistake. That's what happened again, except that Riccardo was in a class of his own. With no one in front of him and his Williams-Renault quicker by far than Senna's McLaren-Honda, he set four fastest laps in the first six, as he rocketed away, and by lap 10 he had built a daunting lead of 14 seconds. It certainly didn't look like Nigel's day. On lap

The end of the road for Stefano Modena's Jordan. In the background lurks Karl Wendlinger's March. The marshals took their time shifting the beached Jordan, and for a while it looked as though the new FISA safety car would be despatched. After a performance that would have taken the gold medal in the Olympic Bureaucratic Bungling event, the organisers eventually left the said vehicle in the pit lane.

Fourth time lucky. Narrowly beaten by Prost (1986), Piquet (1987) and Senna (1991), the culmination of a quest lasting 13 seasons took some time to sink in for the new world champion.

TEAM ANALYSIS

McLAREN

A brilliant win overshadowed by Mansell's championship success. With revised undertray, new rear wing, traction control and benefiting from revised fuel regulations, McLaren reduces gap to Williams but still qualifies 'only' third (Senna) and fifth. Senna/Berger first and second in Sunday warm-up, however. Both make superb starts, passing Mansell to run second and third to Patrese at first corner. Ayrton resists non-stop attack from Mansell from lap eight, taking lead when Patrese spins, lap 39. Runs non-stop, nursing soft-compound tyres and builds lead of over 25s. Has precautionary tyre-stop (6.33s), lap 68, but still wins 35th GP by commanding 40s. A great drive, but he's no longer world champion. Non-stop Berger down to fourth behind Mansell, lap eight, tailed by Schumacher and Brundle. To third after Patrese retirement and finishes there on worn-out tyres — only 3.6s ahead of charging Häkkinen. Team's 14 points lift it back to second, ahead of Benetton, in constructors' championship.

TYRRELL

After problems with semi-active front suspension, de Cesaris and Grouillard qualify 19th and 22nd. Olivier charges up seven places to 15th, lap one, but then retires after colliding with Wendlinger (and also removing Modena). Andrea also makes super start — up to 13th on lap one. Is stuck behind obdurately unyielding Gugelmin for 30 laps but ultimately gets by and finishes eighth, two laps down.

WILLIAMS

Euphoria for Mansell. Misery for Patrese. Riccardo superb in practice; fastest in every session, taking his eighth pole position. Mansell starts second after problems on Friday and going off on Saturday (team's eighth front row monopoly of 1992). Patrese builds massive lead despite distraction of "strange engine noise from lap 20." Spins off, lap 39, but rejoins seventh and obliterates 15s gap to sixth-placed Häkkinen. Retires from seventh, lap 56, losing all hope of World Championship after suffering Renault's first engine failure for two years (it was the much-tested RS4's first race). Mansell passes Berger to take third, lap eight. Ceaselessly attacks Senna but cannot get by. Second after Patrese retirement until lap 62 tyre-stop with puncture. Rejoins sixth. To fifth as Schumacher spins out with detached rear wing. Then brilliantly catches and passes Häkkinen, Brundle and Berger to finish second for the six points which guarantee him his first World Championship in 13 seasons of Formula One — posting fastest (record) lap in the process (1m 18.308s, 113.349 mph). A superb first World Championship for Renault, too.

BRABHAM

Eric van de Poele defects to Fondmetal and is not replaced. Damon Hill stays in garage on Saturday morning, due to team's financial problems, but does well to qualify 25th for his second GP, despite crashing car and having to go out again in spare. With sore neck, drives sensible race to finish — a praiseworthy 11th, four laps down.

FOOTWORK

Alboreto improves from Friday 18th to superb Saturday seventh on grid (Footwork's best yet), gleefully ahead of both Ferraris. After spinning at first corner, drives usual mature race to finish seventh (for the fifth time!), two laps down, and maintain his 100 per cent 1992 finishing record. Suzuki starts 14th and retires, lap 14, after colliding with Bertrand Gachot.

LOTUS

Another bitter/sweet race after Johnny Herbert qualifies 13th and Mika Häkkinen 16th. Johnny out at first corner after being hit by spinning Comas. Mika quite outstanding. Up eight places to eighth by lap nine. In points (sixth, lap 21), after passing Brundle. Finishes superb fourth, only 3.6s behind Berger after setting sixth fastest lap of race.

FONDMETAL

Good practice. Terrible race. Eric van de Poele joins team from Brabham, in place of disgruntled Andrea Chiesa. Pre-qualifies second and qualifies happy 18th for only his third GP in 27 tries. Tarquini pre-qualifies fastest and qualifies well in 12th. Sadly, race an immediate disaster for both drivers. Gabriele out after trying to avoid collision between Ligiers at first corner. Eric spins out, lap three, with tyre grip diminished by dirt picked up in Ligier débâcle.

MARCH

Karl Wendlinger qualifies 23rd and progresses to 16th, lap eight, before colliding with the inevitable Olivier Grouillard, lap 14, and retiring. In his last 1992 GP (no more money) Paul Belmondo out-qualifies Wendlinger to start 17th as the highest Ilmor-engined driver. Then drives his best race yet, setting the 10th fastest lap, to come home an excellent ninth (three laps down) — thus finishing every race he started.

BENETTON

Using the Ford Series VI V8 (better torque), Michael Schumacher brilliantly splits the McLarens on the grid to start an excellent fourth, with Brundle sixth. Magnificent race by both drivers. Schumacher/Brundle run line astern with Berger until Martin passed by Häkkinen on lap 21. Brundle takes Schumacher and Häkkinen, laps 32/33 to run sixth, then fifth until lap 43. Having lost vital sixth gear is passed by Schumacher, but back up to fourth when Michael spins out after losing rear wing (hit by Martin under braking). Brundle runs third, laps 64/66, but finishes disappointed and frustrated fifth after being caught and passed by Mansell and inspired non-stop Häkkinen. After McLaren's first and third in race, Schumacher drops down to fourth and team down to third in their respective championships.

DALLARA

Team Scuderia Italia announces split with Dallara at end of season and formation of exciting partnership with Lola for 1993, using Ferrari engines. To emphasise need for change, Martini qualifies 26th and JJ Lehto fails to do so. Pier-Luigi obstructs lapping Mansell and receives 10s stop/go penalty. Retires lap 40 when aggrieved 14th and last (gearbox).

MINARDI

Awful meeting for team, with both Zanardi and Morbidelli failing to qualify.

LIGIER

With Williams using the Renault RS4 engine for its first race, Ligier "promoted" to the RS3C. Making the most of it Thierry Boutsen and Erik Comas qualify well (eighth and 11th), only to collide and retire at first corner, taking Tarquini and Herbert with them.

FERRARI

For its 500th F1 World Championship race (very much a record) the planet's favourite team hopes for little — and achieves it. "This circuit is bad for the F92A," says designer Harvey Postlethwaite — and he is right. In presence of Ferrari boss Luca di Montezemolo, Alesi and Capelli qualify dispirited ninth and 10th (Ivan still suffering from the after-effects of a massive testing accident at Imola). Alesi an encouraging fourth in Sunday warm-up, but only advances to eighth on lap one. Retires from seventh, lap 15, after spinning and breaking half-shaft. Capelli suffers from understeer and goes off, lap 28.

Rejoins and continues to finish sixth (one lap down) for only his third full race of the year.

VENTURI-LARROUSSE

1991 lap record holder Bertrand Gachot (then in a Jordan-Ford) avoids pre-qualification thanks to there only being one Brabham. Katayama pre-qualifies third for first Hungaroring drive and qualifies well (20th). Bert starts 15th and rockets up to 10th at first corner but tangles with Suzuki and retires, lap 14, after losing part of his rear wing. Katayama damages front wing in startline collision with de Cesaris but progresses to 12th, lap 15, before retiring, lap 35, when engine blows.

JORDAN

In car which is more competitive at Hungaroring, Gugelmin and Modena qualify 21st and 24th. Both start well — Mauricio up seven places to 14th on lap one and Stefano up eight to 16th. Modena soon out thanks to a vintage Grouillard manoeuvre which removes both Stefano and Wendlinger on lap 14. Gugelmin resists irate de Cesaris until lap 43 but finishes 10th, four laps down, as a result of having to stop for work on the fuel system — which makes no difference.

ANDREA MODA

This time the chaotic team goes too far. Moreno uses both cars to pre-qualify as a result of which a furious Perry McCarthy is only able to do one lap and naturally fails again. Moreno does not qualify and team is reprimanded by FISA for not trying hard enough. "Get it right in Belgium or you'll be suspended in Italy." So there.

Overtaking is notoriously difficult at the Hungaroring, but that didn't discourage Brundle and Häkkinen, who had a splendid scrap for fourth place. The Finn's last lap spin proved to be a good tactic, as it forced Brundle off the road and helped the recovering Lotus driver to take three points.

Wishful thinking: Damon Hill did a fine job to finish 11th in his second GP start for Brabham. Catching him, fast, in this shot is Patrese's Williams FW14, the very car that Damon did so much to develop in his role as Williams-Renault's official test driver.

eight, he took Gerhard Berger at the sole passing point, the entry to turn one, to move up to third and close on Senna — but getting past Ayrton was going to be something else.

Cheesed off with having to make do with Brabham's meagre budget, Eric van de Poele defected to Fondmetal. The Belgian qualified respectably, but didn't spend long adapting to the team's reliability record. He spun off on lap two.

Just 2.3s covered second to sixth places: Senna, Mansell, Berger, Schumacher and Brundle, with Martin climbing all over the back of Michael's Benetton and Mansell repeatedly attacking the imperturbable Senna. There were 10 retirements by lap 14, most of them caused by drivers sliding off the resurfaced track and stalling their engines, and on lap 15 there was excitement when the yellow flags and 'SC' boards appeared to signify that the safety car was going out for the first time in a Grand Prix. At least it appeared so, because Stefano Modena's Jordan was stationary on the track minus a rear wheel but, with its rapid removal by the marshals, the Ford Escort Cosworth never left the pit lane. The warring drivers never slowed and the whole episode was a confusing non-event.

Lap 20: no change. Patrese now led by 17s with a mere 2.8s covering the next six. Six, because the enormously impressive Mika Häkkinen, who had started 16th in his Lotus 107, had gained nine places to catch Martin Brundle and was looking for a way past the Benetton. Maybe something would happen soon, because now the leaders were lapping the tail-enders and that's the time when baulking can alter things. Too right! Ahead of the rapidly approaching leaders Damon Hill, Pier-Luigi Martini and Paul Belmondo were battling for 13th place. Patrese got by and so did Senna, but Mansell was held up. Nigel's shaking fist on the TV screens may well have been the reason for the stewards bringing Pier-Luigi in for a 10s stop/go penalty, but by then the Williams was long gone and back on the tail of Senna's McLaren. In the meantime, the inspired Häkkinen took Brundle and sixth place.

Lap 30: still no change. Exciting action but everyone knew it could be better still if someone could break the log jam. On lap 31, someone did. Gerhard Berger slipped past Mansell as Nigel slid wide and down to fourth again. After all that effort. And now the determined Brundle was on a charge. Up to fifth, past Häkkinen and Schumacher — right behind Mansell. Nigel had to finish four points ahead of Patrese to clinch the championship in Hungary and now he was seven points behind him. Not good. Time to attack again! Past Berger for the second

Mansell puts the majestic Senna under pressure. Ayrton ignored the blaze of colour in his rear-view mirror and eventually scored a magnificent victory. For the following Mansell, second place was sufficient reward, guaranteeing him, as it did, the world title.

time to regain third, with Senna now 5.5s up the road. But on lap 38 there was salvation for Nigel and disaster for Riccardo. Patrese fell off!

With a lead of some 30s and the race in the bag, Riccardo slid wide and straddled the kerb. ''There was dirt on the circuit and there was nothing I could do.'' But he'd kept his engine running and regained the track, down to seventh and out of the points. So now Senna led Mansell by 1.5s. Nigel was on course for six points to win the championship if he stayed where he was. But, with Senna on those 'soft Goodyears' and 39 laps still to go, would he be able to stop Mansell getting by to win the title with a ninth victory of the season? There was plenty more to hold the attention, too, as Patrese set about getting back into the points, ideally to fourth place to stop Mansell becoming number one in '93. Closer and closer to Häkkinen's sixth-placed Lotus he got and, with a new lap record on lap 51, he was almost there. Senna led Mansell by six seconds, Nigel was seven ahead of Berger; with no sixth gear, Brundle was down to fifth between

Schumacher and Häkkinen, and Riccardo was bearing down on them. On lap 56 he was out. ''The engine started to go off after about 20 laps and I had a feeling I wasn't going to finish the race.'' Poor Riccardo! It was bitter luck after such a fine drive. It was the first time that the much-tested Renault RS4 V10 had been raced and the company's first failure in the past two years of Formula One.

But Nigel's RS4 ran faultlessly, and all he had to do now was finish in the first three places. With a 12s lead over Berger that should be no problem. Senna could have the race. Second would do nicely! But on lap 62, to groans of dismay, Mansell came into the pits. Puncture! Just 8.7s later he raced out on a new set of Goodyear's soft Ds, but he was down to sixth. Sixth earns one point, and he needed four. That meant third place and he'd got to catch, and pass, Häkkinen, Brundle and Schumacher to get it — in 15 laps. No way, surely? But with never-say-die Mansell you never know. In 1989 he'd won in Hungary for Ferrari from 12th on the grid. If anyone could do it, Nigel could. On lap

NIGEL MANSELL OBE — WORLD CHAMPION
A personal tribute

There are no shades of opinion about Nigel Mansell. People either worship him or they loathe him. To his adoring fans in Britain he is ''Our Nige''. To his fanatical admirers in Italy he is ''Il Leone'' and to countless other aficionados of Formula One all over the world he is what a racing driver ought to be: a gutsy charger and a showman. Others dismiss him as a non-stop whinger who was lucky to be able to exploit a superior car in 1992. Me? I like and admire him immensely, and to the knockers I say ''rubbish!'' No matter how good the car, you've got to have a very special talent to make it win Grands Prix, let alone become world champion in it.

Mansell's self-appointed job in life is to race cars. By 1992 he had been doing so for 30 years, during which time he had devoted himself to it with single-minded determination. He had broken his neck, broken his back twice, sold his house to raise the money to carry on in Formula Three and been financially supported by his greatest helper in life — his charming wife Rosanne. If that isn't dedication, I don't know what is. The result, thanks to his driving brilliance, his natural aggression and his refusal to give up, has been some of the most dramatic and memorable Grand Prix drives of the last 13 years.

Like his 1980 debut in Austria, when he drove his Lotus sitting in a pool of flesh-burning petrol. His crash in the wet at Monaco, leading his first GP. His collapse, pushing his broken Lotus to finish in the searing heat of Dallas. His epic defeats of Williams-Honda team-mate Nelson Piquet at the Brands Hatch and Silverstone Grands Prix of 1986 and '87. His first failure to win the championship, when his tyre blew at Adelaide in 1986, and his second when he crashed in Japan the following year. His sensational second place, in an underpowered Williams-Judd, in the sodden 1988 British Grand Prix. His totally unexpected victory in Brazil in his first race for Ferrari, and his spellbinding pass of Ayrton

Senna to win the 1989 Hungarian race. The black flag for reversing in the pit lane and his subsequent collision with Senna in Portugal '89, and his loss of the 1991 Portuguese race when his Williams wheel went rollabout. His last lap retirement in the lead in Canada, 1991. His superb recovery to finish second in Monaco '92. His record 28th win for a British driver at Silverstone '92 and his championship-clinching second place in Hungary. Those are just some of many emotional Mansell memories.

My reception from Nigel (even when I forgot to turn the microphone on in Brazil for the longest and hottest interview I've ever done!) has never been anything other than friendly, cheerful and helpful. His well-earned success fills me with pleasure and I salute Nigel Mansell — world champion.

Sadly, however, his services have been lost to F1, in the wake of his decision not to defend his title in 1993. Nigel is transferring his racing life, as he has his home, to America. He does so feeling humiliated and frustrated by his failure to continue with the Williams team he has served so well, and which has supported him nobly.

Whatever the rights and wrongs of a complicated situation, it is greatly regretted that Britain has lost its first F1 champion since '76 so soon. We must be content with memories of his stirring achievements and wish him success in his new life. Grand Prix racing and its countless fans will truly miss him.

Murray Walker

Mr and Mrs W Champion: it was as much a triumph for Rosanne Mansell as it was for Nigel. Anyone who agrees to their husband mortgaging the house in exchange for a few F3 drives deserves a break every now and then . . .

63, on his new tyres, he set the fastest lap of the race (1m 18.308s, 113.349 mph). On lap 64 he was up to fifth when Schumacher disappeared as his rear wing flew off. One down. Two to go! And now Berger unwittingly came to Nigel's assistance. Gerhard's softer-compound tyres were shot and he was struggling. Right behind him, Brundle and Häkkinen were jockeying to pass — but they were being held up. Which was all that Nigel needed. On lap 66 he passed Mika and on lap 67 he took Brundle. Third place. Four points. World champion in 10 laps if nothing adverse happened.

On lap 69, Nigel passed Berger for the third time. Six points now. It was in the bag. Ayrton Senna won the 1992 Hungarian Grand Prix in brilliant style because, although he made a safety stop for new tyres (lap 68, a very rapid 6.3s), he was too far ahead to be caught — even if a contented Mansell had been prepared to try. Sadly, though, he never got the credit he deserved because, unsurprisingly, it was Mansell's magnificent charge that had everybody's attention. Nigel lost the race by 40s but no worries, as they say in Australia, he'd finally won the World Championship that had

eluded him for so long. Berger finished third but it was the brilliant Häkkinen who took fourth place when he spun on the last lap, took Brundle off and then saucily passed the Benetton as they recovered!

What a race and what a result! Britain had its first world champion since James Hunt in 1976 and James was there for the BBC, as usual, to honour his successor. Renault had very deservedly won its first World Championship too. There was hardly a dry eye in the house! ''I've been second in the championship twice to Ayrton and once to Alain,'' said Nigel (forgetting that he'd been runner-up to Senna and Nelson Piquet once apiece). ''Sometimes you think you're never going to crack it. It was a hectic race and I have to thank Gerhard for holding up about four cars for me. I wondered how the hell I was going to get through them all, but I did it. I have to admit though that, today, I was only interested in the World Championship!'' At last he'd done it. Nigel Mansell OBE was the world champion of 1992 with five races still to go and, typically Nigel, he'd done it with a charging drive in the face of adversity!

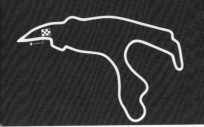

BELGIUM

August 30 1992 Circuit: Spa-Francorchamps

The sublime genius of Ayrton Senna enabled him to continue on slicks in the treacherous conditions. It was a bold gamble by the Brazilian, but ultimately his tactics failed.

It's an exciting experience when you see someone win his first Grand Prix. Especially when that someone has shown, since his first Formula One drive, that he possesses extraordinary talent and has the potential, one day, to be world champion. Gilles Villeneuve was such a man and no one doubted, when he first drove a McLaren at the 1977 British Grand Prix, that he would go on to achieve greatness. Other charismatic naturals (there haven't been many) who spring to mind are Jim Clark, Juan-Manuel Fangio, Ayrton Senna, Stirling Moss, Ronnie Peterson, Alain Prost and Jackie Stewart. And now there's Michael Schumacher, a racing phenomenon if ever there was one.

On his way to the top Michael was champion of everything in Germany — karting, Formula Ford and Formula Three. Mercedes-Benz made him a member of its all-conquering sports car squad and, in 1991, he made his Formula One debut at Spa, driving for Jordan. He qualified seventh, showing maturity way beyond his 22 years. To say that he electrified the hard-bitten and cynical Grand Prix world is a masterpiece of understatement. Tom Walkinshaw wasted no time in recruiting him (amid acrimony!) for

Benetton, and the rest is history. By Spa 1992 he had finished second twice, third three times and earned 37 World Championship points . . . from only 17 races. His first Grand Prix win was only a matter of time. In fact it was to be in Belgium, on the anniversary of his first appearance, after a drive of which any of the past greats would have been proud.

I've said it before and I'll say it again. Spa is the *best* and most demanding Grand Prix circuit in the world. At 4.3 miles long, on public roads

Benetton's Flavio Briatore and Michael Schumacher celebrate the first win of their F1 association with one of the world's more expensive shower gels.

specially closed for the occasion, it winds its picturesque way through pine-clad hills amidst the glorious Ardennes countryside. With gradients galore and every kind of corner, notably the daunting 160 mph plunge down to and through Eau Rouge, it is the ultimate test for a Grand Prix driver. Which is undoubtedly why Ayrton Senna had won there for the last four years.

He didn't look like winning this year though. If ever a circuit suited the Williams-Renault, it was Spa. New world champion Nigel Mansell was hell-bent on winning his ninth 1992 Grand Prix there, to beat the record of eight victories in one season, presently the joint property of himself and Senna. By Sunday lunchtime he looked more than capable of doing so. Fastest in all but one of the five practice sessions, he pulverised the opposition to take his 27th pole position, a demoralising 2.2s faster than the next man — Senna. Schumacher, making his first repeat appearance at a Grand Prix circuit, was third quickest ahead of Patrese, Alesi and Gerhard Berger, who'd had a gigantic crash approaching Eau Rouge in Saturday morning's wet session.

The weather at Spa on Sunday was variable, as usual. One of the circuit's characteristics is that it can be dry one minute, wet the next and drying out again immediately after. Because of that the correct tyre choice can be, and often is, absolutely critical. Never more so than this year. Only 10 minutes before the start the roads were dry, but there was drizzle as the 26 contestants lined up on the curving grid — all on slick-treaded, dry weather Goodyears. With a masterly getaway, Ayrton Senna swept into the lead ahead of Mansell and, miraculously, everybody got round the tight La Source hairpin which immediately follows the start. Well, all bar one. Gerhard Berger's clutch failed on the line and a potential winner was immediately out. First Saturday's accident and now this. Gerhard wouldn't forget Belgium '92 in a hurry.

On lap two the rain began and everybody was automatically on the wrong tyres. In what instantly became a race of tactics, the question was who would change — and when? Mansell and Patrese both passed Senna and, at the end of lap three, Nigel and fifth-placed Alesi pulled out of the leading seven-car snake and into the pits for rain tyres. By lap seven Patrese, Schumacher, Brundle and the inspired Mika Häkkinen, who'd been running sixth, were on wet-weather rubber too. But Senna wasn't. "Gambling on staying out on slicks was my only chance. The others stopped early and I felt, if the drizzle stopped, I would have been in good shape." He would have been, indeed, but it didn't. And then, on lap eight, another possible winner retired when Jean Alesi and Nigel Mansell, contesting second place at La Source, collided and left the Ferrari with a puncture. "His fault," said Jean. "No, his," countered Nigel!

The fact that Senna managed to stay in the lead with a film of water between his smooth tyres and the tarmac is a testimony to his genius. But, lap by lap, the gap shrank and he had to yield to Mansell, Patrese, Schumacher, Brundle, Häkkinen and Capelli. On lap 14 he came in from seventh, changed to rain tyres, and, after a 6.83s stop, emerged from the pit lane down in 13th place. The gamble had failed. But ahead of him the race was a cracker. Mansell led, gradually increasing the gap. By lap 16 he was some four seconds ahead of Patrese, but

the Italian was having to fight every inch of the way. Schumacher was snapping at his gearbox and Brundle was harrying his team-mate with the three of them easing away from Häkkinen's Lotus, the young Finn driving superbly.

That record ninth win looked a foregone conclusion for Nigel as he exploited a superb car and his 13 years of Grand Prix experience. On lap 20 he led by eight seconds. On lap 30 by nine. No worries! Patrese drew away from the warring Benettons, Häkkinen stayed ahead of, first, Capelli and, latterly, Johnny Herbert (both Lotuses in the top six!) after Ivan's Ferrari engine called it a day. Senna grimly set about catching up with all of them. On lap 30 Ayrton was eighth behind JJ Lehto, whose Dallara was handling well for once, when a brief incident transformed the race. Michael Schumacher ran wide at Stavelot and Martin Brundle shot past him into third place.

The rain had stopped and, although it looked likely to begin again at any moment, a dry line was starting to emerge. Ligier's Spa expert Thierry Boutsen had decided it was time to change back to slicks but had done so a bit too early, spinning out of the race on lap 28. But, two laps later, as Schumacher scrambled back

Goodbye Moda team: Brabham's absenteeism dispensed with the need to pre-qualify, allowing Perry McCarthy to attempt GP qualification for the first time. The Andrea Moda team's efforts remained pitiful, however, and in the wake of this race the team was turfed out of F1 for good.

TEAM ANALYSIS

McLAREN

Five-times winner Senna, forecasting a 1993 sabbatical if he cannot drive for Williams, qualifies second after stopping to help Erik Comas in crashed Ligier. Leads at start but passed by Mansell and Patrese. Back to first as both Williams drivers tyre-stop. Brilliantly leads in wet on slicks until lap 11 but slides to seventh. Stops for rain tyres, too late, lap 14. Down to 13th. As course dries but finishes only fifth. Gerhard Berger announces '93 move to Ferrari and qualifies troubled sixth after assorted problems. Has major 160 mph crash in wet at Eau Rouge on Saturday but is, miraculously, unhurt. Transmission locks solid at start, putting Gerhard out immediately. Team's worst Belgian GP for years.

TYRRELL

With handling problems, de Cesaris and Grouillard qualify 13th and 22nd. Olivier furiously condemned by Alboreto for blocking during Sunday warm-up (so what's new?). Collides with Wendlinger, lap two, and retires. Andrea up to seventh by lap five but drops to 13th after tyre stop. Is "stuck behind Senna" (!) for 13 laps and does well to finish eighth (one lap down) after lap 33 spin.

WILLIAMS

Nigel Mansell, chasing record ninth '92 win, starts in 27th pole position for record 177th GP start by a British driver. Riccardo Patrese (going to Benetton in '93) qualifies fourth after spinning on Friday. Mansell/Patrese run at front, laps 11-32, after early changes to rain tyres (Nigel lucky to survive lap eight collision with Alesi when challenging for second). Both outsmarted by astute Michael Schumacher on timing for change to slicks as track dries, and finish second and third to the German, neither able to mount adequate challenge due to power loss (broken exhaust manifolds). But team consoled by 10 points, which clinch its fifth, and Renault's first, constructors' championship — achievements well deserved by superb partnership.

BRABHAM

As result of massive financial problem, team fails to appear in Belgium.

FOOTWORK

Mugen introduces new higher-revving version of V10. On dry Friday Alboreto has set-up problems and Suzuki uses sequential gearbox for first time. Result is 14th and 25th on grid. After lap two stop for rain tyres, Michele up to eighth, lap 15, but has first '92 retirement when gear selection fails, lap 20. Suzuki drives well to finish ninth, one lap down, only 1.2s behind Andrea de Cesaris after two tyre stops and lap five spin.

LOTUS

After team announces re-signing of Johnny Herbert for 1993, both he and Häkkinen qualify impressively — Mika eighth and Johnny 10th. Great race drives by both men. After changing to rain tyres, Mika runs fifth, pressing the two Benettons, laps 13-42, but demoted to sixth at finish by Senna in spite of setting fourth fastest lap of race. Johnny has engine change after Sunday warm-up fire. After switching to rain tyres, lap eight, recovers from 11th to sixth, laps 26-30. Sadly has to retire from seventh, after being passed by Senna, when engine stops, lap 43 (classified 13th). But team well pleased after fourth points-finish in last five races.

FONDMETAL

No Brabhams, so no need to pre-qualify, but team efficiency marred by cash crisis. No testing, no parts and no practice on wet Saturday. But both drivers qualify well — Tarquini 11th and van de Poele highest-ever 15th for home race. Anxious to finish, Tarquini carefully holds strong 10th, lap 21, but frustratedly retires, lap 25 (engine). Van de Poele spins twice and has two tyre stops but delighted to finish 10th in fourth GP (one lap down), despite lack of wet mileage.

MARCH

Money-strapped team, rumoured to be selling, replaces Paul Belmondo with Italian Formula 3000 ace Emanuele Naspetti who does very well to qualify 21st for his first GP — only three places behind Karl Wendlinger. Neither driver goes out during wet Saturday but, despite this, both race very well (Naspetti without a clutch for most of race) in wet/rain GP to finish 11th (Wendlinger) and 12th — both only one lap down.

BENETTON

Sensational success! In only his 18th GP, following 1991 debut with Jordan at Spa, the brilliant Michael Schumacher qualifies third and then races third behind Mansell and Patrese, laps 13-29, after changes to rain tyres. Running wide at Stavelot he is passed by team-mate Martin Brundle, lap 30, but astutely spots need to change back to slicks. Immediately does so, takes lead on lap 34 and retains it to win his first Grand Prix, also setting fastest lap (1m 53.791s, 137.097 mph). This is first full-distance GP win by German driver since 1961 and, at 23, Michael is third youngest GP winner (behind Bruce McLaren and Jacky Ickx). Martin Brundle also outstanding. After qualifying badly (ninth) and wrenching wrist when clobbered by Modena on Saturday, is fourth by lap 13, after tyre stops. Passes Schumacher to third but loses chance of victory when his success distracts him from intention to stop for slicks. After messy lap 31 change, finishes fourth, his disappointment compounded by knowledge that he will be replaced by Patrese in 1993. It's a ruthless world in Formula One. Schumacher back to third in drivers' championship, only one point behind Patrese. Team back to second in constructors' contest, ahead of McLaren, after its first win with new Ford Series VII engine. Benetton only team to have scored points in every '92 GP so far.

DALLARA

With continued nervous handling, Lehto and Martini qualify 16th and 19th. Racing rebuilt car after massive

Christian Fittipaldi returned after missing three races with rib and neck injuries. The Brazilian, destined to stay with Minardi in 1993, felt his way back in gingerly, and failed to qualify.

Saturday off in wet at Eau Rouge, Pier-Luigi spins on lap one, stalls engine and retires. JJ in the points (sixth) laps 34-40, after two perfectly timed tyre stops, but caught and passed by Senna and Herbert. Nevertheless finishes fine full-distance seventh after Herbert's retirement and records sixth fastest lap.

MINARDI

Christian Fittipaldi returns, after missing four races due to French GP practice injury, but fails to qualify (27th). Morbidelli does so (16th), but is detuned by heavy Saturday crash. Switches to spare after race car fails on parade lap and finishes 16th (two laps down).

LIGIER

Erik Comas has major crash on Friday but is, amazingly, unhurt. Doctors advise him not to drive for rest of weekend, however. Boutsen starts excellent seventh in car which is "best it's ever been." After early stop for rain tyres, up to seventh, laps 15-22. Using local knowledge, decides to switch to slicks early, lap 26. Too early. Hits barrier, lap 27, and is out, mercifully unscathed.

FERRARI

Alesi uses new transverse-gearbox version of F92A (the F92AT) to qualify well (fifth). Stops for rain tyres, lap three, and is up to second, lap eight, when he collides with Mansell, punctures and retires (both blame each other, but then drivers always do!). Capelli qualifies old car 12th, complaining of poor handling. Progresses to, and holds, sixth, laps 14-25, but retires, lap 26, when engine

expires. Another black day for Maranello.

VENTURI-LARROUSSE

With non-appearance of Brabhams, no need to pre-qualify. Both Gachot and Katayama have handling problems on Friday and Ukyo is new to circuit. So poor grid positions — 20th (Bertrand) and 26th. Gachot spins twice at La Source but is 11th, laps 32-39. Stops when breakage causes another spin, lap 40 (classified 18th, four laps down). Katayama tyre-stops, laps five and 32, and finishes 17th (two laps down).

JORDAN

Some improvement, with both cars finishing for first time in '92. Modena blots copybook by spinning into Martin Brundle on Saturday, but qualifies 17th — four places ahead of Gugelmin. Mauricio, delayed by Berger's broken McLaren at start, finishes 14th (two laps down), one place ahead of Modena — who completes race for first time in '92. The problem remains with Yamaha's lack of Formula One experience, not the Jordan chassis. Hopefully John Judd's ministrations will put that right.

ANDREA MODA

No pre-qualifying, so Moreno and McCarthy both able to practise for first time. Neither qualifies on dry Friday (28th and 29th) and neither goes out on wet Saturday. Team boss Andrea Sassetti arrested on Saturday for allegedly forging documents in order to placate creditors. Subsequent FISA penalties against team would surprise no one.

107

on to the track behind Brundle, Michael revealed: ''I could see that his tyres were blistered so I knew that was the right moment to change to slicks. It was perfect.'' Indeed it was. In came Michael whilst Brundle, distracted by passing Schumacher, stayed out a lap longer than he had intended. That distraction probably cost him his first Grand Prix victory.

With 13 laps to go, Mansell was first, Patrese second, and Brundle third, all of them on rain tyres. Schumacher was fourth, on slicks, Häkkinen fifth, Lehto an excellent sixth and Herbert seventh with Senna, now slick-shod, closing fast. Very interesting. Schumacher could win! Little did he know it, but he was then helped by confusion in the Williams pit. Mansell had radioed to come in for slicks but

was told to stay out as Patrese was already on his way in. Riccardo changed on lap 32 and Nigel next time round. It was too late. With the fastest lap so far, Schumacher took the lead as Brundle, after a mildly bodged tyre stop, dropped to fourth behind Mansell and Patrese.

But everyone knew what a charger Nigel is. With 10 laps to go and with *his* skill and determination, surely he could demolish the 5.6s gap between himself and Schumacher and go on to victory? Sure enough, he closed on the Benetton. With the fastest lap so far the gap was down to 4.7s. But Schumacher went quicker! Lap 37 was a new lap record for the young German, 0.3s faster than Alain Prost's 1990 Ferrari time — with the track still damp in places. ''I was looking forward to the last seven

Schumacher and Brundle run in team formation. It was a weekend of differing fortunes for the two. Shortly after the German's first F1 win, his British partner was informed that his place in the team was being taken by Riccardo Patrese for 1993.

Spa offers majestic views across the Ardennes. In the distance, the rescue crews are attending to Erik Comas. The Frenchman's participation in the meeting ended with a high-speed accident on Friday morning, though he suffered nothing worse than concussion and a stiff neck.

laps,'' said Mansell. So were we! But our expectations were dashed. ''I had an exhaust problem and lost something like 1,400 revs down the straight. I was still going flat out yet I lost about five seconds a lap.'' And then, on lap 39, Schumacher smashed his own short-lived lap record — 1m 53.791s (137.097 mph) — to extend his lead and clinch a superb first Grand Prix win in only his 18th race. ''I had tears in my eyes at Hockenheim, but I really cried today! I'm happy because this was a good win, one which was the result of my efforts and those of the team. We didn't win because of someone else's problems or an accident. I really feel we deserved it, particularly under such difficult circumstances.''

And so say all of us! Especially Nigel Mansell, who now had to wait for that ninth win. ''I must congratulate Michael and the Benetton team. I think their win is fantastic for

New kid on the block: F3000 graduate Emanuele Naspetti acquitted himself well at March, which gratefully accepted the Italian's sponsorship input.

Formula One." Nigel was right. Michael's brilliant tactical victory was the first by a new GP winner since Thierry Boutsen's at Montreal in 1989. It was the first full-distance win by a German driver since Taffy von Trips at Monza in 1961 (Jochen Mass won the 1975 Spanish GP, but the race had been stopped after a serious accident involving spectators).

Mansell may not have won that coveted ninth victory, but the 10 points that he and third-placed Riccardo Patrese earned were enough to clinch the constructors' championship for Williams and Renault. It was Williams's fifth success but Renault's first in the French company's 200 Grands Prix. "Renault has realised a 15-year dream," said managing director Christian Contzen. "Now we are working for the end of the season and preparing for the next!" A heartbreaking day for Martin Brundle, whose moment of indecision let the race slip through his fingers, and a day of failure for Ayrton Senna, who'd declared that he wouldn't be driving in 1993 unless he could join Alain Prost in the Williams team. But it was another day of joy for Mika Häkkinen, who took a fine sixth place only 0.7s behind Senna.

Most of all, though, a great day for Germany, Great Britain and France. Very international!

Still waiting. World champion elect Nigel Mansell appeared to have a record-breaking ninth win of the season within reach for much of the race. In Belgium, he started his 177th World Championship event, overtaking the late Graham Hill as Britain's most enduring F1 driver.

Eric van de Poele leads Mauricio Gugelmin on his way to 10th place, a reasonable result for the Fondmetal team which, like several of its adversaries, was suffering a cash crisis. The following Jordan came in 14th, the Yamaha's lack of power enabling the Jordans to take the daunting Eau Rouge complex flat out.

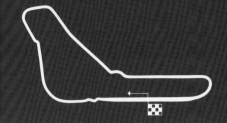

Waved through by the obliging Mansell, Riccardo Patrese looked set for victory on home soil, until waylaid by a hydraulic malfunction. Patrese slipped to fifth while Mansell retired, the world champion also stymied by hopeless hydraulics.

"Due to circumstances beyond my control, I have decided to retire from Formula One at the end of the season. I have made this decision with some regret, but not without a great deal of thought." Nigel Mansell — 11.30am, Monza, September 13 1992.

The Italian Grand Prix is always an exciting and tense occasion, for it is held on the most historic and charismatic circuit of them all and it comes at a time when contract negotiations are at their height. Since 1923 its fabled, fanatical *tifosi* have witnessed legendary drivers such as Nuvolari, Varzi, Caracciola, Rosemeyer, Fangio, Ascari, Moss, Clark, Stewart, Prost and Senna racing for supremacy on its hallowed tarmac, and the fact that such men have competed there generates a very special buzz. But the excitement was greater than ever at Monza '92. It centred upon highly charged speculation concerning the future of the new world champion, Nigel Mansell.

With by far the best car, Williams was in the unique situation of having the world's top three drivers, Alain Prost, Ayrton Senna and Mansell, all jostling to sign for them in 1993. Prost, strongly supported by Renault, was believed to have signed a contract and Senna had made an amazing offer to drive for nothing. But, despite months of negotiation, Mansell and Williams had been unable to agree on pay and conditions. Then, only four hours before the

For most of this lot, the Italian GP ended on lap 13, with the near-simultaneous disappearance of both Ferraris.

race, after he had lapped a full two seconds faster than anyone else in the final half-hour of practice, Mansell made a long and emotional retirement statement to the assembled media.

Did he mean it? Hadn't he done the same thing in 1990? Was it just a negotiation ploy? Would he now drive in the American Indycar series? Who could tell? In a stunned atmosphere, all we knew was that 'Il Leone' appeared rapidly to be approaching the end of his outstanding Grand Prix career. Time would tell, but it would be sad indeed if Formula One's most exciting driver, and Britain's first world champion since 1976, was not around to try and retain his hard won title in 1993.

Almost as an afterthought, we realised that there was a race to be run! As so often in 1992, Mansell had dominated the two days of practice and qualifying, being fastest in every session to secure the 28th pole position of his F1 career. For only the fourth time this season Ayrton Senna was on the front row of the grid, closer than usual to Mansell in terms of time (0.6s adrift). To the delight of the *tifosi*, Jean Alesi was third in a much-revised Ferrari, using a special qualifying engine. Riccardo Patrese, desperately anxious to win his first Grand Prix of the year on his home track before leaving Williams for Benetton in 1993, was fourth ahead of Berger (McLaren), Schumacher (Benetton), Capelli (Ferrari), Boutsen (Ligier) and Brundle (Benetton). Mansell had won in 1991. He clearly had a point to make and, with his record ninth win of the season yet to be achieved, was expected to put the hammer down, clear off and add to his already considerable reputation in Italy on Monza's 70th anniversary.

He certainly cleared off. Straight into the lead ahead of Senna, who was momentarily passed by Alesi on the approach to the first chicane, just after the start. Berger was in trouble though. A complete electrical failure on the grid had obliged him to vacate his race car, jump into the spare which had been set up for Senna, wait for the pedal positions and seat to be changed and then start, last of all, from the pit lane. At the end of lap one he was 21st, at the commencement of a spellbinding drive.

Schumacher was up against it too. After a

bad start he hit Thierry Boutsen's Ligier and had to stop for a new nosecone. For four laps he ran last, but by lap 10, scything his way through the field, he was 16th, with Berger three places ahead of him. At the front Mansell, after a crushing series of fastest laps, was leading Senna by eight seconds — a steady increase of nearly a second a lap. He looked invincible already. Patrese had passed Alesi to take third and was catching Senna, the two Ferraris were fourth and fifth, thanks to a fine drive by Capelli, and Martin Brundle had gained three places to lie sixth. In fact, this was Martin's day. On lap 13 he was fourth, as the *tifosi* despondently started to leave. Both Ferraris were out. The bitterly disappointed, hard-charging Alesi had stuttered into the pits with a broken fuel pump as Capelli, almost simultaneously, spun off when "something locked up at the back." Just what the unfortunate Ivan needed in his last drive for Maranello in Italy.

A lap later Patrese took second from Senna with a daring outbraking manoeuvre at the Rettifilio chicane ("I thought he was going straight into the sand trap!" said Ayrton). Brundle was making no impression on the McLaren ahead, Boutsen was an excellent fifth in his Ligier, Johnny Herbert was a splendid sixth in his Lotus, Berger was up to ninth and Schumacher was right behind him. But not for long. Gerhard is always hard on tyres and today he was especially so, as he passed people off-line. Into the pits then, for a new set of Goodyear's Bs on lap 15, something you can ill afford at Monza where the race time is so short. After a 6.91s stop he rejoined in 12th place, behind the battling Michele Alboreto and Andrea de Cesaris. It would take him 18 laps to get by them both and now Schumacher was ahead of him, up to ninth.

By lap 19 the brilliant German was in the points — sixth, behind Boutsen (Johnny Herbert's Ford V8 had called it a day) — but no sooner had we absorbed that than Patrese was in the lead! In one lap Mansell had lost 12s, but for no apparent reason. He hadn't spun or gone off, his Renault V10 sounded as crisp as ever, only the one lap time had been affected and now he was going as fast as ever. The Renault technicians, glued to their computer screens

Jean Alesi adopts his usual laid-back approach to qualifying. By putting his Ferrari third on the grid, the Frenchman prevented an anticipated 30 per cent slump in ticket sales, had the Ferraris been performing with their habitual mediocrity.

which showed them what Nigel's engine was doing, were mystified and so was everyone else. Speculation was rife, but only later did we find out that Riccardo had asked Mansell if he would help him to win his home Grand Prix, which was so important to the popular Italian. "I was very happy to," said Nigel, "so I let him by and then rode shotgun for him." An astonishingly generous thing to do under the circumstances, and a mark of how well the two team-mates got on with each other.

They were still first and second, but you can never ignore Ayrton Senna. He was well in touch. "I was always able to close the gap in traffic so I kept going at my own pace, sustaining the pressure in the hope that they might crack." How right he was! On lap 30,

After a lengthy absence from the points, Andrea de Cesaris brought his Tyrrell into sixth place.

TEAM ANALYSIS

McLAREN

Both Senna and Berger use active suspension during Friday's free practice but then revert to passive system. Senna starts excellent second on grid and runs third to the two Williams-Renaults until lap 41, when Mansell retires from second place. Takes lead when Patrese also retires and wins 36th GP (Honda's 70th). After qualifying fifth Berger starts from pit lane, in spare set up for Senna, when electrical failure immobilises race car on grid. Makes brilliant recovery, despite lap 15 tyre stop, to finish full-distance fourth. McLaren delight at now being constructor with most points in history of championship tempered by Honda's withdrawal from Formula One at end of season, with resultant need to find new engine supplier. Team announces Michael Andretti as replacement for Gerhard Berger in 1993.

TYRRELL

Neither driver happy with grid position — Grouillard 18th and de Cesaris 21st. Olivier stops for tyres after puncture caused by colliding with Suzuki ''who spun in front of me'' (but see Suzuki's contradictory comment in Footwork team notes!). Rejoins last and retires lap 27 (engine). Andrea stirringly gains five places, lap one, battles with Alboreto for 30 laps, and moves up to fine sixth place on home circuit, lap 42. Stays there (one lap down), well pleased, for fifth point of season.

WILLIAMS

Depressed and disillusioned after months of inconclusive negotiations about his contract renewal, Nigel Mansell announces his retirement from Formula One at the end of the season — having already taken his 28th pole position and been fastest by two seconds in Sunday's warm-up. Patrese, adversely affected by electrical problem and traffic, qualifies fourth. Nigel leads, laps 1-19, before letting Riccardo through, by prior arrangement, hopefully to win his last home race for Williams. Mansell retires from second place, lap 42, stuck in sixth gear (hydraulic failure), having recorded fastest lap (1m 26.119s, 150.655 mph). With failure in suspension hydraulics Riccardo progressively drops to fifth on last lap, furious at loss of 1993 Williams drive after signing for Benetton *prior* to Mansell's announcement.

BRABHAM

Its sale negotiations continuing, the team again fails to appear.

FOOTWORK

Alboreto and Suzuki qualify 16th and 19th. Aguri rammed by Formula One's demolition contractor Olivier Grouillard (''he just hit me up the back'') and retires with broken suspension, lap three. Michele has non-stop contest with de Cesaris for 31 laps, advancing to ninth in process. Then battles with Lehto prior to finishing fine seventh for sixth time in 1992 (''I think there should be a change of rules. We should score points for seventh place!''). ''We are reliable but not fast enough. We must find more speed.'' says Mugen's Tenji Sakai.

Marching out of step. GP new boy Emanuele Naspetti's spirited attempts to keep pace with vaunted team-mate Karl Wendlinger (foreground) earned him only a gravel bath.

LOTUS

Mika Häkkinen re-signs for 1993 and both he and Herbert qualify well. Mika 11th despite accidentally releasing his steering wheel at over 170 mph! Johnny 13th for his first Monza race since 1988 (F3000). Sadly, neither finishes. Häkkinen rockets up to seventh, lap one, but out lap six (engine). Herbert similarly does very well, advancing to sixth, laps 13-18, only to retire, lap 19 (also engine). Nevertheless, another very promising showing.

FONDMETAL

Van de Poele 20th and Tarquini 25th on grid after an engine problem for Gabriele and an undertray-destroying accident for Eric. Both drivers complain of lack of top speed. Van de Poele clutch breaks at start, causing almost immediate retirement. Tarquini 13th, laps 15-19, but then into pits to repair broken gear linkage. Retires from 16th and last, lap 30 (gearbox). Team's future in doubt for financial reasons.

MARCH

After being superb seventh fastest on Saturday morning, Wendlinger qualifies 17th. Impressive Naspetti 12th fastest Friday morning before big off in afternoon. Qualifies 24th in rebuilt car on Saturday. Karl and Emanuele collide, lap 18, when 14th and 15th. Naspetti out immediately and Karl into pits for new nosecone. Finishes 10th, three laps down.

BENETTON

Another great result. Using Ford-Cosworth Series VII engine Schumacher and Brundle qualify sixth and ninth. Both make bad starts. Michael drops to 25th after hitting Boutsen and stopping for new nosecone. Martin sixth by lap seven and then fourth, lap 13, after both Ferraris retire. Third after Mansell retirement and second when Patrese slows. Finishes second for his highest-ever "official" finish (also second in Tyrrell, Detroit 1984, but disallowed due to car irregularity), well pleased in situation where he is looking for 1993 seat. Schumacher storms up through field with brilliant drive, including third fastest lap of race, to finish third and advance to second in drivers' championship in his first full season of GP racing. First time two Benetton drivers on podium since Japan 1990.

DALLARA

Lehto and Martini have contradictory views about value of new undertray. Pier-Luigi likes it and qualifies 22nd for his and team's home race. JJ doesn't and starts 14th, using previous unit. Lehto races spare car after clutch hose problem and is up to fine eighth, laps 13-35. Seventh, lap 42, but then has electrical problem and is classified 11th, six laps down. Martini spins, lap 15, but recovers well to finish eighth, one lap down.

MINARDI

Although revised front aerodynamics improve performance, Monza not a happy home experience for Minardi. Christian Fittipaldi again fails to qualify. Gianni Morbidelli starts 12th, despite being hit by Alesi's Ferrari, but retires from that position with broken crankshaft, lap 13.

LIGIER

Optimistic Thierry Boutsen starts eighth for his 150th GP, pleased with car. Erik Comas fails to find satisfactory balance and starts 15th. Neither finishes. Boutsen up to excellent sixth, laps 1-6, then fifth, laps 13-26, but drops to seventh and retires, lap 42, when fuel management system goes on strike. Comas also well up, running seventh, laps 13-35, but spins out, lap 36, after "Andrea de Cesaris cut across in front of me."

FERRARI

A very negative Italian Grand Prix for Ferrari. It certainly was after Alesi and Capelli, using special qualifying engine for team's most important race of year, achieve best '92 grid positions so far by starting third (Alesi) and seventh. But race a washout. Alesi briefly second after start but down to fourth, laps 2-12, very promisingly followed by Capelli, fifth in first race in transverse-gearbox F92AT. Then both out, lap 13, to heartbroken dismay of Ferrari-mad *tifosi*, when Jean has fuel pump failure and Ivan spins off at Parabolica when "something locked up at the rear." Jean confirms: "It is really a black season for us."

VENTURI-LARROUSSE

After yet another financial restructuring of team, Bertrand Gachot qualifies 10th for his best '92 grid position to date, delighted with new power-boosting Lamborghini V12 cylinder heads. Loses time selecting second gear at start and then has to pit with engine problem, lap 11. Engine fails as he rejoins. Katayama starts 23rd for his first race at Monza and also has difficulty selecting gears. Benefits from reliability to finish ninth (three laps down), equalling best previous finish, despite stopping on last lap with transmission failure.

JORDAN

Judd personnel now working full-time on development of Yamaha V12, whose lack of power is still a major deterrent. Stefano Modena fails to rise above 28th fastest in practice so does not qualify. Mauricio Gugelmin's engine blows on Saturday morning and different-specification replacement is even slower. Nevertheless qualifies 26th — by 0.05s! With virtually zero downforce to maximise straightline speed, runs at rear of field until lap 42 when retires with loss of drive. At least it wasn't the engine! Team thought to be examining other engine possibilities for 1993, despite fact that Yamaha power comes free of charge.

ANDREA MODA

Yet more drama! After team excluded by FISA following Belgian GP for "conduct prejudicial to the sport", unrepentant owner Andrea Sassetti obtains injunction allowing transporters, cars and equipment into Monza paddock pending court hearing. The latter supports FISA's ruling, with subsequent disappearance of team, presumably forever.

His waiting game having paid dividends, Ayrton Senna — complete with jingoistic bunting — leads Martin Brundle on the trek up to the rostrum.

with 23 to go, four seconds covered the front three. They were well ahead of Brundle, who led his team-mate Schumacher by some 24 seconds. And so it continued. As the leaders lapped their rivals, including ninth-placed Gerhard Berger on lap 33, Senna maintained his watching brief. Only 2.8s separated him from nose-to-tail Patrese and Mansell on lap 37. Two laps later Nigel set the fastest lap of the race (1m 26.119s, 150.655 mph — 0.1s off Senna's 1991 lap record, which had been achieved with more potent fuel), and of course he was still content to follow Patrese. On lap 42 the parade ended. Nigel was out. For the first time in 1992 he had a mechanical problem. With the failure of the hydraulic pump, which pressures both the suspension and the gearbox, he was stuck in sixth gear. And it was then we found out why he had been content to stay behind Patrese. "It was a good race and now I hope Riccardo goes on to win it. It means so much to him."

But Patrese was to suffer too. With Senna now second, the Williams in sight and his strategy working, Brundle third, Schumacher fourth, Berger fifth (a lap behind) and de Cesaris up to sixth after Boutsen's demise with an engine problem, Riccardo began to slow. The rear of his undertray was striking huge sparks off the track and the front of his Williams was cocked up in the air. It was obvious that something was amiss with its active suspension. Same problem as Nigel, in fact. A defective

hydraulic pump was affecting the car's posture. "We've only had it once before," said technical director Patrick Head, "and that was in testing. Never in a race and certainly never with both cars!" On lap 48, with only five to go, Senna shot past Patrese who was still going quickly, but not nearly fast enough. On lap 49 Brundle passed Riccardo to take a superb second. On lap 50 Schumacher took third from the hapless Italian and on the very last lap Gerhard Berger, after a brilliant fighting drive, took fourth place (having previously unlapped himself by catching and passing a co-operative Ayrton Senna). Poor Riccardo!

So ended an exciting, eventful and intriguing Italian Grand Prix. A very well deserved win for Senna (his 36th) and a rich reward for hanging on. Brundle's best-ever "official" finish in 91 Grands Prix (he had been second for Tyrrell in the 1984 Detroit GP, but was excluded through no fault of his own), magnificent third and fourth places for Schumacher and Berger, fifth for the unfortunate Patrese and a praiseworthy, lapped, sixth place for de Cesaris in his Tyrrell.

In his first full season of Grand Prix racing a delighted Schumacher was now second in the drivers' championship and a downcast Patrese was bitterly regretting the fact that, having signed for Benetton for 1993, he could not now benefit from Mansell's retirement by retaining his place in the all-conquering Williams team. And Nigel? We waited to hear.

All in all it had been a day to remember!

"What d'you mean, there's none left?" Senna spent almost as much time pitting for tyres as he did racing . . .

Once again the Portuguese Grand Prix was to be the last of the season in Europe. Once again the Formula One regulars looked forward to it. The facilities at Estoril may be lacking compared with those elsewhere, but the track is superb, if bumpy, and it is an occasion that always seems to generate incident and excitement. Good food, good wine, sunshine and rugged coastline scenery compensate for the general shabbiness of Portugal. This year there was the added bonus of continued intrigue about who was to drive for Williams in 1993 and what engine McLaren was to use.

Monza two weeks earlier had seen the first casualty in the battle for a Williams seat, in the form of Nigel Mansell's decision to bale out and drive in America in '93. But there had still been no statement about who would be replacing him and Riccardo Patrese. If the speculative atmosphere had been intense at Monza, it was frantic at Estoril. For four days the Williams motorhome was the scene of non-stop meetings as, surrounded by the frothing media,

Ayrton Senna persistently negotiated to join, or preferably oust, Alain Prost, and alternatives for the second seat were debated. Martin Brundle? Riccardo Patrese (yes, he *had* already signed for Benetton, but that can always be worked out)? Damon Hill? Johnny Herbert? Mika Häkkinen? The paddock was in a frenzied ferment, which was increased by the conviction that McLaren's Ron Dennis was leaving no stone unturned to get Renault engines in an effort to retain Senna. There was hardly time to get another lobster dinner.

On Sunday morning came the belated announcement that Prost would be driving for Williams in 1993, a statement which drew savage and insulting condemnation from Senna, who had been trying so hard to achieve what Alain had. Then, just as in Monza, came the realisation that what everyone was really here for was to watch a Grand Prix and, especially, to see whether Nigel Mansell could break what was one of the few records left to him — more than eight wins in one season.

It was going to be a very demanding race. There had been some heavy rain on Friday and Saturday night. On Sunday morning the track had only dried out at the end of the half-hour warm-up and the result was that it was 'green' — virgin tarmac with no rubber coating from the five practice periods. Goodyear's slick tyres were only available in the medium C compound. ''A pit stop will be necessary, because otherwise in the latter part of the race the tyres of most drivers would be close to worn out,'' explained the tyre technicians. And that was what they expected in 'normal' circumstances, when the track was coated in rubber.

There hadn't been any surprises in qualifying. Polemeister Mansell was up front for the 12th time in 14 races, team-mate Riccardo Patrese was second on the grid again and it was the Williams team's ninth front row monopoly of the year. With the advantage their perfected active suspension gave them over Estoril's notoriously bumpy surface, they should walk it, allowing Nigel that ninth win he wanted so much. (So

long as there was no repetition of the hydraulic pump failure that had, as in Italy, collapsed Mansell's suspension in practice.) For who was to stop them? McLaren's Senna and Berger from row two? They were well off the pace. Benetton's Schumacher and Brundle from row three? They were a second slower than the McLarens. The Lotuses of Mika Häkkinen and Johnny Herbert? They were an excellent seventh and ninth, sandwiching Michele Alboreto's Footwork, but most unlikely victors. And certainly not the Ferraris of Alesi and Capelli, who were almost in shock over the handling of their F92ATs. Prancing Horse was the right description. So light the lights! Start the race and we'd see!

Schumacher had made things rather more difficult for himself by stalling on the dummy grid and having to start from the back as Mansell led away from Patrese, with Berger temporarily up to third ahead of Senna, Häkkinen, exploiting the gap left by Schumacher's absence, and Brundle. Poor Johnny Herbert was out. At the second corner he was nudged into Alboreto by Alesi, broke his suspension and retired for the 11th time in 14 races.

As we'd thought, it was no contest for the lead. ''Having taken pole position my main motivation is to win and get away from here,'' a dispirited Mansell had said before the race, and he was certainly responding to it. ''I drove the first few laps like qualifying laps,'' and the result was that, by lap 10, his lead was a massive nine seconds. With Patrese a further four seconds ahead of Senna it looked as though we were in for a boring procession. So thank heavens for Schumacher! The young German was scything his way through the field from his tail-end start and, as Nigel started lap 11, Michael was up to 13th — stuck behind de Cesaris, Gachot, Boutsen and Comas. But not for long.

After Portugal, Ivan Capelli (right) would be forced to follow GP racing via the small screen. His place at Ferrari was to be taken by Nicola Larini. In his farewell appearance, the unfortunate Italian retired . . . again.

Gerhard Berger (left) achieved something which proved to be beyond all other drivers: he completed as many racing laps as Mansell.

TEAM ANALYSIS

McLAREN

A tense, politically charged meeting as Senna ceaselessly and doggedly tries to get Williams drive for 1993 and Ron Dennis negotiates for Renault engines in effort to retain Ayrton. Senna qualifies third fastest (1.2s slower than Mansell), despite engine problem on Friday and rear wing collapse on Saturday. Berger fourth on grid with severe back pain after clouting kerb on Friday. Ayrton follows Mansell/Patrese for 19 laps but up to second, laps 25-56, after tyre change. Has three more tyre stops, laps 43, 57 and 63, with "car feeling really strange" (later found to be caused by front wing endplate support wire problem). Finishes third, one lap down, having set fastest lap of race (1m 16.272s, 127.579 mph). Berger down to sixth from third after lap 21 tyre stop. Regains third, lap 25, but is caught and repeatedly challenged by Patrese. Enormous crash, lap 44, when Riccardo's right front tyre hits Gerhard's left rear as Berger slows to enter pit lane for second tyre stop. "He gave no signal at all," says Riccardo. "It was a misunderstanding which I really regret. It was the fault of neither of us," says Gerhard, who finishes second. Senna and McLaren regain second places in their championships amidst unhappy and sullen atmosphere.

TYRRELL

Using new front wing, plus developed traction-control and ride-height systems, Grouillard and de Cesaris start 12th and 15th. Andrea up to ninth, laps 1-12, and then to seventh, laps 27/28, delighted with car until ride-height battery fails. After race-long battle with Alboreto, finishes ninth, two laps down, following second tyre stop with puncture from Patrese crash debris. Grouillard improves to ninth, laps 23-26, but retires, lap 27, with gearbox failure.

WILLIAMS

Team motorhome scene of high drama as non-stop meetings try to resolve who drives for Williams in 1993. Belated statement on Sunday that Alain Prost will be number one, but who will partner him? Earlier seven-day Estoril test results provide perfect suspension set-up, which enables Mansell to take 12th pole position of season with Patrese second. But Nigel also suffers another active suspension failure due to FISA-inspired new fuel spec causing vibration in Renault RS4 engine, which breaks component in hydraulic pump. On Sunday a low-key Nigel is never challenged and wins his record ninth GP of the year — his last in Europe before switching to Indycar racing in 1993. In doing so he achieves the RS4's first win and raises his season points score to a record 108 with two races still to go. Patrese not so lucky. Tyre-stops from second, lap 24. Rejoins fifth. Catches third-placed Gerhard Berger and repeatedly tries to pass until gigantic crash, lap 44, when he hits McLaren's rear wheel as Berger slows to enter pit lane. Riccardo, miraculously unhurt, angrily blames Gerhard for not giving signal. Anxious Berger says it's nobody's fault.

BRABHAM

In deep financial trouble, team sadly withdraws after 30 years in Formula One, 399 Grands Prix and 35 victories. Since it is for sale, however, it will hopefully re-appear.

FOOTWORK

With a new-spec Mugen V10 whose high torque suits the Estoril track, a very happy Michele Alboreto qualifies an

Katayama fends off Fittipaldi and Suzuki. After the former spun out, the Brazilian put up his best display since returning from injury. He eventually ceded to Suzuki, but set seventh fastest race lap on his way to 12th.

excellent ninth. Has an equally good race, firstly resisting Alesi and then a charging Schumacher. Breaks seventh place jinx by finishing sixth for first point since Imola. Suzuki qualifies 17th but starts from pit lane after fuel pressure problem on grid. Races well to finish 10th, three laps down.

LOTUS

Another great race for Mika. Another terrible one for Johnny. Häkkinen starts seventh from his best-yet qualifying position. Herbert ninth and both delighted with race set-up. But poor Herbert out for 11th time in 14 races when second-corner contact with Alesi and Alboreto breaks suspension. In underdeveloped car, inspired Häkkinen races close fifth behind Berger until lap 19. Then, benefiting from tyre stops of rivals, progresses to astounding second, lap 24. After own lap 25 tyre change has great battle with Brundle which gearbox trouble forces him to concede. Nevertheless finishes fifth, one lap down, for his sixth 1992 points finish. The tightly-budgeted Lotus team now only three points behind mega-rich Ferrari in constructors' championship.

FONDMETAL

Financially-strapped team fails to show, but hopes to be back for Japan and Australia.

MARCH

In car which handles badly over Estoril's bumps, Wendlinger and Naspetti do well to qualify 22nd and 23rd (Karl for his last race with March before joining new Sauber team for 1993). Wendlinger up to 14th before lap 26 tyre stop, after which advances to 13th before oil cooler breaks, causing lap 49 retirement with overheated gearbox — and great discomfort for battling Häkkinen and Brundle who he coats with oil. Naspetti has another impressive drive. Races with Karl until lap 21 tyre stop. Drives strongly thereafter to beat Fittipaldi to 11th place (three laps down) by 0.2s.

BENETTON

Team concerned that, with Mobil fuel, they suffer more from revised FISA spec. Schumacher and Brundle qualify fifth and sixth but Michael starts from back after stalling on grid. Brundle, hoping for second Williams drive in 1993, battles with superb Häkkinen until lap 24 tyre stop from fourth place. Back to fine fourth, laps 44-62. Runs third, laps 63-67 after Senna's fourth stop, but caught and passed by Ayrton, lap 68. Finishes fourth, in points for ninth time. Schumacher up to 20th, lap one, and 14th, lap five. Stuck behind Comas until lap 16, but up to amazing seventh laps 29-43, after lap 19 tyre stop. Has two further stops to change punctured tyre and nosecone (Patrese debris) and to check for damage but still finishes seventh (two laps down), having set fourth fastest lap of race. But, disappointingly, Schumacher and team down to third in respective championships.

DALLARA

New front wing improves aerodynamics but Lehto/Martini still only qualify 19th/21st. JJ unwell on race day. Zaps up to 14th, lap one, and improves further to 11th, laps 44-47,

after tyre stop. But out (and very lucky to survive), lap 52, when driveshaft from Patrese crash penetrates chassis right between JJ's legs. Pier-Luigi races 17th/18th until lap 20 tyre stop. Up to 14th, laps 31-43, in battle with Lehto and Wendlinger, but retires, lap 44, after puncturing two tyres on Patrese debris.

MINARDI

Christian Fittipaldi starts 26th for first GP at Estoril. Runs towards rear of field for first 20 laps but benefits from decision to make late tyre change. Up to 10th, lap 46, but down three places after lap 52 stop. Charges hard to a confidence-building 12th, three laps down, only 0.2s behind Naspetti, with fine seventh fastest lap of race. Gianni Morbidelli tries, and very much likes, new Lamborghini V12 cylinder heads. Qualifies 18th but has big off on Saturday. Tyre-stops from 16th, lap 24, and then drops to rear of field after second stop with puncture from Patrese debris. Finishes 14th, three laps down.

LIGIER

Amidst rumours that team being bought by McLaren to gain access to Renault engines in 1993, Boutsen and Comas qualify 11th and 14th (amidst further rumours that they are to be replaced by Martin Brundle and Mark Blundell next year!). Optimistic Boutsen fifth fastest in Sunday warm-up. Thierry and Erik race together up to 10th/11th, lap 15. After tyre stops Boutsen in again, lap 42, with sticking throttle. Despite further trouble with broken shock absorber finishes eighth, two laps down. Comas, battling with de Cesaris, runs 10th, laps 27-43, then up to eighth, laps 44-47, only to retire, lap 48, when over-revved engine expires.

FERRARI

''This is the worst circuit of the year for us. The race will be very difficult,'' says Jean Alesi. He is right. With inadequate power and suspension unsuited to Estoril's bumps he qualifies only 10th despite usual herculean efforts, whilst Ivan Capelli starts lowly 16th. Neither finishes the race. Alesi spins out from eighth, lap 13, and Capelli engine blows, lap 34, when 16th. ''We are now concentrating all our effort into preparing the engine and chassis for next year,'' says Harvey Postlethwaite. Quite.

VENTURI-LARROUSSE

Bertrand Gachot 13th on grid. Up to 10th, and then ninth, chasing de Cesaris, until lap 22. Tyre stops, lap 24. Slides back with failing fuel pressure. Retires, lap 26. First-timer Ukyo Katayama fails to set time on Friday (transmission failure). Qualifies 25th on Saturday and is up to 16th, lap 25. Rejoins 22nd and last after tyre stop. Spins out, lap 47.

JORDAN

Engine wizard John Judd's work on Yamaha V12, notably new engine cover and airbox, improves power but not driveability. Gugelmin and Modena start 20th and 24th. This time Mauricio fails to finish, retiring from 20th, lap 20 (electrics). Modena soldiers on. After lap 32 tyre stop advances to 10th (out of 14), laps 52-56, but then suffers reduced fuel pressure. Finishes, for only second time in 14 races, in 13th place, three laps down.

On your marks . . . a few hours after Williams had finally confirmed that it had signed Alain Prost for 1993, Nigel Mansell prepares to set another new statistical record — nine GP victories in a single season.

By lap 18 he was 11th, having gained a very impressive 14 places, when he came into the pits for new Goodyears. He left 6.71s later, down to 15th but having made an excellent tactical move. And now came the other initial tyre changes. Senna, lap 20 (5.1s!). Berger, lap 21 (also 5.1s!). Patrese, lap 23. His was a bad one though, for the rear jack broke: 19.31s, and that dropped him down to fourth behind Berger. But Mansell, cannily getting as much mileage as possible out of his first set, in an effort to avoid a second change, didn't come in until lap 29. After a steady and undramatic 9.45s (with everyone mindful of his team's disastrous race-losing wheel change the previous year), he rejoined the track still in the lead. And that was the last his pursuing rivals saw of him.

Behind Nigel, after their tyre stops, Senna was second, Berger was third and Patrese fourth — charging to regain his second place after his unfortunate stop — followed by a terrific scrap for fifth between Häkkinen and Brundle. In fact, Mika was driving an inspired race in his comparatively undeveloped and under-funded Lotus 107. At one time, as others stopped for tyres, he had been up to a superb second driving steadily, safely and very quickly. A man to watch. So, too, was Riccardo Patrese!

As Brundle and Häkkinen swapped places, with Martin up to fifth for four laps, Riccardo had been closing on Berger's McLaren. By lap 40 he was swarming all over its gearbox, looking for a way past which Gerhard consistently, and fairly, denied him. Time and time again Patrese tried but every time he failed. On lap 43 the McLaren and the Williams were as one as they exited the right-hander before the pits straight at some 160 mph. Gerhard moved into the centre of the track, as he had before, but this time he kept going to the right and backed off to enter the pit lane for a second tyre stop. Riccardo's right front tyre climbed Gerhard's left rear and immediately the Williams was horrifically airborne, arching backwards into a half-loop. Just missing an overhead gantry, it flew for over 100 metres before crashing to the ground on its left rear corner, sliding along the pit wall and shedding debris all over the track as it ground to a standstill. Unbelievably, Patrese was unharmed and groggily climbed out of his cockpit. "No signal!" he said. "He gave no signal! I could have been killed!" Indeed he could, and was very lucky not to have been seriously injured. "It was the result of a complete misunderstanding," said a very upset Gerhard Berger, one of Formula One's nice guys. "You can't put your hand up coming out of that fast right hander because of the G-forces. I was sure that he was going to overtake me on the left as I went into the pits. I don't want to say it was my mistake or his mistake. It was just something that went wrong. Thank God that nothing worse happened."

As an incredulous Riccardo stumbled away, Berger rejoined the race third, between Senna and Martin Brundle, now fourth thanks to gearbox trouble for Häkkinen. The race was far from over though.

Patrese's debris caused mayhem, claiming the retirements of Martini (two punctures), Morbidelli (one puncture) and Lehto (Williams driveshaft through his Dallara chassis, right between his legs!). It also necessitated two more pit stops for Schumacher. Michael had worked his way up to a brilliant seventh but now had to stop, firstly for a tyre and nosecone change and then for a chassis-damage check. Then it was Senna's turn for trouble.

Having abandoned any thought of winning he was brought in for a precautionary second tyre stop but "doing my best in second place, the car felt really strange — as though it was on three wheels." That led to a third stop and then, incredibly, a fourth — which dropped him to fourth place behind Martin Brundle. With a determined charge, including the fastest lap of the race (1m 16.272s, 127.579 mph) the freshly-tyred Ayrton retook his third place on lap 68, but when he finished (lapped by Mansell) he discovered he had a puncture.

Although he had long since re-signed for Lotus, the excellent Mika Häkkinen was reputed to be on Williams' hit-list. The Finn enhanced his reputation further in Portugal, with a fine drive to fifth place.

So Nigel Mansell did what he'd come to do in Portugal, winning his ninth Grand Prix of the year to create a new record and increase his 1992 World Championship points score to 108 — another record. It had been an exciting, incident-packed, enjoyable and memorable weekend — marred principally by the grubby political machinations before the race. Senna had moved back to second in the drivers' championship and, with 10 points for second and third places, McLaren to second in the constructors' contest. Fine drives to fourth and fifth by Brundle and Häkkinen and so, too,

were those of Michele Alboreto, who at last broke his seventh place jinx by finishing a worthy sixth, and Michael Schumacher who, despite all his problems, still managed to take seventh.

But the abiding memory of Portugal 1992 was the heart-stopping sight of Riccardo Patrese's Williams barrelling through the air, smashing itself to pieces and sliding to a halt without even scratching its popular driver. Formula One is a hard and cruel sport, but sometimes miracles happen. Thank heavens, this was just such an occasion.

"All of a sudden I was cruising at 30,000 feet . . ." Patrese (left) had a lucky escape. Williams' Adrian Newey (centre) and Patrick Head pay heed.

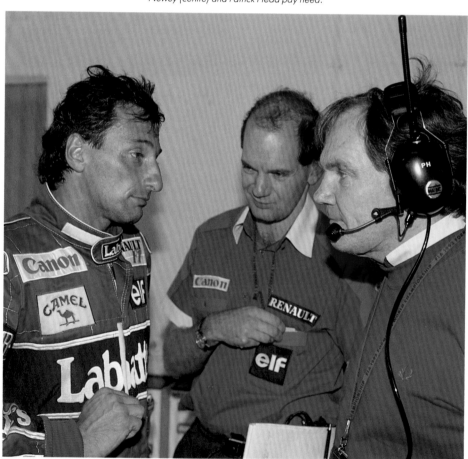

"'After you...'' Having let Patrese through, Mansell pushed his Italian team-mate hard enough to reduce the latter's lap times by two seconds.

The fanatical enthusiasm for Grand Prix racing in Japan is almost frightening. Numerous magazines cover it, anything commercial sells in vast quantities, the lesser drivers are revered and the top few are gods. Jackets, watches, videos — even carbon fibre notebooks — carrying Nigel Mansell's signature command mammoth price tags, spectators at Suzuka wear expensive Ayrton Senna replica helmets and, amazingly, nearly *seven million* people applied for the 120,000 tickets to this year's Grand Prix. Much of this dedication derives from the fact that Honda has devoted seemingly bottomless resources to achieving and retaining dominance in Formula One, a vital part of its worldwide marketing strategy to build awareness and create a hi-tech and sporty image for its road cars. It is a tactic that has worked to perfection, for in 10 years the company's commercial success had coincided with the winning of five successive drivers' and constructors' championships with Williams and McLaren.

Japan has been lucky with its slot in the Grand Prix calendar. For the last five years, the drivers' championship had been decided there, but not this year. Nigel Mansell, Williams and Renault had already been world champions for over two months when they arrived at Suzuka — a bitter pill for Honda who, to use its own word, was ''suspending'' Formula One involvement at the end of 1992. Having won only two of the five Japanese Grands Prix it had contested, the Japanese giant was anxious to go out on a high note by winning its last race on home ground. It was to be disappointed, but not for lack of trying.

When Senna and Berger drove their McLarens out of the pit lane for the first qualifying session, they were equipped with yet another evolution of the Honda V12. This was designed to overcome Renault's season-long superiority and to give McLaren its fifth win of the year. But this time Renault had a 'qualifying' V10 for Mansell and Patrese. One of the reasons for re-entering Formula One with

Senna fans come in all shapes and sizes. This particular model was even smaller than Honda's realistic hopes of success.

Williams in 1989 had been to demonstrate that Europe in general, and Renault in particular, could take on and beat the best from Japan. It had never won there and where better to do so, to underline its 1992 dominance, than at Suzuka, the track owned by Honda?

Suzuka has a unique configuration. At 3.66 miles long it is a distorted figure of eight, with the track crossing itself at the centre. It is bumpy, demanding and the drivers like and respect it. Except that, like Monaco, South Africa and Hungary, it is almost impossible to pass. So, even more than usual, being on the front row of the grid is vital. Its characteristics might have been designed specifically for the actively-suspended Williams with its semi-automatic gearbox and torquey Renault engine, and Mansell and Patrese revelled in it. Japan was one of the few Grands Prix that Nigel hadn't won and, since this would be his last appearance at Suzuka, he was expected to go all-out for victory number 31. Little did we know!

After Friday's qualifying session, with the aid of his 'rocket' engine, he was in the provisional pole position, nearly a full second faster than his team-mate Riccardo Patrese. Senna was 'only' third, despite having driven the wheels off his McLaren. Berger was fourth, Schumacher fifth and the Lotus 107s of Johnny Herbert and Mika Häkkinen were a magnificent sixth and seventh ahead of Erik Comas's Ligier. Much loss of face for Honda, who had occupied seven out of the eight front row places over the last four years. And, to its dismay, Friday's grid order was Sunday's, too, because on Saturday it rained so heavily that the final session had to be stopped.

So, on Sunday, the circuit was 'green', just as it had been at Estoril after similar heavy rain. Which meant it would be tough on tyres. Another plus for Williams and another minus for McLaren, with its heavier V12 and its need for a greater fuel load.

Senna blew an engine in the warm-up and Mansell went off, damaging the floor of his Williams. But all was well when the lights turned to green — especially for Nigel. In front of the bizarre hordes of Japanese Mansell-devotees clad in Union Jacks, he just disappeared. At the end of the first lap he was over three seconds

Choreography O-level failures. Gachot and sidekick Katayama suffer an outbreak of synchronised embarrassment.

ahead of Patrese. Senna was third, leading a four-car train of Berger, Schumacher, Herbert and Häkkinen. On lap three they were reaching for their swords at Honda as Senna rolled to a standstill with a blown engine — the end of his passionate desire to win for the people who had done so much for him. Berger now lay third, albeit well behind Patrese as Mansell pulverised the opposition, drawing further and further away with every lap.

Herbert and Häkkinen were harrying Schumacher's Benetton every inch of the way, a superb achievement considering the respective team budgets and the fact that Lotus had Series V Ford engines whilst Benetton had

the more powerful Series VII. Behind them, but getting closer, was an equally impressive Martin Brundle. Martin had been suffering from food poisoning since Thursday, had gone off on Friday after qualifying 13th, and had been in bed throughout Saturday. But now, with the adrenalin surging through his system, he forgot his malaise as he forced his way up the field. He was 11th by lap one, 10th by lap two, ninth by lap three, seventh by lap nine and sixth, in the points, by lap 13!

It wasn't just because he was charging so hard, but also because Schumacher had joined Senna as a retiree when his gearbox failed. Now the man ahead of Brundle in fifth place

TEAM ANALYSIS

McLAREN

At its last Japanese GP with McLaren, Honda produces further evolution of V12 in determined effort to beat Renault — but fails even to make front row of grid. Senna, fighting to retain second place in championship, starts third, a second slower than Mansell, despite monumental effort. Blows engine in race warm-up and retires from third place on lap three with another engine failure. Down to third in championship with 1993 plans still a mystery. Berger qualifies fourth after gearbox problem and "not enough power" (from Honda!). Opts for two tyre stops in effort to push Williams drivers but is only able to run third behind Patrese until Mansell's lap 45 retirement. Finishes second 23s adrift of Riccardo.

TYRRELL

Excellent performance by Andrea de Cesaris who qualifies ninth, praising new traction control. He advances to sixth by lap 16. Down to seventh, fighting Comas, after tyre stop. Benefits from retirements to finish fourth, one lap down. Heartening for team believed to be running Ukyo Katayama with big-budget Japanese backing and Yamaha (rebadged Judd) V10 engine in 1993. Olivier Grouillard, probably in last race for team, starts 21st and spins out on lap eight.

WILLIAMS

Great, although disappointingly incomplete, result for team, winning its first Japanese GP with Renault in Hondaland. Mansell fastest in all four Friday/Saturday sessions and, using special qualifying V10 for first time, takes 13th pole position of season to equal Senna's record. Patrese second on grid to give team 10th front row of 1992. Nigel builds massive 20s lead after lap 23 tyre stop (6.72s) and then, as in Italy, unselfishly slows to let Patrese lead on lap 36. "Riccardo was very low and I wanted to help him regain second place in the championship." Then closes on Patrese, pushing hard, but staying second, until lap 45 when engine blows one lap after he set a new record (1m 40.646s, 130.332s). Nigel thus maintains 100 per cent failure to finish in Japan. Patrese happily wins first GP of '92, and sixth of career, to move back to second in championship.

FOOTWORK

Jack Oliver announces very welcome 1993 return of Derek Warwick to act as team leader at expense of Michele Alboreto, who can only qualify 24th for Footwork's 'home' race with clutch trouble. Aguri Suzuki fails to appear before countrymen for wet Saturday qualifying but starts 16th and races strongly. Up to 10th, lap 38, after tyre stop, battling with Modena, Fittipaldi and Alesi. Has engine cut-out problem and drops back but still finishes eighth (one lap down). Michele has miserable race in unbalanced car. Flogs along at back of field to finish 15th (two laps down).

LOTUS

Superb qualifying and race achievements by both Herbert and Häkkinen but no resultant reward. Relaunched team's best yet qualifying (despite use of lesser-performance Series V Ford HB V8) with Herbert sixth and Häkkinen seventh. Johnny even better in warm-up: fourth fastest. Following Senna/Schumacher retirements and Berger tyre stop, Herbert/Häkkinen third/fourth, laps 13-15, but jinxed Johnny retires for 12th time in 15 races when gearbox fails. Mika takes over until passed by Berger, lap 22. Races excellent fourth, laps 22-44 (after briefly regaining third when Mansell retires) until lap 45 retirement with over-revved engine following gearchange problem. Whole team deserves better after cruel luck.

MARCH

Dutchman Jan Lammers, who last drove in F1 for Theodore team in 1982, takes Karl Wendlinger's place. Qualifies 23rd, three places ahead of team-mate Naspetti, and is outstanding sixth in wet Saturday morning session. Runs 20th prior to gear selection problem, lap 28 clutch failure, and retirement. Naspetti, in first drive at Suzuka, finishes 17th (two laps down) despite loss of clutch and third gear. Team believed to have landed major sponsor for 1993.

BENETTON

Michael Schumacher starts fifth, behind Williams and McLarens. After Senna's retirement races fourth, laps 3-11, chasing Berger. To third, lap 12, with then Gerhard tyre-stops, only to retire next lap when gearbox fails. Down to fourth in championship after fourth 1992 failure to finish. Martin Brundle, suffering from food poisoning, qualifies 13th on Friday despite going off. Stays in bed all Saturday which, fortunately for him, is wet. Eighth in Sunday warm-up, still feeling ill. Charges hard to excellent sixth, lap 13. Up to fifth after first tyre stop, lap 15, and retains place after second tyre change, lap 31. Deservedly inherits third after Mansell/Häkkinen retirements and stays there to finish 1.2s behind Berger ("adrenalin is a marvellous thing!") for his 10th points finish in last 11 races. Team maintains proud record of having scored in every race of season.

DALLARA

Both JJ Lehto and Pier-Luigi Martini continue to be very unhappy with car's handling. Martini starts 19th and Lehto 22nd before racing with each other to finish ninth (JJ) and 10th, both one lap down, after Pier-Luigi hits Mauricio Gugelmin crash debris on lap 23.

MINARDI

Car much improved by handling improvements from recently-joined Gustav Brunner and further evolution of Lamborghini V12. Christian Fittipaldi starts 12th for first race in Japan, with Gianni Morbidelli 14th. Christian, obviously having regained all his confidence after worrying French GP practice crash, drives magnificent race. Has non-stop battle with Alesi's Ferrari and progresses to ninth by lap 14. Charges again after lap 21 tyre stop, still with Alesi. In points for first time on lap 45 and stays there to finish sixth, one lap down, for first ever

Turning back the clock. Young Jan Lammers, 36, made his F1 return after a decade's abstinence. The Dutchman gave a good account of himself.

point (and team's first since Portugal 1991, 19 races ago). Morbidelli finishes 14th, two laps down.

LIGIER

With McLaren's Ron Dennis continuing to try to buy Ligier's Renault engine deal for 1993, Erik Comas and Thierry Boutsen qualify eighth and 10th. Disenchanted (long ago!) Thierry has fourth gear seize on lap one and gearbox fail on lap three, but Comas lasts longer and does better. Battling with de Cesaris, is sixth and in the points, laps 25-35, but retires from seventh with engine failure, lap 36, after being passed by Andrea.

FERRARI

Dishearteningly for all enthusiasts, the awful Ferrari inadequacy saga continues at Suzuka. Team tester Nicola Larini, returning to Formula One in place of Ivan Capelli, drives much-revised, actively-suspended F92A to qualify 11th. Despairing Jean Alesi only 15th in passive, down on power F92AT, which is actually slower than last year's 643 over Suzuka's bumps. Nicola spoils impressive practice by stalling at green light and having to be push-started. Hard-charger Alesi up to seventh by lap 22, battling with Bertrand Gachot's Larrousse. After lap 23 tyre stop Jean leads four-car train with Fittipaldi, Modena and Suzuki, moving up to finish drained fifth, one lap

down, depressed at his V12's lack of power. Meantime Larini races at tail of field to finish 12th, one lap down.

VENTURI-LARROUSSE

Disappointing race for Bertrand Gachot who qualifies 18th, complaining of traffic, but is fine seventh fastest in warm-up. Racing hard, is up to excellent sixth on lap 24, having gained 12 places at tortuous Suzuka. Dreadful lap 24 tyre stop drops him to 13th behind team-mate Katayama — with whom he collides, lap 40, trying to pass at notorious chicane. Bert retires whilst livid Ukyo, having started 20th for his first home GP, rejoins track to finish 11th, one lap down after stop to fix radiator damage. Team renews contract to use Lamborghini V12 engine, this time exclusively, in 1993.

JORDAN

Jordan and Yamaha unsurprisingly announce that they will not be with each other in 1993. Relieved team believed to have done deal to use very promising new Hart V10. Modena has best race of season so far. Qualifies 17th and races with Alesi and Fittipaldi to finish seventh, almost scoring team's first point of 1992. Mauricio Gugelmin starts 25th after damaging car on Friday. Advances to 13th, lap 22, but crashes out of race, lap 23, due to suspected breakage.

was Berger. Before the race began, Gerhard felt that his only chance of beating the two Williams-Renaults would be to go for a double tyre-change — in a bid to press them on softer rubber. But the Didcot cars were so superior that not only did his strategy fail, but he had to stop as early as lap 11 — when Herbert and Häkkinen moved up to third and fourth, by far the best placing that the Hethel team had held in 1992. Sadly, it wasn't to last.

On lap 16 Herbert retired for the 12th time in 15 races when his engine gave up. Cruel luck, for he seemed destined for his first, well-deserved podium finish. As Johnny suffered, Mika benefited. Now he was third, with Berger closing up as Brundle went in for tyres and Mansell and Patrese continued to pull away up front. By the time the leaders had completed their tyre stops, on lap 26 out of 53, Mansell was a commanding 16s ahead of Patrese, with Berger third, Häkkinen fourth, Brundle fifth, Erik Comas sixth and Andrea de Cesaris seventh — leading a superb battle between Jean Alesi, Christian Fittipaldi and Stefano Modena. A

Jordan-Yamaha was almost in the points!

In came Berger and Brundle for second sets of Goodyears, without losing their places in what was not, to be honest, a gripping race. Until lap 36! Suddenly, with a lead of some 20s, Mansell slowed at the chicane. Patrese shot past into the lead and Nigel picked up speed again to follow him. I had spent three days with Nigel at his Florida home just before Japan, and he had told me that he intended to let Patrese win one of the two remaining races if he got the chance. ''Riccardo has been a superb team-mate to me. We've both worked very hard to develop the car to its dominant pitch and he deserves a win — especially as he is very low after his awful crash in Portugal.'' Nigel's sudden slowdown looked inexplicable at the time, but that was the reason. And a generous gesture it was. Not many drivers would do it once, but now Nigel had done it twice, in Italy and Japan.

Having done so, he closed right up on Riccardo, pushing him very hard but making no effort to pass, and on lap 44 he set the fastest

Nicola Larini gave Ferrari's actively-suspended F92A its race debut, though it was hard to find anything truly 'active' about the Prancing Horse in Japan.

The sound of silence. Ayrton's Honda screamed its last as early as lap three.

lap of the race (1m 40.646s, 130.332 mph). Ironically though, with only eight laps to go, the back of his Williams suddenly burst into flames as his engine blew in a big way. Renault's race wasn't quite going to be perfect. But on went Patrese, mightily relieved not to have the harrying Mansell on his gearbox. Although Nigel had said he was going to help Riccardo to regain his championship second place, the Italian wasn't at all sure that the hard time he had been getting wasn't Nigel wanting the lead back!

Almost at the same time that Mansell was pulling off the circuit, poor Häkkinen was doing the same. For a short, glorious time he was third again, as Berger moved up to second but, like Herbert, Mika had his engine blow after buzzing it when he had gearchange problems.

Raw fish be damned. Martin Brundle put food poisoning to the back of his mind, and finished a superb third.

Berger leads Schumacher and the spirited Lotus twins. Only the Austrian was still running at the end.

So Patrese won his first Grand Prix of 1992, the sixth in his 239-race Formula One career, and it couldn't have happened to a nicer bloke. There to meet and embrace him in the parc fermé, wearing his ''signed by Nigel Mansell'' £1,000 leather jacket, was the man himself, obviously delighted that Riccardo had not only won the race but moved back to second in the championship. Berger was second in his last Japanese GP for McLaren-Honda and Brundle took third place (''adrenalin is a marvellous thing!''). But the happiest chap in the paddock was the youngest man in the race, Christian Fittipaldi. Christian had lost confidence after his neck-breaking accident before the French Grand Prix, but he had fought back in Portugal to finish 12th. Here in Japan, though, he had driven his best Grand Prix yet, taking sixth place. It was his first World Championship point in his ninth Grand Prix, and he finished only seconds behind Jean Alesi's Ferrari, with which he had battled for most of the race. A star in the making.

Just one race left now. Australia, the best of the year, at Adelaide in two weeks' time. Nigel had never won there, either, and we wagered that he wouldn't be giving this one away!

AUSTRALIA

November 8 1992 Circuit: Adelaide

A farewell to arms? In what might, for the time being, have been both drivers' final F1 Grand Prix, Senna and Mansell scrapped mightily prior to their controversial collision, which sparked off petty recriminations.

Australia was to be the jewel in Nigel Mansell's 1992 crown. World champion already, and the holder of almost every record in the book for a season of Formula One racing, he was aiming for two more unique achievements before departing Grand Prix racing to take up a new Indycar career in America. He wanted to be the first driver to win 10 Grands Prix and the first to take 14 pole positions in one season. The latter would be especially sweet, because he shared the current record 13 with his arch-rival Ayrton Senna — and Nigel would like nothing more than to deprive the Brazilian of the honour!

There didn't seem to be any good reason why he shouldn't achieve both objectives. He was in top form with his confidence high, his Williams-Renault was by far the best car and he had a special incentive: in seven tries he had never won in Australia, and it was at Adelaide that his memorable tyre blowout had deprived him of the World Championship in 1986.

Where better, then, to go out on a high note?

It is as well that Adelaide is always the last Grand Prix of the year, for it is by far the best. The city of churches with its wide, open streets, its beautiful parks, its essentially "English" atmosphere, its excellent restaurants and its relaxed, cheerful and welcoming inhabitants is a joy to visit. The superb street circuit has admirable facilities and leaves nothing to be desired for the teams, the drivers and the media. When you throw in blazing sunshine in November and some of the world's finest wines (not to mention Mr Foster's amber nectar!), it is no wonder that everyone looks forward to finishing their year there.

Despite all that, its Formula One visitors had a slightly apprehensive air when they disembarked, bleary-eyed and jet-lagged, at Adelaide airport. Was the weather going to be kind this year? More often than not it had been, but November marks the turn of the seasons in Australia, with winter just giving way to spring. Last year's race had been cut short, in torrential rain, after only 14 laps. No worries this year though, mate. It's going to be a beaut. And so it was. On Friday and Saturday, anyway.

Friday was hot and sunny when the 26 attendees (Fondmetal was again absent, due to shortage of money) left the pit lane to see what had been done to the 2.35-mile circuit since last year. The answer was that the Jack Brabham straight, whose waterlogged surface had caused so much trouble in 1991, had been resurfaced and recontoured. Excellent! The track was still very slippery though, and still very

tough on drivers, brakes, engines and fuel consumption. But they could cope with that. Especially Nigel Mansell, who scorched round in 1m 13.732s (114.380 mph) on race tyres to beat Senna's 1991 pole position time set on qualifiers. And this was only day one on a green track! Tomorrow should be sensational.

But when tomorrow came the temperature was 85 degrees, with a clear blue sky and the searing sun we'd all been hoping for. That meant the times would be less spectacular — and they were. Nearly everyone was at least a second slower — except for Ayrton Senna and Gerhard Berger. Their times were very close to Friday's, and it was clear that McLaren and Honda had done a better job than their rivals for their last race together. So Nigel had his coveted 14th pole position, a superb achievement and half of his longed-for 'double'.

Senna was second on the grid for his last race with Honda power, Patrese third for his last scheduled race with Williams, Berger fourth for his last race with McLaren and Michael Schumacher fifth. With no team orders, everything to go for and a lot of scores to be settled, the eighth Australian F1 Grand Prix had the makings of a fizzer. It was.

Using all the road, and a fraction more, Michael Schumacher hustled to the very end. One more lap and he might have won...

Gerhard Berger signed off his Mclaren career in fine style, the Austrian's timely tyre stop proving to be decisive.

TEAM ANALYSIS

McLAREN

Team uses Honda V12 Japanese GP-spec engine and qualifies well with Senna strong second on grid (fastest in Saturday qualifying) and Berger fourth. Senna has furious battle with Mansell for 18 laps after briefly leading on lap one. Breaks record, lap 12, and closes right up on Mansell as Nigel laps Nicola Larini. Controversially rams Mansell at hairpin to remove both cars from race. As usual each driver blames the other. Berger makes poor start, dropping to fifth behind Schumacher. Passes Michael to fourth, laps 3-18, behind Patrese but becomes close second to Riccardo after leaders collide. Tyre-stops at perfect moment, lap 35, and rejoins third behind Schumacher. To second lap 43, when Michael tyre-stops and then leads after Patrese retirement (lap 51). Brilliantly paces himself to conserve fuel and wins his second Australian GP (and last for McLaren) by 0.7s from charging Schumacher. Honda thus wins its last GP ''for the time being.'' McLaren finishes second in constructors' championship but still appears to have no engine for 1993. Senna down to fourth in drivers' contest with no stated intentions for next season.

TYRRELL

Team officially announces two-year deal with Yamaha to use rebadged Judd V10 from 1993. Andrea de Cesaris, delighted with semi-active front suspension, qualifies in best-of-season seventh place but is demoted to eighth, lap one, by Martin Brundle. Collides with Häkkinen, lap four, but is unscathed. In points (sixth) laps 19-29, but retires with rear of car in flames when fuel pressure fails, lap 30. Olivier Grouillard starts 13th in spare car after race car suffers an engine problem. Overdoes it at green light, spins, collides with Herbert and Martini, and immediately retires. Not expected to be with Tyrrell in 1993!

WILLIAMS

Using Renault RS4 qualifying engine, Nigel Mansell takes a record 14th pole position of season with Patrese third on grid after Friday balance and traffic problems. Hoping for record 10th win of season at race where he has yet to finish first, Mansell has tremendous fight for lead with Senna for 18 laps but is rammed by the Brazilian on lap 19 and forced to retire. Makes furious protest to stewards but is ignored. Ends outstanding GP career as hurt and rejected world champion, having broken almost every record (see *During 1992*). Riccardo Patrese takes over lead ahead of charging Gerhard Berger and is happily controlling things at front when fuel pressure fails on lap 51. Out of race but finishes second in drivers' championship, strongly rumoured to be staying with team instead of joining Benetton. Renault's joy at 1992 success unbounded.

FOOTWORK

Michele Alboreto qualifies 11th for last race with team but spins out of contention, lap one, after having suspension damaged when hit by unknown assailant at first corner. Aguri Suzuki starts 18th, rockets up to 11th, laps 5-11, and has almost race-long scrap with Morbidelli and Häkkinen. Does well to finish eighth, two laps down.

LOTUS

Car and drivers well suited to Adelaide track. Häkkinen qualifies 10th and Herbert 12th after Johnny had spun three times on Saturday, damaging race car. But then bad luck strikes. Herbert hits spinning Grouillard at start and has to pit for new nosecone. Loses three laps and rejoins very much last. Typically gets head down and finishes 13th (four laps down), setting eighth fastest lap of race. Mika catches de Cesaris on lap three but spins and drops to 22nd when Andrea runs wide (''What he did was idiotic''). Then charges magnificently to finish seventh, one lap down. Takes fine eighth place in drivers' championship. Team praiseworthy fifth in constructors' championship and confidently looks forward to 1993 with excellent car and unchanged driver line-up.

MARCH

Only two cars, as at Japan. Both Lammers and Naspetti, new to track, have problems on Friday and qualify 23rd (Naspetti) and 25th with Saturday times. Emanuele loses clutch on lap four and flat-spots tyres due to locking brakes. Spins after tyre change and retires with broken gearbox, lap 56. Jan Lammers has steady race to finish 12th (three laps down). Team still hopeful of finding major sponsor in 1993.

BENETTON

A marvellous ending to a superb season, Schumacher qualifies fifth with Brundle eighth after usual problem of trying to get best out of car on low fuel load (Martin sixth fastest on full tanks in Sunday warm-up). Michael closely pursues Patrese/Berger struggle for third until lap 21 becomes third himself after Mansell/Senna collision. Second laps 35-42, following Berger tyre stop, but then down to third after his own tyre stop. Second again on lap 51 when Patrese retires. Then begins thrilling charge to catch fuel-conserving Berger. Breaks lap record on laps 61, 63, 64, 66 and 68 to finish magnificent second, 0.7s behind Gerhard, and takes third place in drivers' championship ahead of Senna and Berger. Record 68th lap is fastest of race (1m 16.978s, 111.144 mph), over two seconds faster than Mansell's 1990 record. Martin Brundle also outstanding in last drive for the team (or was it?). Up to fourth on lap 19 then third, lap 51, when Patrese out. Stays there, with fifth fastest lap of race, for ninth consecutive points finish and sixth place in championship, hopefully to stay with team in 1993 if rumour that Patrese is to stay with Williams is correct. Team finishes third in constructors' championship having scored points in every race — the first time that this has been done since Lotus and BRM did so in 1963.

DALLARA

A poor finish to disappointing season. Pier-Luigi Martini qualifies 14th but clobbered by errant Grouillard at first corner and retires. JJ Lehto starts 24th for last Dallara drive

After a lacklustre season, Stefano Modena finished 1992 on a more positive note, giving Jordan its only point of the campaign. Eddie Jordan threw a party to celebrate the following Tuesday... Johnny Herbert follows, the Englishman several laps down after a first lap incident.

(with Sauber in 1993). Progresses well to 12th, laps 19/20. Chases Morbidelli, Fittipaldi and Larini until lap 71 retirement from 12th place with broken gearbox. Team now to develop new association with Lola and Ferrari.

MINARDI

Morbidelli and Fittipaldi, very closely matched, qualify 16th and 17th only 0.03s apart. Gianni a fine eighth, laps 30-42, before spinning down to 10th. Races just ahead of Fittipaldi until lap 66 when passed by Christian who finishes ninth, one second behind Suzuki, to end excellent first season as youngest driver in F1, 13 seconds ahead of Morbidelli (both two laps down).

LIGIER

Delighted Erik Comas starts ninth praising car's balance which "has never been so good." Dispirited Thierry Boutsen (the 1989 winner for Williams) qualifies 22nd on Friday, having had shock-absorber problems, and cannot improve in slower Saturday session. Frustrated Erik retires from ninth place, lap five, when gearbox breaks. In contrast Boutsen has best race of year. Charges through field to sixth, lap 31, and improves to fifth, lap 51, after Patrese retirement. Stays there for his first points finish (one lap down) in 32 races. His pleasure marred by fact that he has no 1993 drive organised.

FERRARI

Jean Alesi, driving the wheels off ill-handling car, qualifies sixth and declares intention to drive conservatively in view of inability to keep up with main rivals. Then drives usual blinder! Fifth, laps 19-50 after Mansell/Senna retirements and then fourth to end of race (one lap down), after Patrese stops. Nicola Larini qualifies and races overweight

active-suspension car for the second time in order to accelerate development of 1993 system. Qualifies 19th (ninth fastest in warm-up), but starts at back of grid for second successive race after clutch drag problem on parade lap. From 19th on lap one improves to finish 11th, two laps down. "One of the most difficult seasons in the history of Ferrari," says team manager Harvey Postlethwaite. "Now we will work very hard on a major development programme for next year."

VENTURI-LARROUSSE

In midst of yet more management problems, ill-fated team drivers Bertrand Gachot and Ukyo Katayama qualify 21st and 26th (Katayama for his first race in Australia). Bert races up through field with Larini, chasing Fittipaldi and Lehto. Retires from 12th, lap 52, when Lamborghini engine gives up. Katayama races at tail of field until retiring from 17th, lap 36, when differential fails.

JORDAN

Team's last race with Yamaha is its best. Stefano Modena qualifies a contented 15th with Mauricio Gugelmin 20th — both concerned with the ability of their thirsty V12 engine's ability to go the distance on a tank of fuel. Gugelmin has brake failure at end of fast Brabham straight, lap eight, and crashes heavily into barrier. Suspects having cut brake line running over Alboreto accident debris on lap two. Modena races up to seventh by lap 19, battling with de Cesaris. Up to sixth when Andrea retires, lap 30. Is passed by Boutsen but regains place when Patrese retires and finishes sixth to give team first point of year. Jordan now thankfully abandons unloved Yamaha power and prepares new design to accommodate Hart V10 in 1993.

It might look like a promotional board, but it's actually used for measuring the depth of puddles. This year, happily, it wasn't needed until after the race.

Senna's determination to lead was awesome. At Racetrack Hairpin, some three-quarters of the way round the lap, he thrust his McLaren ahead of Mansell's Williams, only to run wide and be passed by Nigel on the exit. This was a battle of the Titans and they drew away from the similar contest for third place between Patrese, Schumacher and Berger. By lap four the two leaders were six seconds ahead of Patrese with Berger past Schumacher to fourth as Mansell and Senna fought for supremacy. Could this go on?

On lap nine Nigel, on almost full tanks, broke his own 1990 lap record. He broke it again on lap 14 and Senna replied with an even faster time on lap 15. The two world champions were now 12 seconds ahead of Patrese. What a pace! Behind them, Berger was all over the gearbox of Patrese's Williams with Riccardo refusing to yield and Schumacher calmly holding a watching brief just two seconds down the road.

On lap 19 it happened. Mansell was closing rapidly on Nicola Larini's Ferrari, looking for a way past the actively-suspended Italian. He

Sunday was cooler with a high wind in heavy, overcast conditions. "A 50/50 chance of rain," said the forecasters. Oh no, not again! No problems in the warm-up though. Patrese was fastest this time, followed by Mansell, Senna and Berger with four-tenths of a second covering them. "The active suspension gives no real advantage here," said Nigel, whilst Senna's view was that if he could get to the first corner first he had a good chance of winning. He didn't.

Mansell may not like the Williams traction control system, which is designed to avoid wheelspin, but it worked better than McLaren's and Our Nige was into the chicane after the start ahead of the Brazilian, with Patrese third, Schumacher up to fourth ahead of Berger and Alesi sixth.

found it, as did Senna, and at Foster's Hairpin, the end of the lap, Ayrton closed on the Williams at a seemingly impossible pace. It was impossible. Straight into the back of the Williams he went, ripping off his nearside front wheel and smashing Mansell into retirement. Who was to blame? "All I know is I felt an impact and someone hit me at about 40 or 50 miles per hour up the back as I was turning into the corner," said Mansell. "I could not stop the car when he braked early," said Senna. Take your pick. The popular view was that this was another of Senna's kamikaze passing manoeuvres that hadn't come off. Either way, the result was the same. What had been a thrilling and enthralling battle between two of the world's best drivers was over amidst familiar, and tiresome, acrimony.

As both of them moved away breathing outrage, the leader was now Patrese, winner of the previous race in Japan, with Berger as close to him as Senna had been to Mansell. Lap after lap Gerhard tried to pass Patrese at the end of the long straight, but every time he was repelled by the experienced Italian. Just once, on lap

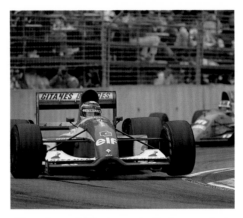

Thierry Boutsen's fifth place marked his first points finish for 32 races. Gearbox trouble accounted for the following Emanuele Naspetti.

20, Gerhard scrambled into the lead, but he lost it at the exit of the corner in exactly the same way that Senna had to Mansell earlier. With Schumacher third, a mere 2.2s behind, it was still anybody's race as Patrese started to lap the tail-enders. On lap 33 the top three were together in this fascinating race and, on lap 35, Berger pulled his master stroke. He stopped for new tyres.

It didn't seem to be a bright move at the time as Schumacher advanced to second, for it was felt that this was just another indication of how hard the Austrian is on his tyres. But we were wrong. "I was amazed that Riccardo didn't stop too," said Gerhard later. His view was justified as, on grippy new rubber, he started to catch Schumacher, who had closed to within 1.2s of the leader before losing time behind Häkkinen's Lotus. On lap 43 he passed him as Michael too stopped for a new set of Goodyears. Schumacher retained his third place, but was now some way back. Was Patrese going to stop, or was he going to try to stave off the charging McLaren and Benetton behind him on his original set of Goodyears?

We never found the answer because, with Berger in second place, breaking the lap record

If David Brabham's plan to race for Tyrrell had borne fruit, this might never have happened... Pier-Luigi Martini was barged off at the first corner by Tyrrell's trainee demolition expert Olivier Grouillard.

and only some five seconds behind him, Patrese suddenly stopped! "The car was very good and everything went dead." His fuel pressure was zero and Riccardo was out. Cruel luck after a fine drive, with a second successive victory possibly within his reach.

Berger now led by some 20s from Schumacher, with Martin Brundle a fine third, Alesi fourth, a lapped Thierry Boutsen fifth in his Ligier and Stefano Modena sixth, giving Jordan a points place for the first time in 1992. With exactly 30 laps to go, Gerhard's cushion seemed to be more than enough, but it wasn't as far as the gutsy Schumacher was concerned!

He just got his head down and charged — past all the people he had overtaken before his tyre stop, and he kept it up as though he knew that Berger had a problem. Which he had. After his terrific effort at the start, Gerhard was marginal on fuel. So he deliberately and calmly began to pace himself whilst Schumacher remorselessly closed in. Driving superbly, Michael broke the lap record again and again. Lap 61, lap 63, lap 64, lap 66 and lap 68 (the fastest of the race: 1m 16.078s, 111.144mph). With 10 laps to go Berger was less than 10s ahead of the Benetton. And still it closed.

When Gerhard crossed the line to start his last lap he was 5.2s ahead of Schumacher and he won by the closest margin in the history of the Australian GP, 0.7s! "It doesn't matter whether you win by 20 seconds or one second," said Gerhard afterwards. He was right, of course, but it was close!

It had been a great race, with Brundle third (the last to go the whole distance), and the lapped Alesi, Boutsen and Modena fourth, fifth and sixth — Thierry's first points for 32 races and Stefano and Jordan's first of the season. A good result, but how much better it would have been if Mansell and Senna had been able to fight it out to the end. But Patrese had finished second in the championship, as he so fervently desired, and Benetton had maintained its superb record of finishing in the points in every race of the season — the first manufacturer to do so since Lotus and BRM in 1963.

All in all it had been another great season. Would 1993 be as good with the prospect of no Mansell and no Senna — and Prost possibly dominating in the even-better Williams-Renault FW15? Time would tell! As we mused about it, down came the rain, almost as heavily as in 1991. Nothing changes!

Team shot : has anybody told Ayrton that it's not actually sunny?

In an age of increasing hostility between team-mates, the mutual respect of Patrese and Mansell is a thing to behold. Here, they celebrate yet another 1-2 in Mexico.

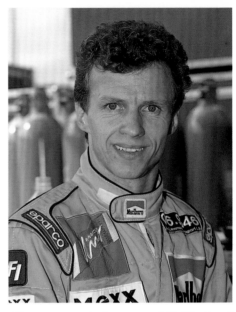

Never say never... Jan Lammers, a sprightly 36, returned to F1 in Japan, after 10 seasons away from the sport's highest echelon.

When Grand Prix historians look back on 1992 they will recall three things in particular. The overwhelming dominance of the Williams-Renault team, a year of outstanding success for Nigel Mansell and the establishment of a bright new superstar, Michael Schumacher.

For four years the McLaren team, in partnership with its Japanese ally Honda, had dominated both the drivers' and the constructors' championships. Williams' technical director Patrick Head had always said: ''We will never beat McLaren on organisation and administration — we must build a better car.'' Painstakingly, he proceeded to do that, very ably assisted by his brilliant chief designer Adrian Newey. The first move, in 1989, was to form an alliance with Renault, who put as much into the patient development of its V10 engine as Williams put into producing the right

chassis and perfecting its innovative semi-automatic gearbox and active suspension. When Nigel Mansell was persuaded to change his mind about retiring at the end of 1990, the team had all the elements it needed for success, but it still had to weld them together. The main problem was debugging the initially troublesome semi-automatic gearbox but, by the sixth race of 1991, it had been done and Williams won seven of the last 11 races, with Mansell in contention for the championship right up to his unfortunate course-departure in Japan.

After much testing, but no racing, the team's decision to use its active suspension in 1992 was a brave move that resulted in a car vastly superior to anything else, including the new McLaren MP4/7A with its revised Honda V12 and semi-automatic gearbox. With an unprecedented run of success, Nigel Mansell achieved his first World Championship by the 11th race of the year, and Williams won its fifth constructors' championship at a canter — well deserved rewards for both of them and, of course, for Renault, who had attained its objective of demonstrating that Europe could beat the very best from Japan. But Renault's joy was Honda's misery. No one could have put more into Formula One than it had and, after winning six constructors' championships with Williams and McLaren since 1987, plus five drivers' championships, it decided to suspend its Grand Prix involvement at the end of the year. Naturally, it wanted to go out on a high note but the Williams-Renault success denied them the

ability to retire at the top. Even so, Honda's achievement had been immense and everyone hoped that the rumour that they would be returning in 1994 to race a car of its own construction was true.

Sadly, Nigel Mansell's immense and richly deserved success, after 13 years of effort, was denigrated by some. Their attitude was that anyone could have driven such a superb car to victory after victory and that, somehow, it ''wasn't fair'' that he should have been so dominant. However, this viewpoint conveniently overlooked the fact that, every season, it is usual for one team to dominate its rivals in Formula One. Alfa Romeo, Ferrari, Mercedes-Benz, Cooper, Lotus, Brabham, McLaren, Williams and others had all done so since the World Championship series began in 1950, and now it was Williams' turn to do so again. That being so, either Mansell or Patrese had the best chance of winning the most races in 1992 and Nigel made a better job of mastering the actively-suspended Williams than Riccardo did. Whilst it was doubtless true that Senna could have been equally successful in the 1992 Williams, the fact was that he had chosen to deny himself the opportunity. Ayrton had negotiated to join Williams in 1990 and '91 but insiders had always felt that he was doing so to enhance his value to McLaren rather than seriously intending to drive elsewhere. That being so, he was hoist on his own petard in 1992 whilst Mansell reaped the reward of helping to develop the year's top car.

If Mansell was the star of 1992, the star of the future certainly seemed to be Michael Schumacher, for seldom has a newcomer to Formula One made such an impact in his first full season. It was ace talent-spotter Eddie Jordan who introduced the young German to the Grand Prix world when he recruited him to replace Bertrand Gachot for the Belgian race in 1991. Schumacher's seventh place on the grid immediately established him as a man with great potential and, in very contentious circumstances, Tom Walkinshaw wasted no time in signing him for Benetton. The fur certainly flew but, since Eddie's legal arrangements weren't watertight, Benetton now had Michael. It earned a massive dividend from its investment

Murray thinks that the return to South Africa is good news, for some reason or other...

Applicants for the number two Williams seat were queuing up to see Frank all season.

If his Indycar plans flop, Mansell is tipped to be joining Kim Wilde's support band as backing vocalist.

for, in 1992, he showed not only that he was a superb driver but that he had a very mature head on his 23 year-old shoulders. He wasn't just blindingly fast, he was also sensible, tactically astute, amazingly unflurried and, with it all, a cheerful, approachable chap. In short a credit to himself, his country (which, for years, had been longing for a Grand Prix superstar), his team and Formula One. His win in Belgium was the first full-distance Grand Prix victory by a German driver since Wolfgang von Trips won at Aintree in 1961 and, after the Italian Grand Prix, he had been second in the championship. Ahead of Senna. Ahead of Berger and ahead of Patrese. In his first season! Germany eagerly looked forward to having its first-ever world champion in the not so distant future.

So, a great season for Williams and Renault, a depressing one for McLaren and Honda and an enormously satisfying one for Benetton and Ford (thanks not only to Schumacher but also to many fine drives by Martin Brundle). It was an awful season for Ferrari though. Everyone wants to see the great Maranello team do well. It has more charisma and racing tradition than all the others put together, but the last time it won was in Spain, 1990. Would the exciting new F92A, with its unique twin-floor aerodynamics, put them back on top? It would not! In fact it was a failure which seemed to get worse and worse as the season progressed. New boss Luca di Montezemolo, realising that a complete re-organisation of the politics-ridden team was required, appointed the great Niki Lauda as consultant and re-appointed Englishman John Barnard as the team's

technical director, with previous designer Harvey Postlethwaite as team manager. In time this combination, backed by the might and money of Fiat, will hopefully take Ferrari back to the top but, in 1992, they could only grimly do the best they could with a totally inadequate car/engine combination. And it wasn't nearly good enough.

This was the year that the worldwide financial recession finally hit Formula One. Brabham teetered on the brink for a long time and disappeared after Hungary. Fondmetal went missing after Italy, where the Andrea Moda team was excluded from the World Championship having disgraced it all season. The underfunded March team was struggling all season, as was Minardi. Lotus too was far from flush but, under the administrative and technical direction of Peter Collins and Peter Wright, the team did an absolutely superb job, thanks to an excellent Chris Murphy-designed car, the admirable Ford-Cosworth HB V8 engine and two magnificent drivers in Johnny Herbert and Mika Häkkinen. Despite the team not having enough money to go testing, it proudly achieved a string of points positions and finished well ahead of amply-funded rivals in the constructors' championship, an achievement which should help it progress.

1992 may have been largely a Williams benefit but that doesn't mean to say that it wasn't rich in exciting memories. The return of Formula One to South Africa. Nigel Mansell's opening string of five successive victories. His magnificent charge in the closing stages of the Monaco GP, with his non-stop efforts to get past

"Right. We've got fourpence-halfpenny to see us through the next three races." Peter Collins discloses Lotus's perilous financial position to Johnny Herbert. The Hethel team achieved marvels on a limited budget.

Ayrton Senna, and his emotion-laden first World Championship in Hungary. Michael Schumacher's dramatic first win in Belgium of which, in future years, people will be proud to say "I was there!" Riccardo Patrese's terrifying accident in Portugal. Martin Brundle's superb response to his first real opportunity to succeed in Grand Prix racing, especially his brave third place in Japan after being struck down for three days with food poisoning. The little appreciated, but very real, talent of Karl Wendlinger, whose driving of the underfunded and underdeveloped March was most impressive. And, of course, the heroic efforts of Ayrton Senna to keep up with the superior Williams-Renaults. For the whole season, Ayrton never failed to emphasise that he was doing the best he could "with the available equipment", with which he was clearly underwhelmed. His best was nothing less than magnificent as he constantly demonstrated that his is a very special talent. His wins in Monaco and Hungary were vintage Senna.

So it is a gloomy thought that we may not be able to enjoy that talent next year. For the perfectionist Ayrton, the best is only *just* good enough and, with little chance of either being able to join his ex-McLaren team-mate, Alain Prost, at Williams, or to drive a car capable of beating an even better new Williams-Renault FW15, he seems likely to be taking a sabbatical. In fact Williams' 1992 dominance caused enormous controversy, ill-feeling and political uproar in Formula One.

With the world's three best drivers, Prost, Senna and Mansell, vying to sit in the two 1993 Williams seats there was a most unhappy result when Mansell became a casualty and decided to go Indycar racing instead. Nigel is Britain's first world champion since 1976 and, whatever the rights and wrongs of his move, it is very sad indeed that he will not be defending his title in 1993. It is just as sad that Senna seems unlikely to be racing against Prost — and even sadder that all three of them won't be competing.

So what are the prospects for the new season? Not, I have to say, as enticing as they have been in the past, unless there are dramatic developments on the top driver front — which seems unlikely. Welcome as the return of the likeable Alain Prost is, he can be expected to have things very much his own way in an even better Williams-Renault, without competition from Senna and Mansell. Having him win race after race would be no more exciting than having anyone else dominate the season. But, looking on the bright side, there will be lots of things that are different and, therefore, potentially exciting. Like America's CART racing champion, Michael Andretti, driving for McLaren, the very welcome return of sportscar world champion Derek Warwick, the prospects of Lotus coming-men Johnny Herbert and Mika Häkkinen achieving stardom, Benetton's Michael Schumacher and Riccardo Patrese battling with the Williams drivers and the sight of Gerhard Berger back in a Ferrari. And there will be much to observe on the technical front, too. The new tyre and aerodynamic regulations could well result in the racing being a lot more competitive and spectacular. There will be new V10 engines from Hart and Yamaha (a rebadged Judd but, heaven knows, Yamaha needs success to build some credibility after two awful years with its V12), more teams with semi-automatic gearboxes, active suspension and even ABS brakes. Hopefully, the return of Ferrari to the front with a Barnard car and the prospect of three new teams — the Swiss Sauber team, the reformed Scuderia Italia with Lola chassis and Ferrari engines and, hopefully, from Britain, Keith Wiggins' Pacific team.

On reflection, recession or no recession, it looks pretty good to me!

1992 FORMULA ONE GRAND PRIX
ROUND ONE

SOUTH AFRICA

Kyalami, Johannesburg

March 1, 1992

Circuit Length: 2.648 mls/4.261 km

Laps: 72

Johnny Herbert: wonderful drive in ancient Lotus.

Official Starting Grid

Driver / Team	Time	No.		Driver / Team	Time
Mansell *Williams*	(1.15.486)	**5**			
Berger *McLaren*	(1.16.672)	**2**	**1**	Senna *McLaren*	(1.16.227)
Alesi *Ferrari*	(1.17.208)	**27**	**6**	Patrese *Williams*	(1.16.989)
Wendlinger *March*	(1.18.115)	**16**	**19**	Schumacher *Benetton*	(1.17.635)
Capelli *Ferrari*	(1.18.387)	**28**	**20**	Brundle *Benetton*	(1.18.327)
Herbert *Lotus*	(1.18.626)	**12**	**4**	de Cesaris *Tyrrell*	(1.18.544)
Comas *Ligier*	(1.19.200)	**26**	**3**	Grouillard *Tyrrell*	(1.18.749)
Tarquini *Fondmetal*	(1.19.305)	**15**	**25**	Boutsen *Ligier*	(1.19.296)
Alboreto *Footwork*	(1.19.571)	**9**	**10**	Suzuki *Footwork*	(1.19.532)
Morbidelli *Minardi*	(1.19.636)	**24**	**30**	Katayama *Venturi*	(1.19.621)
Häkkinen *Lotus*	(1.19.672)	**11**	**23**	Fittipaldi *Minardi*	(1.19.641)
Gugelmin *Jordan*	(1.20.120)	**33**	**29**	Gachot *Venturi*	(1.20.039)
Martini *Dallara*	(1.20.203)	**22**	**21**	Lehto *Dallara*	(1.20.126)
			7	van de Poele *Brabham*	(1.20.488)

Race Classification

Pos.	Driver	No.	Nat.	Car	Laps	Time/retirement
1	Nigel Mansell	5	GB	Williams-Renault	72	1h36m 45.320s
2	Riccardo Patrese	6	I	Williams-Renault	72	1h37m 09.680s
3	Ayrton Senna	1	BR	McLaren-Honda	72	1h37m 19.995s
4	Michael Schumacher	19	D	Benetton-Ford	72	1h37m 33.183s
5	Gerhard Berger	2	A	McLaren-Honda	72	1h37m 58.954s
6	Johnny Herbert	12	GB	Lotus-Ford	71	
7	Erik Comas	26	F	Ligier-Renault	71	
8	Aguri Suzuki	10	J	Footwork-Mugen	70	
9	Mika Häkkinen	11	SF	Lotus-Ford	70	
10	Michele Alboreto	9	I	Footwork-Mugen	70	
11	Mauricio Gugelmin	33	BR	Jordan-Yamaha	70	
12	Ukyo Katayama	30	J	Venturi-Lamborghini	68	
13	Eric van de Poele	7	B	Brabham-Judd	68	
R	Olivier Grouillard	3	F	Tyrrell-Ilmor	62	Clutch
R	Thierry Boutsen	25	B	Ligier-Renault	60	Engine
R	Pier-Luigi Martini	22	I	Dallara-Ferrari	56	Clutch
R	Gianni Morbidelli	24	I	Minardi-Lamborghini	55	Engine
R	JJ Lehto	21	SF	Dallara-Ferrari	46	Final drive
R	Christian Fittipaldi	23	BR	Minardi-Lamborghini	43	Electrics
R	Andrea de Cesaris	4	I	Tyrrell-Ilmor	41	Engine
R	Jean Alesi	27	F	Ferrari	40	Engine
R	Ivan Capelli	28	I	Ferrari	28	Engine
R	Gabriele Tarquini	15	I	Fondmetal-Ford	23	Engine
R	Karl Wendlinger	16	A	March-Ilmor	13	Overheating
R	Bertrand Gachot	29	B	Venturi-Lamborghini	8	Suspension damage
R	Martin Brundle	20	GB	Benetton-Ford	1	Clutch

Fastest lap: Mansell, on lap 70, 1m 17.578s, 122.865 mph/197.731 km/h (record)

Drivers' World Championship

Pos.	Driver	Total
1	Nigel Mansell	10
2	Riccardo Patrese	6
3	Ayrton Senna	4
4	Michael Schumacher	3
5	Gerhard Berger	2
6	Johnny Herbert	1

Constructors' World Championship

Pos.	Team	Total
1	Williams	16
2	McLaren	6
3	Benetton	3
4	Lotus	1

Non Qualifiers

No.	Name	Car
17	Belmondo	March
14	Chiesa	Fondmetal
32	Modena	Jordan
8	Amati	Brabham

Non Pre-Qualifiers

Pre-qualifying was cancelled following the exclusion from the meeting of the Andrea Moda team.

1992 FORMULA ONE GRAND PRIX
ROUND TWO

MEXICO

Autodromo Hermanos Rodriguez,
Magdalena Mixhuca, Mexico City

Circuit Length: 2747 mls/4.421 km

Laps: 69

Andrea de Cesaris' brilliant recovery drive bagged him a brace of points.

Official Starting Grid

Driver	Time	No.		Driver	Time
Mansell *Williams*	(1.16.346)	5	6	Patrese *Williams*	(1.16.362)
Schumacher *Benetton*	(1.17.292)	19	20	Brundle *Benetton*	(1.18.588)
Berger *McLaren*	(1.18.589)	2	1	Senna *McLaren*	(1.18.791)
Lehto *Dallara*	(1.19.111)	21	33	Gugelmin *Jordan*	(1.19.355)
Martini *Dallara*	(1.19.378)	22	27	Alesi *Ferrari*	(1.19.417)
de Cesaris *Tyrrell*	(1.19.423)	4	12	Herbert *Lotus*	(1.19.509)
Gachot *Venturi*	(1.19.743)	29	15	Tarquini *Fondmetal*	(1.19.769)
Modena* *Jordan*	(1.19.957)	32	3	Grouillard *Tyrrell*	(1.19.961)
Fittipaldi *Minardi*	(1.20.042)	23	11	Häkkinen *Lotus*	(1.20.145)
Wendlinger *March*	(1.20.200)	16	28	Capelli *Ferrari*	(1.20.223)
Morbidelli *Minardi*	(1.20.227)	24	25	Boutsen *Ligier*	(1.20.395)
Chiesa *Fondmetal*	(1.20.845)	14	30	Katayama *Venturi*	(1.20.935)
Alboreto *Footwork*	(1.21.064)	9	26	Comas *Ligier*	(1.21.122)

*Started from pit lane

Race Classification

Pos.	Driver	No.	Nat.	Car	Laps	Time/retirement
1	Nigel Mansell	5	GB	Williams-Renault	69	1h 31m 53.587s
2	Riccardo Patrese	6	I	Williams-Renault	69	1h 23m 06.558s
3	Michael Schumacher	19	D	Benetton-Ford	69	1h 32m 15.016s
4	Gerhard Berger	2	A	McLaren-Honda	69	1h 32m 26.934s
5	Andrea de Cesaris	4	I	Tyrrell-Ilmor	68	
6	Mika Häkkinen	11	SF	Lotus-Ford	68	
7	Johnny Herbert	12	GB	Lotus-Ford	68	
8	JJ Lehto	21	SF	Dallara-Ferrari	68	
9	Erik Comas	26	F	Ligier-Renault	67	
10	Thierry Boutsen	25	B	Ligier-Renault	67	
11	Bertrand Gachot	29	B	Venturi-Lamborghini	66	
12	Ukyo Katayama	30	J	Venturi-Lamborghini	66	
13	Michele Alboreto	9	I	Footwork-Mugen	65	
R	Martin Brundle	20	GB	Benetton-Ford	47	Overheating
R	Gabriele Tarquini	15	I	Fondmetal-Ford	45	Clutch
R	Andrea Chiesa	14	CH	Fondmetal-Ford	37	Spun off
R	Pier-Luigi Martini	22	I	Dallara-Ferrari	36	Handling
R	Jean Alesi	27	F	Ferrari	31	Engine
R	Gianni Morbidelli	24	I	Minardi-Lamborghini	29	Spun off
R	Stefano Modena	32	I	Jordan-Yamaha	17	Gearbox
R	Olivier Grouillard	3	F	Tyrrell-Ilmor	12	Engine
R	Ayrton Senna	1	BR	McLaren-Honda	11	Transmission
R	Christian Fittipaldi	23	BR	Minardi-Lamborghini	2	Spun off
R	Mauricio Gugelmin	33	BR	Jordan-Yamaha	1	Engine
R	Karl Wendlinger	16	A	March-Ilmor	0	Startline collision
R	Ivan Capelli	28	I	Ferrari	0	Startline collision

Fastest lap: Berger, on lap 60, 1m 17.711s, 127.260 mph/204.805 km/h.

Drivers' World Championship

Pos.	Driver	Total
1	Nigel Mansell	20
2	Riccardo Patrese	12
3	Michael Schumacher	7
4	Gerhard Berger	5
5	Ayrton Senna	4
6	Andrea de Cesaris	2
7 =	Mika Häkkinen	1
7 =	Johnny Herbert	1

Constructors' World Championship

Pos.	Team	Total
1	Williams	32
2	McLaren	9
3	Benetton	7
4 =	Lotus	2
4 =	Tyrrell	2

Non Qualifiers

No.	Name	Car
10	Suzuki	Footwork
17	Belmondo	March
7	van de Poele	Brabham
8	Amati	Brabham

Non Pre-Qualifiers

Pre-qualifying was cancelled following the withdrawal of the Andrea Moda Formula entries of Alex Caffi and Enrico Bertaggia, which could not be readied in time.

1992 FORMULA ONE GRAND PRIX ROUND THREE

BRAZIL

Interlagos, Sao Paulo

April 5, 1992

Circuit Length: 2.687 mls/4.325 km

Laps: 71

Michele Alboreto scored Footwork's first point for quite some time.

Official Starting Grid

Mansell	(1.15.703)	**5**			
Williams			**6** Patrese		(1.16.894)
Senna	(1.17.902)	**1**	Williams		
McLaren			**2** Berger		(1.18.416)
Schumacher	(1.18.541)	**19**	McLaren		
Benetton			**27** Alesi		(1.18.647)
Brundle	(1.18.711)	**20**	Ferrari		
Benetton			**22** Martini		(1.18.953)
Wendlinger	(1.19.007)	**16**	Dallara		
March			**25** Boutsen		(1.19.038)
Capelli	(1.19.300)	**28**	Ligier		
Ferrari			**32** Modena		(1.19.314)
de Cesaris	(1.19.343)	**4**	Jordan		
Tyrrell			**9** Alboreto		(1.19.533)
Comas	(1.19.537)	**26**	Footwork		
Ligier			**21** Lehto		(1.19.834)
Grouillard	(1.19.849)	**3**	Dallara		
Tyrrell			**29** Gachot		(1.19.927)
Tarquini	(1.19.993)	**15**	Venturi		
Fondmetal			**23** Fittipaldi		(1.20.133)
Gugelmin	(1.20.266)	**33**	Minardi		
Jordan			**10** Suzuki		(1.20.435)
Morbidelli	(1.20.445)	**24**	Footwork		
Minardi			**11** Häkkinen		(1.20.577)
Katayama	(1.20.648)	**30**	Lotus		
Venturi			**12** Herbert		(1.20.650)
			Lotus		

Race Classification

Pos.	Driver	No.	Nat.	Car	Laps	Time/retirement
1	Nigel Mansell	5	GB	Williams-Renault	71	1h 36m 51.856s
2	Riccardo Patrese	6	I	Williams-Renault	71	1h 37m 21.186s
3	Michael Schumacher	19	D	Benetton-Ford	70	
4	Jean Alesi	27	F	Ferrari	70	
5	Ivan Capelli	28	I	Ferrari	70	
6	Michele Alboreto	9	I	Footwork-Mugen	70	
7	Gianni Morbidelli	24	I	Minardi-Lamborghini	69	
8	JJ Lehto	21	SF	Dallara-Ferrari	69	
9	Ukyo Katayama	30	J	Venturi-Lamborghini	68	
10	Mika Häkkinen	11	SF	Lotus-Ford	67	
R	Gabriele Tarquini	15	I	Fondmetal-Ford	62	Overheating
R	Karl Wendlinger	16	A	March-Ilmor	55	Clutch
R	Christian Fittipaldi	23	BR	Minardi-Lamborghini	54	Gearbox
R	Olivier Grouillard	3	F	Tyrrell-Ilmor	52	Engine
R	Erik Comas	26	F	Ligier-Renault	42	Engine
R	Johnny Herbert	12	GB	Lotus-Ford	36	Eliminated by Boutsen/Comas
R	Thierry Boutsen	25	B	Ligier-Renault	36	Collision with Comas
R	Mauricio Gugelmin	33	BR	Jordan-Yamaha	36	Gearbox
R	Martin Brundle	20	GB	Benetton-Ford	30	Collision with Alesi
R	Pier-Luigi Martini	22	I	Dallara-Ferrari	24	Clutch
R	Bertrand Gachot	29	B	Venturi-Lamborghini	23	Rear suspension
R	Andrea de Cesaris	14	CH	Tyrrell-Ilmor	21	Electrics
R	Ayrton Senna	1	BR	McLaren-Honda	17	Electrics
R	Gerhard Berger	2	A	McLaren-Honda	4	Overheating
R	Aguri Suzuki	10	J	Footwork-Mugen	2	Oil system
R	Stefano Modena	32	I	Jordan-Yamaha	1	Gearbox

Fastest lap: Patrese, on lap 34, 1m 19.490s 121.710 mph/195.874 km/h (record).

Drivers' World Championship

Pos.	Driver	Total
1	Nigel Mansell	30
2	Riccardo Patrese	18
3	Michael Schumacher	11
4	Gerhard Berger	5
5	Ayrton Senna	4
6	Jean Alesi	3
7=	Andrea de Cesaris	2
7=	Ivan Capelli	2
8=	Mika Häkkinen	1
8=	Johnny Herbert	1
8=	Michele Alboreto	1

Constructors' World Championship

Pos.	Team	Total
1	Williams	48
2	Benetton	11
3	McLaren	9
4	Ferrari	5
5=	Lotus	2
5=	Tyrrell	2
7	Footwork	1

Non Qualifiers

No.	Name	Car
14	Chiesa	Fondmetal
17	Belmondo	March
7	van de Poele	Brabham
8	Amati	Brabham

Non Pre-Qualifiers

No.	Name	Car
34	Moreno	Andrea Moda

1992 FORMULA ONE GRAND PRIX
ROUND FOUR

SPAIN

Circuit de Catalunya, Barcelona

May 3, 1992

Circuit Length: 2.949 mls/4.747 km

Laps: 65

Pier-Luigi Martini scored Dallara's first point of the year.

Official Starting Grid

Driver	Time	No.		Driver	Time
Mansell	(1.20.190)	5			
Williams			19	Schumacher	(1.21.195)
Senna	(1.21.209)	1		*Benetton*	
McLaren			6	Patrese	(1.21.534)
Capelli	(1.22.413)	28		*Williams*	
Ferrari			20	Brundle	(1.22.529)
Berger	(1.22.711)	2		*Benetton*	
McLaren			27	Alesi	(1.22.746)
Wendlinger	(1.23.121)	16		*Ferrari*	
March			26	Comas	(1.23.593)
de Cesaris	(1.23.723)	4		*Ligier*	
Tyrrell			21	Lehto	(1.24.054)
Martini	(1.24.236)	22		*Dallara*	
Dallara			25	Boutsen	(1.24.583)
Grouillard	(1.24.608)	3		*Ligier*	
Tyrrell			9	Alboreto	(1.24.634)
Gugelmin	(1.24.671)	33		*Footwork*	
Jordan			15	Tarquini	(1.24.800)
Suzuki	(1.24.940)	10		*Fondmetal*	
Footwork			14	Chiesa	(1.24.963)
Häkkinen	(1.25.202)	11		*Fondmetal*	
Lotus			23	Fittipaldi	(1.25.315)
Belmondo	(1.25.467)	17		*Minardi*	
March			29	Gachot	(1.25.700)
Morbidelli	(1.25.786)	24		*Venturi*	
Minardi			12	Herbert	(1.25.786)
				Lotus	

Race Classification

Pos.	Driver	No.	Nat.	Car	Laps	Time/retirement
1	Nigel Mansell	5	GB	Williams-Renault	65	1h 56m 10.674s
2	Michael Schumacher	19	D	Benetton-Ford	65	1h 56m 34.588s
3	Jean Alesi	27	F	Ferrari	65	1h 56m 37.136s
4	Gerhard Berger	2	A	McLaren-Honda	65	1h 57m 31.321s
5	Michele Alboreto	9	I	Footwork-Mugen	64	
6	Pier-Luigi Martini	22	I	Dallara-Ferrari	63	
7	Aguri Suzuki	10	J	Footwork-Mugen	63	
8	Karl Wendlinger	16	A	March-Ilmor	63	
9	Ayrton Senna	1	BR	McLaren-Honda	62	Spun off
10	Ivan Capelli	28	I	Ferrari	62	Spun off
11	Christian Fittipaldi	23	BR	Minardi-Lamborghini	61	
12	Paul Belmondo	17	F	March-Ilmor	61	
R	JJ Lehto	21	SF	Dallara-Ferrari	56	Spun off
R	Gabriele Tarquini	15	I	Fondmetal-Ford	56	Spun off
R	Mika Häkkinen	11	SF	Lotus-Ford	56	Spun off
R	Erik Comas	26	F	Ligier-Renault	55	Spun off
R	Bertrand Gachot	29	B	Venturi-Lamborghini	35	Engine
R	Olivier Grouillard	3	F	Tyrrell-Ilmor	30	Spun off
R	Gianni Morbidelli	24	I	Minardi-Lamborghini	26	Handling
R	Mauricio Gugelmin	33	BR	Jordan-Yamaha	24	Spun off
R	Andrea Chiesa	14	CH	Fondmetal-Ford	22	Spun off
R	Riccardo Patrese	6	I	Williams-Renault	19	Spun off
R	Johnny Herbert	12	GB	Lotus-Ford	13	Spun off
R	Thierry Boutsen	25	B	Ligier-Renault	11	Engine
R	Martin Brundle	20	GB	Benetton-Ford	4	Spun off
R	Andrea de Cesaris	4	I	Tyrrell-Ilmor	2	Oil pressure

Fastest lap: Mansell, on lap 10, 1m 42.503s, 103.594 mph/166.719 km/h.

Drivers' World Championship

Pos.	Driver	Total
1	Nigel Mansell	40
2	Riccardo Patrese	18
3	Michael Schumacher	17
4	Gerhard Berger	8
5	Jean Alesi	7
6	Ayrton Senna	4
7	Michele Alboreto	3
8=	Andrea de Cesaris	2
8=	Ivan Capelli	2
10=	Mika Häkkinen	1
10=	Johnny Herbert	1
10=	Pier-Luigi Martini	1

Constructors' World Championship

Pos.	Team	Total
1	Williams	58
2	Benetton	17
3	McLaren	12
4	Ferrari	9
5	Footwork	3
6=	Lotus	2
6=	Tyrrell	2
8	Dallara	1

Non Qualifiers

No.	Name	Car
30	Katayama	Venturi
7	van de Poele	Brabham
32	Modena	Jordan
8	Hill	Brabham

Non Pre-Qualifiers

No.	Name	Car
34	Moreno	Andrea Moda
35	McCarthy	Andrea Moda

1992 FORMULA ONE GRAND PRIX
ROUND FIVE

SAN MARINO

Imola, Italy

May 17, 1992

Circuit Length: 3.132 mls/5.040 km

Laps: 60

A finish at last! Imola came as quite a relief for Martin Brundle.

Official Starting Grid

Mansell *Williams*	(1.21.842)	**5**	
		6 Patrese *Williams*	(1.22.895)
Senna *McLaren*	(1.23.086)	**1**	
		2 Berger *McLaren*	(1.23.418)
Schumacher *Benetton*	(1.23.701)	**19**	
		20 Brundle *Benetton*	(1.23.904)
Alesi *Ferrari*	(1.23.970)	**27**	
		28 Capelli *Ferrari*	(1.24.192)
Alboreto *Footwork*	(1.24.706)	**9**	
		25 Boutsen *Ligier*	(1.25.043)
Suzuki *Footwork*	(1.25.134)	**10**	
		16 Wendlinger *March*	(1.25.483)
Comas *Ligier*	(1.25.543)	**26**	
		4 de Cesaris *Tyrrell*	(1.25.637)
Martini *Dallara*	(1.25.838)	**22**	
		21 Lehto *Dallara*	(1.25.865)
Katayama *Venturi*	(1.25.982)	**30**	
		33 Gugelmin *Jordan*	(1.26.056)
Gachot *Venturi*	(1.26.182)	**29**	
		3 Grouillard *Tyrrell*	(1.26.404)
Morbidelli *Minardi*	(1.26.681)	**24**	
		15 Tarquini *Fondmetal*	(1.26.765)
Modena* *Jordan*	(1.26.774)	**32**	
		17 Belmondo *March*	(1.27.194)
Fittipaldi *Minardi*	(1.27.229)	**23**	
		12 Herbert *Lotus*	(1.27.270)

*Started from pit lane

Race Classification

Pos.	Driver	No.	Nat.	Car	Laps	Time/retirement
1	Nigel Mansell	5	GB	Williams-Renault	60	1h 28m 40.927s
2	Riccardo Patrese	6	I	Williams-Renault	60	1h 28m 50.378s
3	Ayrton Senna	1	BR	McLaren-Honda	60	1h 29m 29.911s
4	Martin Brundle	20	GB	Benetton-Ford	60	1h 29m 33.934s
5	Michele Alboreto	9	I	Footwork-Mugen	59	
6	Pier-Luigi Martini	22	I	Dallara-Ferrari	59	
7	Mauricio Gugelmin	33	BR	Jordan-Yamaha	58	
8	Olivier Grouillard	3	F	Tyrrell-Ilmor	58	
9	Erik Comas	26	F	Ligier-Renault	58	
10	Aguri Suzuki	10	J	Footwork-Mugen	58	
11	JJ Lehto	21	SF	Dallara-Ferrari	57	Engine cut out
12	Karl Wendlinger	16	A	March-Ilmor	57	
13	Paul Belmondo	17	F	March-Ilmor	57	
14	Andrea de Cesaris	4	I	Tyrrell-Ilmor	55	Fuel pressure
R	Ukyo Katayama	30	J	Venturi-Lamborghini	40	Spun off
R	Jean Alesi	27	F	Ferrari	39	Collision with Berger
R	Gerhard Berger	2	A	McLaren-Honda	39	Collision with Alesi
R	Bertrand Gachot	29	B	Venturi-Lamborghini	32	Spun off
R	Thierry Boutsen	25	B	Ligier-Renault	29	Engine cut out
R	Stefano Modena	32	I	Jordan-Yamaha	25	Gearbox
R	Gianni Morbidelli	24	I	Minardi-Lamborghini	24	Transmission
R	Gabriele Tarquini	15	I	Fondmetal-Ford	24	Overheating
R	Michael Schumacher	19	D	Benetton-Ford	20	Spun/suspension
R	Ivan Capelli	28	I	Ferrari	11	Spun off
R	Christian Fittipaldi	23	BR	Minardi-Lamborghini	8	Transmission
R	Johnny Herbert	12	GB	Lotus-Ford	8	Gearbox

Fastest lap: Patrese, on lap 60, 1m 26.100s, 130.943 mph/210.732 km/h (record).

Drivers' World Championship

Pos.	Driver	Total
1	Nigel Mansell	50
2	Riccardo Patrese	24
3	Michael Schumacher	17
4=	Gerhard Berger	8
4=	Ayrton Senna	8
6	Jean Alesi	7
7	Michele Alboreto	5
8	Martin Brundle	3
9=	Andrea de Cesaris	2
9=	Ivan Capelli	2
9=	Pier-Luigi Martini	2
12=	Johnny Herbert	1
12=	Mika Häkkinen	1

Constructors' World Championship

Pos.	Team	Total
1	Williams	74
2	Benetton	20
3	McLaren	16
4	Ferrari	9
5	Footwork	5
6=	Lotus	2
6=	Tyrrell	2
6=	Dallara	2

Non Qualifiers

No.	Name	Car
11	Häkkinen	Lotus
14	Chiesa	Fondmetal
8	Hill	Brabham
7	van de Poele	Brabham

Non Pre-Qualifiers

No.	Name	Car
34	Moreno	Andrea Moda
35	McCarthy	Andrea Moda

1992 FORMULA ONE GRAND PRIX ROUND SIX

MONACO

Circuit de Monaco,

Monte Carlo

May 31, 1992

Circuit Length: 2.068 mls/3.328 km

Laps: 78

Bertrand Gachot: a rare, but welcome, point for Venturi.

Official Starting Grid

Mansell	(1.19.495)	**5**	
Williams			
Senna	(1.20.608)	**1**	
McLaren			
Berger	(1.21.224)	**2**	
McLaren			
Brundle	(1.22.068)	**20**	
Benetton			
Herbert	(1.22.579)	**12**	
Lotus			
Alboreto	(1.22.671)	**9**	
Footwork			
Gugelmin	(1.22.863)	**33**	
Jordan			
Gachot	(1.23.122)	**29**	
Venturi			
Fittipaldi	(1.23.487)	**23**	
Minardi			
Suzuki	(1.23.641)	**10**	
Footwork			
Modena	(1.23.890)	**32**	
Jordan			
Comas	(1.23.974)	**26**	
Ligier			
Tarquini	(1.24.479)	**15**	
Fondmetal			

6	Patrese	(1.20.368)	
	Williams		
27	Alesi	(1.20.895)	
	Ferrari		
19	Schumacher	(1.21.831)	
	Benetton		
28	Capelli	(1.22.119)	
	Ferrari		
4	de Cesaris	(1.22.647)	
	Tyrrell		
24	Morbidelli	(1.22.733)	
	Minardi		
11	Häkkinen	(1.22.886)	
	Lotus		
16	Wendlinger	(1.23.264)	
	March		
22	Martini	(1.23.508)	
	Dallara		
21	Lehto	(1.23.862)	
	Dallara		
25	Boutsen	(1.23.909)	
	Ligier		
3	Grouillard	(1.23.990)	
	Tyrrell		
34	Moreno	(1.24.945)	
	Andrea Moda		

Race Classification

Pos.	Driver	No.	Nat.	Car	Laps	Time/retirement
1	Ayrton Senna	1	BR	McLaren-Honda	78	1h 50m 59.372s
2	Nigel Mansell	5	GB	Williams-Renault	78	1h 50m 59.587s
3	Riccardo Patrese	6	I	Williams-Renault	78	1h 51m 31.215s
4	Michael Schumacher	19	D	Benetton-Ford	78	1h 51m 38.666s
5	Martin Brundle	20	GB	Benetton-Ford	78	1h 52m 20.719s
6	Bertrand Gachot	29	B	Venturi-Lamborghini	77	
7	Michele Alboreto	9	I	Footwork-Mugen	77	
8	Christian Fittipaldi	23	BR	Minardi-Lamborghini	77	
9	JJ Lehto	21	SF	Dallara-Ferrari	76	
10	Erik Comas	26	F	Ligier-Renault	76	
11	Aguri Suzuki	10	J	Footwork-Mugen	76	
12	Thierry Boutsen	25	B	Ligier-Renault	75	
R	Ivan Capelli	28	I	Ferrari	60	Spun off
R	Gerhard Berger	2	A	McLaren-Honda	32	Gearbox
R	Mika Häkkinen	11	SF	Lotus-Ford	30	Clutch
R	Jean Alesi	27	F	Ferrari	28	Gearbox
R	Mauricio Gugelmin	33	BR	Jordan-Yamaha	18	Transmission
R	Johnny Herbert	12	GB	Lotus-Ford	17	Accident
R	Roberto Moreno	34	BR	Andrea Moda-Judd	11	Engine
R	Andrea de Cesaris	4	I	Tyrrell-Ilmor	9	Gearbox
R	Stefano Modena	32	I	Jordan-Yamaha	6	Accident
R	Gabriele Tarquini	15	I	Fondmetal-Ford	6	Overheating
R	Olivier Grouillard	3	F	Tyrrell-Ilmor	4	Gearbox
R	Karl Wendlinger	16	A	March-Ilmor	1	Flat battery
R	Gianni Morbidelli	24	I	Minardi-Lamborghini	1	Flat battery
R	Pier-Luigi Martini	22	I	Dallara-Ferrari	0	Accident

Fastest lap: Mansell, on lap 74, 1m 21.598s, 91.234 mph/146.827 km/h (record).

Drivers' World Championship

Pos.	Driver	Total
1	Nigel Mansell	56
2	Riccardo Patrese	28
3	Michael Schumacher	20
4	Ayrton Senna	18
5	Gerhard Berger	8
6	Jean Alesi	7
7=	Michele Alboreto	5
7=	Martin Brundle	5
9=	Andrea de Cesaris	2
9=	Ivan Capelli	2
9=	Pier-Luigi Martini	2
12=	Johnny Herbert	1
12=	Mika Häkkinen	1
12=	Betrand Gachot	1

Constructors' World Championship

Pos.	Team	Total
1	Williams	84
2	McLaren	26
3	Benetton	25
4	Ferrari	9
5	Footwork	5
6=	Lotus	2
6=	Tyrrell	2
6=	Dallara	2
9	Venturi	1

Non Qualifiers

No.	Name	Car
7	van de Poele	Brabham
8	Hill	Brabham
14	Chiesa	Fondmetal
17	Belmondo	March

Non Pre-Qualifiers

No.	Name	Car
30	Katayama	Venturi
35	McCarthy	Andrea Moda

1992 FORMULA ONE GRAND PRIX
ROUND SEVEN

CANADA
Gilles Villeneuve
June 14, 1992
Circuit Length: 2.752 mls/4.430 km
Laps: 69

Karl Wendlinger: terrific drive gave March a fillip.

Official Starting Grid

Senna *McLaren*	(1.19.775)	1				
			6	Patrese *Williams*	(1.19.872)	
Mansell *Williams*	(1.19.948)	5				
			2	Berger *McLaren*	(1.20.145)	
Schumacher *Benetton*	(1.20.456)	19				
			12	Herbert *Lotus*	(1.21.645)	
Brundle *Benetton*	(1.21.738)	20				
			27	Alesi *Ferrari*	(1.21.777)	
Capelli *Ferrari*	(1.22.297)	28				
			11	Häkkinen *Lotus*	(1.22.360)	
Katayama *Venturi*	(1.22.510)	30				
			16	Wendlinger *March*	(1.22.566)	
Morbidelli *Minardi*	(1.22.594)	24				
			4	de Cesaris *Tyrrell*	(1.22.635)	
Martini *Dallara*	(1.22.850)	22				
			9	Alboreto *Footwork*	(1.22.878)	
Modena *Jordan*	(1.23.023)	32				
			15	Tarquini *Fondmetal*	(1.23.063)	
Gachot *Venturi*	(1.23.138)	29				
			17	Belmondo *March*	(1.23.189)	
Boutsen *Ligier*	(1.23.203)	25				
			26	Comas *Ligier*	(1.23.212)	
Lehto *Dallara*	(1.23.249)	21				
			33	Gugelmin *Jordan*	(1.23.431)	
Fittipaldi *Minardi*	(1.23.433)	23				
			3	Grouillard *Tyrrell*	(1.23.469)	

Drivers' World Championship

Pos.	Driver	Total
1	Nigel Mansell	56
2	Riccardo Patrese	28
3	Michael Schumacher	26
4=	Ayrton Senna	18
4=	Gerhard Berger	18
6	Jean Alesi	11
7=	Michele Alboreto	5
7=	Martin Brundle	5
9	Andrea de Cesaris	4
10	Karl Wendlinger	3
11=	Ivan Capelli	2
11=	Pier-Luigi Martini	2
13=	Johnny Herbert	1
13=	Mika Häkkinen	1
13=	Bertrand Gachot	1
13=	Erik Comas	1

Constructors' World Championship

Pos.	Team	Total
1	Williams	84
2	McLaren	36
3	Benetton	31
4	Ferrari	13
5	Footwork	5
6	Tyrrell	4
7	March	3
8=	Dallara	2
8=	Lotus	2
10=	Venturi	1
10=	Ligier	1

Race Classification

Pos.	Driver	No.	Nat.	Car	Laps	Time/retirement
1	Gerhard Berger	2	A	McLaren-Honda	69	1h 37m 08.299s
2	Michael Schumacher	19	D	Benetton-Ford	69	1h 37m 20.700s
3	Jean Alesi	27	F	Ferrari	69	1h 38m 15.626s
4	Karl Wendlinger	16	A	March-Ilmor	68	
5	Andrea de Cesaris	4	I	Tyrrell-Ilmor	68	
6	Erik Comas	26	F	Ligier-Renault	68	
7	Michele Alboreto	9	I	Footwork-Mugen	68	
8	Pier-Luigi Martini	22	I	Dallara-Ferrari	68	
9	JJ Lehto	21	SF	Dallara-Ferrari	68	
10	Thierry Boutsen	25	B	Ligier-Renault	67	
11	Gianni Morbidelli	24	I	Minardi-Lamborghini	67	
12	Olivier Grouillard	3	F	Tyrrell-Ilmor	67	
13	Christian Fittipaldi	23	BR	Minardi-Lamborghini	65	
14	Paul Belmondo	17	F	March-Ilmor	64	
R	Ukyo Katayama	30	J	Venturi-Lamborghini	61	Engine
R	Martin Brundle	20	GB	Benetton-Ford	45	Final drive
R	Riccardo Patrese	6	I	Williams-Renault	43	Gearbox
R	Ayrton Senna	1	BR	McLaren-Honda	37	Electrics
R	Stefano Modena	32	I	Jordan-Yamaha	36	Transmission
R	Mika Häkkinen	11	SF	Lotus-Ford	35	Gearbox
R	Johnny Herbert	12	GB	Lotus-Ford	34	Clutch
R	Ivan Capelli	28	I	Ferrari	18	Crash
R	Nigel Mansell	5	GB	Williams-Renault	14	Spun off
R	Mauricio Gugelmin	33	BR	Jordan-Yamaha	14	Transmission
R	Bertrand Gachot	29	B	Venturi-Lamborghini	14	Disqualified for push-start
R	Gabriele Tarquini	15	I	Fondmetal-Ford	0	Gearbox

Fastest lap: Berger, on lap 61, 1m 22.325s, 120.372 mph/193.720 km/h (record).

Non Qualifiers

No.	Name	Car
10	Suzuki	Footwork
7	van de Poele	Brabham
14	Chiesa	Fondmetal
8	Hill	Brabham

Non Pre-Qualifiers

No.	Name	Car
34	Moreno	Andrea Moda
35	McCarthy	Andrea Moda

1992 FORMULA ONE GRAND PRIX
ROUND EIGHT

FRANCE

Magny-Cours, Nevers

July 5, 1992

Circuit Length: 2.64 mls/4.25km

Laps: 69

Jean Alesi: stupendous effort on slicks in the wet.

Official Starting Grid

Mansell *Williams*	(1.13.864)	**5**				
				6 Patrese *Williams*	(1.14.332)	
Senna *McLaren*	(1.15.199)	**1**				
				2 Berger *McLaren*	(1.15.316)	
Schumacher *Benetton*	(1.15.569)	**19**				
				27 Alesi *Ferrari*	(1.16.118)	
Brundle *Benetton*	(1.16.151)	**20**				
				28 Capelli *Ferrari*	(1.16.443)	
Boutsen *Ligier*	(1.16.806)	**25**				
				26 Comas *Ligier*	(1.16.938)	
Häkkinen *Lotus*	(1.16.999)	**11**				
				12 Herbert *Lotus*	(1.17.257)	
Gachot *Venturi*	(1.17.442)	**29**				
				9 Alboreto *Footwork*	(1.17.508)	
Suzuki *Footwork*	(1.17.548)	**10**				
				24 Morbidelli *Minardi*	(1.17.667)	
Lehto *Dallara*	(1.17.677)	**21**				
				30 Katayama *Dallara*	(1.17.709)	
de Cesaris *Tyrrell*	(1.17.868)	**4**				
				32 Modena *Jordan*	(1.17.901)	
Wendlinger *March*	(1.17.937)	**16**				
				3 Grouillard *Tyrrell*	(1.17.989)	
Tarquini *Fondmetal*	(1.17.993)	**15**				
				33 Gugelmin *Jordan*	(1.18.337)	
Martini *Dallara*	(1.18.586)	**22**				
				14 Chiesa *Fondmetal*	(1.18.701)	

Drivers' World Championship

Pos.	Driver	Total
1	Nigel Mansell	66
2	Riccardo Patrese	34
3	Michael Schumacher	26
4=	Ayrton Senna	18
4=	Gerhard Berger	18
6	Jean Alesi	11
7	Martin Brundle	9
8	Michele Alboreto	5
9=	Andrea de Cesaris	4
9=	Mika Häkkinen	4
11=	Karl Wendlinger	3
11=	Erik Comas	3
13=	Ivan Capelli	2
13=	Pier-Luigi Martini	2
13=	Johnny Herbert	2
16	Bertrand Gachot	1

Constructors' World Championship

Pos.	Team	Total
1	Williams	100
2	McLaren	36
3	Benetton	35
4	Ferrari	13
5	Lotus	6
6	Footwork	5
7	Tyrrell	4
8=	March	3
8=	Ligier	3
10	Dallara	2
11	Venturi	1

Race Classification

Pos.	Driver	No.	Nat.	Car	Laps	Time/retirement
1	Nigel Mansell	5	GB	Williams-Renault	69	1h 38m 08.459s
2	Riccardo Patrese	6	I	Williams-Renault	69	1h 38m 54.906s
3	Martin Brundle	20	GB	Benetton-Ford	69	1h 39m 21.038s
4	Mika Häkkinen	11	SF	Lotus-Ford	68	
5	Erik Comas	26	F	Ligier-Renault	68	
6	Johnny Herbert	12	GB	Lotus-Ford	68	
7	Michele Alboreto	9	I	Footwork-Mugen	68	
8	Gianni Morbidelli	24	I	Minardi-Lamborghini	68	
9	JJ Lehto	21	SF	Dallara-Ferrari	67	
10	Pier-Luigi Martini	22	I	Dallara-Ferrari	67	
11	Olivier Grouillard	3	F	Tyrrell-Ilmor	66	
R	Jean Alesi	27	F	Ferrari	61	Engine
R	Andrea de Cesaris	4	I	Tyrrell-Ilmor	51	Spun off
R	Ukyo Katayama	30	J	Venturi-Lamborghini	49	Engine
R	Thierry Boutsen	25	B	Ligier-Renault	46	Spun off
R	Ivan Capelli	28	I	Ferrari	38	Engine
R	Karl Wendlinger	16	A	March-Ilmor	33	Gearbox
R	Stefano Modena	32	I	Jordan-Yamaha	25	Engine
R	Aguri Suzuki	10	J	Footwork-Mugen	20	Slid off
R	Michael Schumacher	19	D	Benetton-Ford	17	Accident
R	Gerhard Berger	2	A	McLaren-Honda	10	Engine
R	Gabriele Tarquini	15	I	Fondmetal-Ford	6	Throttle cable
R	Bertrand Gachot	29	F	Venturi-Lamborghini	0	Collision damage
R	Mauricio Gugelmin	33	BR	Jordan-Yamaha	0	Collision damage
R	Andrea Chiesa	14	CH	Fondmetal-Ford	0	Collision damage
R	Ayrton Senna	1	BR	McLaren-Honda	0	Collision damage

Fastest lap: Mansell, on lap 37, 1m 17.070s, 123.355 mph/198.521 km/h.

Non Qualifiers

No.	Name	Car
17	Belmondo	March
23	Fittipaldi	Minardi
7	van de Poele	Brabham
8	Hill	Brabham

Non Pre-Qualifiers

No pre-qualifying session held following non-arrival of Andrea Moda team.

1992 FORMULA ONE GRAND PRIX
ROUND NINE

GREAT BRITAIN

Silverstone

12 July, 1992

Circuit Length: 3.247 mls/5.225 km

Laps: 59

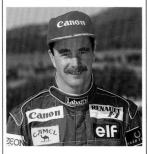

*Mansell: home advantage
increased his factor of invincibility*

Official Starting Grid

Mansell	(1.18.965)	**5**				
Williams				**6**	Patrese	(1.20.884)
Senna	(1.21.706)	**1**			Williams	
McLaren				**19**	Schumacher	(1.22.066)
Berger	(1.22.296)	**2**			Benetton	
McLaren				**20**	Brundle	(1.23.489)
Herbert	(1.23.605)	**12**			Benetton	
Lotus				**27**	Alesi	(1.23.723)
Häkkinen	(1.23.813)	**11**			Ferrari	
Lotus				**26**	Comas	(1.23.957)
Gachot	(1.24.065)	**29**			Ligier	
Venturi				**9**	Alboreto	(1.24.198)
Boutsen	(1.24.545)	**25**			Footwork	
Ligier				**28**	Capelli	(1.24.558)
Tarquini	(1.24.761)	**15**			Ferrari	
Fondmetal				**30**	Katayama	(1.24.851)
Suzuki	(1.24.924)	**10**			Venturi	
Footwork				**4**	de Cesaris	(1.24.984)
Lehto	(1.25.037)	**21**			Tyrrell	
Dallara				**3**	Grouillard	(1.25.096)
Wendlinger	(1.25.123)	**16**			Tyrrell	
March				**22**	Martini	(1.25.221)
Modena	(1.25.362)	**32**			Dallara	
Jordan				**33**	Gugelmin	(1.25.988)
Morbidelli	(1.25.998)	**24**			Jordan	
Minardi				**8**	Hill	(1.26.378)
					Brabham	

Drivers' World Championship

Pos.	Driver	Total
1	Nigel Mansell	76
2	Riccardo Patrese	40
3	Michael Schumacher	29
4	Gerhard Berger	20
5	Ayrton Senna	18
6	Martin Brundle	13
7	Jean Alesi	11
8=	Michele Alboreto	5
8=	Mika Häkkinen	5
10	Andrea de Cesaris	4
11=	Karl Wendlinger	3
11=	Erik Comas	3
13=	Ivan Capelli	2
13=	Pier-Luigi Martini	2
13=	Johnny Herbert	2
16	Bertrand Gachot	1

Constructors' World Championship

Pos.	Team	Total
1	Williams	116
2	Benetton	42
3	McLaren	38
4	Ferrari	13
5	Lotus	7
6	Footwork	5
7	Tyrrell	4
8=	March	3
8=	Ligier	3
10	Dallara	2
11	Venturi	1

Race Classification

Pos.	Driver	No.	Nat.	Car	Laps	Time/retirement
1	Nigel Mansell	5	GB	Williams-Renault	59	1h 25m 42.991s
2	Riccardo Patrese	6	I	Williams-Renault	59	1h 26m 22.085s
3	Martin Brundle	20	GB	Benetton-Ford	59	1h 26m 31.386s
4	Michael Schumacher	19	D	Benetton-Ford	59	1h 26m 36.258s
5	Gerhard Berger	2	A	McLaren-Honda	59	1h 27m 38.786s
6	Mika Häkkinen	11	SF	Lotus-Ford	59	1h 27m 03.129s
7	Michele Alboreto	9	I	Footwork-Mugen	58	
8	Erik Comas	26	F	Ligier-Renault	58	
9	Ivan Capelli	28	I	Ferrari	58	
10	Thierry Boutsen	25	B	Ligier-Renault	57	
11	Olivier Grouillard	3	F	Tyrrell-Ilmor	57	
12	Aguri Suzuki	10	J	Footwork-Mugen	57	
13	JJ Lehto	21	SF	Dallara-Ferrari	57	
14	Gabriele Tarquini	15	I	Fondmetal-Ford	57	
15	Pier-Luigi Martini	22	I	Dallara-Ferrari	56	
16	Damon Hill	8	GB	Brabham-Judd	55	
17	Gianni Morbidelli	24	I	Minardi-Lamborghini	53	Engine
R	Ayrton Senna	1	BR	McLaren-Honda	52	Transmission
R	Andrea de Cesaris	4	I	Tyrrell-Ilmor	46	Suspension/spun off
R	Jean Alesi	27	F	Ferrari	43	Fire extinguisher discharged
R	Stefano Modena	32	I	Jordan-Yamaha	43	Engine
R	Mauricio Gugelmin	33	BR	Jordan-Yamaha	37	Engine
R	Bertrand Gachot	29	F	Venturi-Lamborghini	32	Rear wheel bearing
R	Johnny Herbert	12	GB	Lotus-Ford	31	Gearbox
R	Karl Wendlinger	16	A	March-Ilmor	27	Gearbox
R	Ukyo Katayama	30	J	Venturi-Lamborghini	27	Gear linkage

Fastest lap: Mansell, on lap 57, 1m 22.539s 141.633 mph/227.936 km/h (record)

Non Qualifiers

No.	Name	Car
23	Zanardi	Minardi
17	Belmondo	March
14	Chiesa	Fondmetal
7	van de Poele	Brabham

Non Pre-Qualifiers

No.	Name	Car
34	Moreno	Andrea Moda
35	McCarthy	Andrea Moda

1992 FORMULA ONE GRAND PRIX
ROUND TEN

GERMANY

Hockenheim-Ring

July 26, 1992

Circuit Length: 4.234 mls/6.815km

Laps: 45

Michael Schumacher: sending the fans home happy.

Official Starting Grid

Mansell	(1.37.960)	**5**		
Williams			**6** Patrese	(1.38.310)
Senna	(1.39.106)	**1**	*Williams*	
McLaren			**2** Berger	(1.39.716)
Alesi	(1.40.959)	**27**	*McLaren*	
Ferrari			**19** Schumacher	(1.41.132)
Comas	(1.41.942)	**26**	*Benetton*	
Ligier			**25** Boutsen	(1.42.112)
Brundle	(1.42.136)	**20**	*Ligier*	
Benetton			**16** Wendlinger	(1.42.357)
Herbert	(1.42.645)	**12**	*March*	
Lotus			**28** Capelli	(1.42.748)
Häkkinen	(1.42.749)	**11**	*Ferrari*	
Lotus			**3** Grouillard	(1.42.797)
Suzuki	(1.42.838)	**10**	*Tyrrell*	
Footwork			**30** Katayama	(1.43.079)
Alboreto	(1.43.171)	**9**	*Venturi*	
Footwork			**22** Martini	(1.43.556)
Tarquini	(1.43.777)	**15**	*Dallara*	
Fondmetal			**4** de Cesaris	(1.43.790)
Lehto	(1.43.931)	**21**	*Tyrrell*	
Dallara			**17** Belmondo	(1.44.130)
Gugelmin	(1.44.521)	**33**	*March*	
Jordan			**23** Zanardi	(1.44.593)
Gachot	(1.44.596)	**29**	*Minardi*	
Venturi			**24** Morbidelli	(1.44.763)
			Minardi	

Drivers' World Championship

Pos.	Driver	Total
1	Nigel Mansell	86
2	Riccardo Patrese	40
3	Michael Schumacher	33
4	Ayrton Senna	24
5	Gerhard Berger	20
6	Martin Brundle	16
7	Jean Alesi	13
8=	Michele Alboreto	5
8=	Mika Häkkinen	5
10=	Andrea de Cesaris	4
10=	Erik Comas	4
12	Karl Wendlinger	3
13=	Ivan Capelli	2
13=	Pier-Luigi Martini	2
13=	Johnny Herbert	2
16	Bertrand Gachot	1

Constructors' World Championship

Pos.	Team	Total
1	Williams	126
2	Benetton	49
3	McLaren	44
4	Ferrari	15
5	Lotus	7
6	Footwork	5
7=	Tyrrell	4
7=	Ligier	4
9	March	3
10	Dallara	2
11	Venturi	1

Race Classification

Pos.	Driver	No.	Nat.	Car	Laps	Time/retirement
1	Nigel Mansell	5	GB	Williams-Renault	45	1h 18m 22.032s
2	Ayrton Senna	1	BR	McLaren-Honda	45	1h 18m 26.532s
3	Michael Schumacher	19	D	Benetton-Ford	45	1h 18m 56.494s
4	Martin Brundle	20	GB	Benetton-Ford	45	1h 18m 58.991s
5	Jean Alesi	27	F	Ferrari	45	1h 19m 34.639s
6	Erik Comas	26	F	Ligier-Renault	45	1h 19m 58.530s
7	Thierry Boutsen	25	B	Ligier-Renault	45	1h 19m 59.212s
8	Riccardo Patrese	6	I	Williams-Renault	44	Spun off
9	Michele Alboreto	9	I	Footwork-Mugen	44	
10	JJ Lehto	21	SF	Dallara-Ferrari	44	
11	Pier-Luigi Martini	22	I	Dallara-Ferrari	44	
12	Gianni Morbidelli	24	I	Minardi-Lamborghini	44	
13	Paul Belmondo	17	F	March-Ilmor	44	
14	Bertrand Gachot	29	F	Venturi-Lamborghini	44	
15	Mauricio Gugelmin	33	BR	Jordan-Yamaha	43	
16	Karl Wendlinger	16	A	March-Ilmor	42	
R	Gabriele Tarquini	15	I	Fondmetal-Ford	33	Engine
R	Andrea de Cesaris	4	I	Tyrrell-Ilmor	25	Engine
R	Johnny Herbert	12	GB	Lotus-Ford	23	Engine cut out
R	Ivan Capelli	28	I	Ferrari	21	Engine
R	Mika Häkkinen	11	SF	Lotus-Ford	21	Engine
R	Gerhard Berger	2	A	McLaren-Honda	16	Misfire
R	Olivier Grouillard	3	F	Tyrrell-Ilmor	8	Overheating
R	Ukyo Katayama	30	J	Venturi-Lamborghini	8	Accident
R	Aguri Suzuki	10	J	Footwork-Mugen	1	Spun off
R	Alessandro Zanardi	23	I	Minardi-Lamborghini	1	Clutch

Fastest lap: Patrese, on lap 36, 1m 41.591s, 150.060 mph/241.498 km/h.

Non Qualifiers

No.	Name	Car
32	Modena	Jordan
7	van de Poele	Brabham
14	Chiesa	Fondmetal
8	Hill	Brabham

Non Pre-Qualifiers

No.	Name	Car
34	Moreno	Andrea Moda
35	McCarthy	Andrea Moda

1992 FORMULA ONE GRAND PRIX
ROUND ELEVEN

HUNGARY

Hungaroring, Budapest

August 16, 1992

Circuit Length: 2.465 mls/3.968 km

Laps: 77

Champion at last: Nigel Mansell had spent 13 F1 seasons chasing the world title.

Official Starting Grid

Driver	Time	No.		Driver	Time
Patrese *Williams*	(1.15.476)	6			
			5	Mansell *Williams*	(1.15.643)
Senna *McLaren*	(1.16.267)	1			
			19	Schumacher *Benetton*	(1.16.524)
Berger *McLaren*	(1.17.277)	2			
			20	Brundle *Benetton*	(1.18.148)
Alboreto *Footwork*	(1.18.604)	9			
			25	Boutsen *Ligier*	(1.18.618)
Alesi *Ferrari*	(1.18.665)	27			
			28	Capelli *Ferrari*	(1.18.765)
Comas *Ligier*	(1.18.902)	26			
			15	Tarquini *Fondmetal*	(1.19.123)
Herbert *Lotus*	(1.19.143)	12			
			10	Suzuki *Footwork*	(1.19.200)
Gachot *Venturi*	(1.19.365)	29			
			11	Häkkinen *Lotus*	(1.19.587)
Belmondo *March*	(1.19.626)	17			
			14	van de Poele *Fondmetal*	(1.19.776)
de Cesaris *Tyrrell*	(1.19.867)	4			
			30	Katayama *Venturi*	(1.19.990)
Gugelmin *Jordan*	(1.20.023)	33			
			3	Grouillard *Tyrrell*	(1.20.063)
Wendlinger *March*	(1.20.315)	16			
			32	Modena *Jordan*	(1.20.707)
Hill *Brabham*	(1.20.781)	8			
			22	Martini *Dallara*	(1.20.988)

Drivers' World Championship

Pos.	Driver	Total
1	Nigel Mansell	92
2	Riccardo Patrese	40
3	Ayrton Senna	34
4	Michael Schumacher	33
5	Gerhard Berger	24
6	Martin Brundle	18
7	Jean Alesi	13
8	Mika Häkkinen	8
9	Michele Alboreto	5
10=	Andrea de Cesaris	4
10=	Erik Comas	4
12=	Karl Wendlinger	3
12=	Ivan Capelli	3
14=	Pier-Luigi Martini	2
14=	Johnny Herbert	2
16	Bertrand Gachot	1

Constructors' World Championship

Pos.	Team	Total
1	Williams	132
2	McLaren	58
3	Benetton	51
4	Ferrari	16
5	Lotus	10
6	Footwork	5
7=	Tyrrell	4
7=	Ligier	4
9	March	3
10	Dallara	2
11	Venturi	1

Race Classification

Pos.	Driver	No.	Nat.	Car	Laps	Time/retirement
1	Ayrton Senna	1	BR	McLaren-Honda	77	1h 46m 19.216s
2	Nigel Mansell	5	GB	Williams-Renault	77	1h 46m 59.355s
3	Gerhard Berger	2	A	McLaren-Honda	77	1h 47m 09.998s
4	Mika Häkkinen	11	SF	Lotus-Ford	77	1h 47m 13.529s
5	Martin Brundle	20	GB	Benetton-Ford	77	1h 47m 16.714s
6	Ivan Capelli	28	I	Ferrari	76	
7	Michele Alboreto	9	I	Footwork-Mugen	75	
8	Andrea de Cesaris	4	I	Tyrrell-Ilmor	75	
9	Paul Belmondo	17	F	March-Ilmor	74	
10	Mauricio Gugelmin	33	BR	Jordan-Yamaha	73	
11	Damon Hill	8	GB	Brabham-Judd	73	
R	Michael Schumacher	19	D	Benetton-Ford	63	Rear wing/spun off
R	Riccardo Patrese	6	I	Williams-Renault	55	Engine
R	Pier-Luigi Martini	22	I	Dallara-Ferrari	40	Gearbox
R	Ukyo Katayama	30	J	Venturi-Lamborghini	35	Engine
R	Jean Alesi	27	F	Ferrari	14	Spun off
R	Bertrand Gachot	29	F	Venturi-Lamborghini	13	Collision with Suzuki
R	Aguri Suzuki	10	J	Footwork-Mugen	13	Collision with Gachot
R	Olivier Grouillard	3	F	Tyrrell-Ilmor	13	Collision with Wendlinger
R	Karl Wendlinger	16	A	March-Ilmor	13	Collision with Grouillard
R	Stefano Modena	32	I	Jordan-Yamaha	13	Hit by Grouillard
R	Eric van de Poele	7	B	Brabham-Judd	2	Spun off
R	Erik Comas	26	F	Ligier-Renault	0	Collision with Boutsen
R	Thierry Boutsen	25	B	Ligier-Renault	0	Collision with Comas
R	Johnny Herbert	12	GB	Lotus-Ford	0	Spun off avoiding Comas/Boutsen
R	Gabriele Tarquini	15	I	Fondmetal-Ford	0	Spun off avoiding Comas/Boutsen

Fastest lap: Mansell, on lap 63, 1m 18.308s, 113.349 mph/182.418 km/h (record)

Non Qualifiers

No.	Name	Car
24	Morbidelli	Minardi
21	Lehto	Dallara
23	Zanardi	Minardi
34	Moreno	Andrea Moda

Non Pre-Qualifiers

No.	Name	Car
35	McCarthy	Andrea Moda

1992 FORMULA ONE GRAND PRIX
ROUND TWELVE

BELGIUM

Circuit de Spa-Francorchamps

August 30, 1992

Circuit Length: 4.3123 mls/6.940 km

Laps: 44

Michael Schumacher: F1's first 'new' winner since 1989.

Official Starting Grid

Mansell *Williams*	(1.50.545)	5			
Schumacher *Benetton*	(1.53.221)	19	1	Senna *McLaren*	(1.52.743)
Alesi *Ferrari*	(1.54.438)	27	6	Patrese *Williams*	(1.53.557)
Boutsen *Ligier*	(1.54.654)	25	2	Berger *McLaren*	(1.54.642)
Brundle *Benetton*	(1.54.973)	20	11	Häkkinen *Lotus*	(1.54.812)
Tarquini *Fondmetal*	(1.55.965)	15	12	Herbert *Lotus*	(1.54.812)
de Cesaris *Tyrrell*	(1.56.111)	4	28	Capelli *Ferrari*	(1.56.075)
van de Poele *Fondmetal*	(1.56.674)	14	16	Alboreto *March*	(1.56.809)
Modena *Jordan*	(1.56.889)	32	21	Lehto *Dallara*	(1.56.809)
Martini *Dallara*	(1.57.267)	22	16	Wendlinger *March*	(1.57.039)
Naspetti *March*	(1.57.974)	17	29	Gachot *Venturi*	(1.57.330)
Morbidelli *Minardi*	(1.58.126)	24	3	Grouillard *Tyrrell*	(1.57.818)
Suzuki *Footwork*	(1.58.826)	10	33	Gugelmin *Jordan*	(1.58.499)
			30	Katayama *Venturi*	(1.59.383)

Drivers' World Championship

Pos.	Driver	Total
1	Nigel Mansell	98
2	Riccardo Patrese	44
3	Michael Schumacher	43
4	Ayrton Senna	36
5	Gerhard Berger	24
6	Martin Brundle	21
7	Jean Alesi	13
8	Mika Häkkinen	9
9	Michele Alboreto	5
10=	Andrea de Cesaris	4
10=	Erik Comas	4
12=	Karl Wendlinger	3
12=	Ivan Capelli	3
14=	Pier-Luigi Martini	2
14=	Johnny Herbert	2
16	Bertrand Gachot	1

Constructors' World Championship

Pos.	Team	Total
1	Williams	142
2	Benetton	64
3	McLaren	60
4	Ferrari	16
5	Lotus	11
6	Footwork	5
7=	Tyrrell	4
7=	Ligier	4
9	March	3
10	Dallara	2
11	Venturi	1

Race Classification

Pos.	Driver	No.	Nat.	Car	Laps	Time/retirement
1	Michael Schumacher	19	D	Benetton-Ford	44	1h 36m 10.721s
2	Nigel Mansell	5	GB	Williams-Renault	44	1h 36m 47.316s
3	Riccardo Patrese	6	I	Williams-Renault	44	1h 36m 54.618s
4	Martin Brundle	20	GB	Benetton-Ford	44	1h 36m 56.780s
5	Ayrton Senna	1	BR	McLaren-Honda	44	1h 37m 19.090s
6	Mika Häkkinen	11	SF	Lotus-Ford	44	1h 37m 20.751s
7	JJ Lehto	21	SF	Dallara-Ferrari	44	1h 37m 48.958s
8	Andrea de Cesaris	4	I	Tyrrell-Ilmor	43	
9	Aguri Suzuki	10	J	Footwork-Mugen	43	
10	Eric van de Poele	7	B	Fondmetal-Ford	43	
11	Karl Wendlinger	16	A	March-Ilmor	43	
12	Emanuele Naspetti	17	I	March-Ilmor	43	
13	Johnny Herbert	12	GB	Lotus-Ford	42	Engine
14	Mauricio Gugelmin	33	BR	Jordan-Yamaha	42	
15	Stefano Modena	32	I	Jordan-Yamaha	42	
16	Gianni Morbidelli	24	I	Minardi-Lamborghini	42	
17	Ukyo Katayama	30	J	Venturi-Lamborghini	42	
18	Bertrand Gachot	29	B	Venturi-Lamborghini	40	Spun off
R	Thierry Boutsen	25	B	Ligier-Renault	27	Accident
R	Ivan Capelli	28	I	Ferrari	25	Engine
R	Gabriele Tarquini	15	I	Fondmetal-Ford	25	Engine
R	Michele Alboreto	9	I	Footwork-Mugen	20	Gearbox
R	Jean Alesi	27	F	Ferrari	7	Spun off
R	Olivier Grouillard	3	F	Tyrrell-Ilmor	1	Spun off
R	Pier-Luigi Martini	22	I	Dallara-Ferrari	0	Spun off
R	Gerhard Berger	2	A	McLaren-Honda	0	Transmission

Fastest lap: Schumacher, on lap 39, 1m 53.791s, 137.097 mph/220.636 km/h (record)

Non Qualifiers

No.	Name	Car
23	Fittipaldi	Minardi
34	Moreno	Andrea Moda
35	McCarthy	Andrea Moda
26	Comas	Ligier

Non Pre-Qualifiers

No pre-qualifying session held due to the absence of the Brabham team.

1992 FORMULA ONE GRAND PRIX
ROUND THIRTEEN

ITALY

Autodromo Nazionale di Monza

September 13, 1992

Circuit Length: 3.6039 mls/5.80 km

Laps: 53

On the market: Martin Brundle offered a timely reminder of his ability.

Drivers' World Championship

Pos.	Driver	Total
1	Nigel Mansell	98
2	Michael Schumacher	47
3 =	Riccardo Patrese	46
3 =	Ayrton Senna	46
5 =	Gerhard Berger	27
5 =	Martin Brundle	27
7	Jean Alesi	13
8	Mika Häkkinen	9
9 =	Michele Alboreto	5
9 =	Andrea de Cesaris	5
11	Erik Comas	4
12 =	Karl Wendlinger	3
12 =	Ivan Capelli	3
14 =	Pier-Luigi Martini	2
14 =	Johnny Herbert	2
16	Bertrand Gachot	1

Constructors' World Championship

Pos.	Team	Total
1	Williams	144
2	Benetton	74
3	McLaren	73
4	Ferrari	16
5	Lotus	11
6 =	Footwork	5
6 =	Tyrrell	5
8	Ligier	4
9	March	3
10	Dallara	2
11	Venturi	1

Official Starting Grid

Driver / Team	Time	No.	No.	Driver / Team	Time
Mansell *Williams*	(1.22.221)	5	1	Senna *McLaren*	(1.22.822)
Alesi *Ferrari*	(1.22.976)	27	6	Patrese *Williams*	(1.23.022)
Berger *McLaren*	(1.23.112)	2	19	Schumacher *Benetton*	(1.23.629)
Capelli *Ferrari*	(1.24.321)	28	25	Boutsen *Ligier*	(1.24.413)
Brundle *Benetton*	(1.24.551)	20	29	Gachot *Venturi*	(1.24.654)
Häkkinen *Lotus*	(1.24.807)	11	24	Morbidelli *Minardi*	(1.24.912)
Herbert *Lotus*	(1.25.140)	12	21	Lehto *Dallara*	(1.25.145)
Comas *Ligier*	(1.25.178)	26	9	Alboreto *Footwork*	(1.25.234)
Wendlinger *March*	(1.25.343)	16	3	Grouillard *Tyrrell*	(1.25.354)
Suzuki *Footwork*	(1.25.374)	10	15	Tarquini *Fondmetal*	(1.25.420)
de Cesaris *Tyrrell*	(1.25.425)	4	22	Martini *Dallara*	(1.25.528)
Katayama *Venturi*	(1.26.174)	30	17	Naspetti *March*	(1.26.279)
van de Poele *Fondmetal*	(1.26.407)	14	33	Gugelmin *Jordan*	(1.26.463)

Race Classification

Pos.	Driver	No.	Nat.	Car	Laps	Time/retirement
1	Ayrton Senna	1	BR	McLaren-Honda	53	1h 18m 15.349s
2	Martin Brundle	20	GB	Benetton-Ford	53	1h 18m 32.399s
3	Michael Schumacher	19	D	Benetton-Ford	53	1h 18m 39.722s
4	Gerhard Berger	2	A	McLaren-Honda	53	1h 19m 40.839s
5	Riccardo Patrese	6	I	Williams-Renault	53	1h 19m 48.507s
6	Andrea de Cesaris	4	I	Tyrrell-Ilmor	52	
7	Michele Alboreto	9	I	Footwork-Mugen	52	
8	Pier-Luigi Martini	22	I	Dallara-Ferrari	52	
9	Ukyo Katayama	30	J	Venturi-Lamborghini	50	Transmission/spun off
10	Karl Wendlinger	16	A	March-Ilmor	50	
11	JJ Lehto	21	SF	Dallara-Ferrari	47	Electrics/engine cut out
R	Mauricio Gugelmin	33	BR	Jordan-Yamaha	46	Transmission
R	Nigel Mansell	5	GB	Williams-Renault	41	Hydraulics/gearbox
R	Thierry Boutsen	25	B	Ligier-Renault	41	Electronics
R	Erik Comas	26	F	Ligier-Renault	35	Spun off
R	Gabriele Tarquini	15	I	Fondmetal-Ford	30	Gearbox
R	Olivier Grouillard	3	F	Tyrrell-Ilmor	26	Engine
R	Johnny Herbert	12	GB	Lotus-Ford	18	Engine
R	Emanuele Naspetti	17	I	March-Ilmor	17	Collision with Wendlinger
R	Jean Alesi	27	F	Ferrari	12	Fuel pressure
R	Ivan Capelli	28	I	Ferrari	12	Spun off
R	Gianni Morbidelli	24	I	Minardi-Lamborghini	12	Engine
R	Bertrand Gachot	29	B	Venturi-Lamborghini	11	Engine
R	Mika Häkkinen	11	SF	Lotus-Ford	5	Electrics
R	Aguri Suzuki	10	J	Footwork-Mugen	2	Spun off
R	Eric van de Poele	7	B	Fondmetal-Ford	0	Clutch

Fastest lap: Mansell, on lap 39, 1m 26.119s, 150.655 mph/242.455 km/h

Non Qualifiers

No.	Name	Car
23	Fittipaldi	Minardi
32	Modena	Jordan

Non Pre-Qualifiers

No pre-qualifying session held due to the absence of the Brabham team and the exclusion of Andrea Moda Formula.

1992 FORMULA ONE GRAND PRIX
ROUND FOURTEEN

PORTUGAL
Autodromo do Estoril

September 27, 1992

Circuit Length: 2.703 mls/4.350 km

Laps: 71

Mika Häkkinen: yet another splendid effort for Lotus.

Official Starting Grid

Mansell *Williams*	(1.13.041)	**5**		
			6 Patrese *Williams*	(1.13.672)
Senna *McLaren*	(1.14.258)	**1**		
			2 Berger *McLaren*	(1.15.068)
Schumacher *Benetton*	(1.15.356)	***19**		
			20 Brundle *Benetton*	(1.16.084)
Häkkinen *Lotus*	(1.16.173)	**11**		
			9 Alboreto *Footwork*	(1.16.282)
Herbert *Lotus*	(1.16.628)	**12**		
			27 Alesi *Ferrari*	(1.16.884)
Boutsen *Ligier*	(1.16.930)	**25**		
			4 de Cesaris *Tyrrell*	(1.17.240)
Gachot *Venturi*	(1.17.250)	**29**		
			26 Comas *Ligier*	(1.17.264)
Grouillard *Tyrrell*	(1.17.277)	**3**		
			28 Capelli *Ferrari*	(1.17.287)
Suzuki *Footwork*	(1.17.361)	****10**		
			24 Morbidelli *Minardi*	(1.17.387)
Lehto *Dallara*	(1.17.474)	**21**		
			33 Gugelmin *Jordan*	(1.17.631)
Martini *Dallara*	(1.17.661)	**22**		
			16 Wendlinger *March*	(1.18.060)
Naspetti *March*	(1.18.092)	**17**		
			32 Modena *Jordan*	(1.18.318)
Katayama *Venturi*	(1.18.592)	**30**		
			23 Fittipaldi *Minardi*	(1.18.615)

* Started from back of grid   ** Started from pit lane

Drivers' World Championship

Pos.	Driver	Total
1	Nigel Mansell	108
2	Ayrton Senna	50
3	Michael Schumacher	47
4	Riccardo Patrese	46
5	Gerhard Berger	33
6	Martin Brundle	30
7	Jean Alesi	13
8	Mika Häkkinen	11
9	Michele Alboreto	6
10	Andrea de Cesaris	5
11	Erik Comas	4
12=	Karl Wendlinger	3
12=	Ivan Capelli	3
14=	Pier-Luigi Martini	2
14=	Johnny Herbert	2
16	Bertrand Gachot	1

Race Classification

Pos.	Driver	No.	Nat.	Car	Laps	Time/retirement
1	Nigel Mansell	5	GB	Williams-Renault	71	1h 34m 46.659s
2	Gerhard Berger	2	A	McLaren-Honda	71	1h 35m 24.192s
3	Ayrton Senna	1	BR	McLaren-Honda	70	
4	Martin Brundle	20	GB	Benetton-Ford	70	
5	Mika Häkkinen	11	SF	Lotus-Ford	70	
6	Michele Alboreto	9	I	Footwork-Mugen	70	
7	Michael Schumacher	19	D	Benetton-Ford	69	
8	Thierry Boutsen	25	B	Ligier-Renault	69	
9	Andrea de Cesaris	4	I	Tyrrell-Ilmor	69	
10	Aguri Suzuki	10	J	Footwork-Mugen	68	
11	Emanuele Naspetti	17	I	March-Ilmor	68	
12	Christian Fittipaldi	23	BR	Minardi-Lamborghini	68	
13	Stefano Modena	32	I	Jordan-Yamaha	68	
14	Gianni Morbidelli	24	I	Minardi-Lamborghini	68	
R	JJ Lehto	21	SF	Dallara-Ferrari	51	Accident damage
R	Karl Wendlinger	16	A	March-Ilmor	48	Oil cooler/gearbox
R	Erik Comas	26	F	Ligier-Renault	47	Engine over-revved
R	Ukyo Katayama	30	J	Venturi-Lamborghini	46	Spun off
R	Riccardo Patrese	6	I	Williams-Renault	43	Collision with Berger
R	Pier-Luigi Martini	22	I	Dallara-Ferrari	43	Damage from Patrese debris
R	Ivan Capelli	28	I	Ferrari	34	Engine
R	Olivier Grouillard	3	F	Tyrrell-Ilmor	27	Gearbox
R	Bertrand Gachot	29	B	Venturi-Lamborghini	25	Fuel pressure
R	Mauricio Gugelmin	33	BR	Jordan-Yamaha	19	Electrics
R	Jean Alesi	27	F	Ferrari	12	Spun off
R	Johnny Herbert	12	GB	Lotus-Ford	2	Bent steering arm

Fastest lap: Senna, on lap 66, 1m 16.272s, 127.579 mph/205.318 km/h (record)

Constructors' World Championship

Pos.	Team	Total
1	Williams	154
2	McLaren	83
3	Benetton	77
4	Ferrari	16
5	Lotus	13
6	Footwork	6
7	Tyrrell	5
8	Ligier	4
9	March	3
10	Dallara	2
11	Venturi	1

Non Qualifiers

None. Only 26 cars present.

Non Pre-Qualifiers

No pre-qualifying session held due to the absence of the Brabham, Andrea Moda and Fondmetal teams.

1992 FORMULA ONE GRAND PRIX
ROUND FIFTEEN

JAPAN

Suzuka International Racing Course

October 25, 1992

Circuit Length: 3.641 mls/5.859 km

Laps: 53

Christian Fittipaldi: following in uncle's footsteps?

Official Starting Grid

Driver	Time	Pos		Driver	Time
Mansell *Williams*	(1.37.360)	5			
			6	Patrese *Williams*	(1.38.219)
Senna *McLaren*	(1.38.375)	1			
			2	Berger *McLaren*	(1.40.296)
Schumacher *Benetton*	(1.40.922)	19			
			12	Herbert *Lotus*	(1.41.030)
Häkkinen *Lotus*	(1.41.415)	11			
			26	Comas *Ligier*	(1.42.187)
de Cesaris *Tyrrell*	(1.42.361)	4			
			25	Boutsen *Ligier*	(1.42.428)
Larini *Ferrari*	(1.42.488)	28			
			23	Fittipaldi *Minardi*	(1.42.617)
Brundle *Benetton*	(1.42.626)	20			
			24	Morbidelli *Minardi*	(1.42.627)
Alesi *Ferrari*	(1.42.824)	27			
			10	Suzuki *Footwork*	(1.43.029)
Modena *Jordan*	(1.43.117)	32			
			29	Gachot *Venturi*	(1.43.156)
Martini *Dallara*	(1.43.251)	22			
			30	Katayama *Venturi*	(1.43.488)
Grouillard *Tyrrell*	(1.43.941)	3			
			21	Lehto *Dallara*	(1.44.037)
Lammers *March*	(1.44.075)	16			
			9	Alboreto *Footwork*	(1.44.149)
Gugelmin *Jordan*	(1.44.253)	33			
			17	Naspetti *March*	(1.47.303)

Drivers' World Championship

Pos.	Driver	Total
1	Nigel Mansell	108
2	Riccardo Patrese	56
3	Ayrton Senna	50
4	Michael Schumacher	47
5	Gerhard Berger	39
6	Martin Brundle	34
7	Jean Alesi	15
8	Mika Häkkinen	11
9	Andrea de Cesaris	8
10	Michele Alboreto	6
11	Erik Comas	4
12 =	Karl Wendlinger	3
12 =	Ivan Capelli	3
14 =	Pier-Luigi Martini	2
14 =	Johnny Herbert	2
16 =	Bertrand Gachot	1
16 =	Christian Fittipaldi	1

Constructors' World Championship

Pos.	Team	Total
1	Williams	164
2	McLaren	89
3	Benetton	81
4	Ferrari	18
5	Lotus	13
6	Tyrrell	8
7	Footwork	6
8	Ligier	4
9	March	3
10	Dallara	2
11 =	Venturi	1
11 =	Minardi	1

Race Classification

Pos.	Driver	No.	Nat.	Car	Laps	Time/retirement
1	Riccardo Patrese	6	I	Williams-Renault	53	1h 33m 09.553s
2	Gerhard Berger	2	A	McLaren-Honda	53	1h 33m 23.282s
3	Martin Brundle	20	GB	Benetton-Ford	53	1h 34m 25.056s
4	Andrea de Cesaris	4	I	Tyrrell-Ilmor	52	
5	Jean Alesi	27	F	Ferrari	52	
6	Christian Fittipaldi	23	BR	Minardi-Lamborghini	52	
7	Stefano Modena	32	I	Jordan-Yamaha	52	
8	Aguri Suzuki	10	J	Footwork-Mugen	52	
9	JJ Lehto	21	SF	Dallara-Ferrari	52	
10	Pier-Luigi Martini	22	I	Dallara-Ferrari	52	
11	Ukyo Katayama	30	J	Venturi-Lamborghini	52	
12	Nicola Larini	28	I	Ferrari	52	
13	Emanuele Naspetti	17	I	March-Ilmor	51	
14	Gianni Morbidelli	24	I	Minardi-Lamborghini	51	
15	Michele Alboreto	9	I	Footwork-Mugen	51	
R	Nigel Mansell	5	GB	Williams-Renault	44	Engine
R	Mika Häkkinen	11	SF	Lotus-Ford	44	Engine
R	Bertrand Gachot	29	B	Venturi-Lamborghini	39	Collided with Katayama
R	Erik Comas	26	F	Ligier-Renault	36	Engine
R	Jan Lammers	16	NL	March-Ilmor	27	Clutch
R	Mauricio Gugelmin	33	BR	Jordan-Yamaha	22	Accident
R	Johnny Herbert	12	GB	Lotus-Ford	15	Gearbox
R	Michael Schumacher	19	D	Benetton-Ford	13	Gearbox
R	Olivier Grouillard	3	F	Tyrrell-Ilmor	6	Accident
R	Thierry Boutsen	25	B	Ligier-Renault	3	Gearbox
R	Ayrton Senna	1	BR	McLaren-Honda	2	Engine

Fastest lap: Mansell, on lap 44, 1m 40.646s, 130.332 mph/209.749 km/h (record)

Non Qualifiers

None. Only 26 cars present.

Non Pre-Qualifiers

No pre-qualifying session held due to the absence of the Brabham, Andrea Moda and Fondmetal teams.

1992 FORMULA ONE GRAND PRIX
ROUND SIXTEEN

AUSTRALIA
Adelaide

November 8, 1992

Circuit Length: 2.347 mls/3.778 km

Laps: 81

Stefano Modena: convincing performance after a lacklustre season.

Official Starting Grid

Mansell	(1.13.732)	5				
Williams			**1**	Senna	(1.14.202)	
Patrese	(1.14.370)	6		*McLaren*		
Williams			**2**	Berger	(1.15.114)	
Schumacher	(1.15.210)	19		*McLaren*		
Benetton			**27**	Alesi	(1.16.091)	
de Cesaris	(1.16.440)	4		*Ferrari*		
Tyrrell			**20**	Brundle	(1.16.562)	
Comas	(1.16.727)	26		*Benetton*		
Ligier			**11**	Häkkinen	(1.16.863)	
Alboreto	(1.16.937)	9		*Lotus*		
Footwork			**12**	Herbert	(1.16.944)	
Grouillard	(1.17.037)	3		*Lotus*		
Tyrrell			**22**	Martini	(1.17.047)	
Modena	(1.17.231)	32		*Dallara*		
Jordan			**24**	Morbidelli	(1.17.333)	
Fittipaldi	(1.17.367)	23		*Minardi*		
Minardi			**10**	Suzuki	(1.17.409)	
Larini	(1.17.465)	28		*Footwork*		
Ferrari			**33**	Gugelmin	(1.17.805)	
Gachot	(1.17.808)	29		*Jordan*		
Venturi			**25**	Boutsen	(1.17.957)	
Naspetti	(1.18.138)	17		*Ligier*		
March			**21**	Lehto	(1.18.565)	
Lammers	(1.18.843)	16		*Dallara*		
March			**30**	Katayama	(1.18.862)	
				Venturi		

Drivers' World Championship

Pos.	Driver	Total
1	Nigel Mansell	108
2	Riccardo Patrese	56
3	Michael Schumacher	53
4	Ayrton Senna	50
5	Gerhard Berger	49
6	Martin Brundle	38
7	Jean Alesi	18
8	Mika Häkkinen	11
9	Andrea de Cesaris	8
10	Michele Alboreto	6
11	Erik Comas	4
12=	Karl Wendlinger	3
12=	Ivan Capelli	3
14=	Pier-Luigi Martini	2
14=	Johnny Herbert	2
14=	Thierry Boutsen	2
17=	Bertrand Gachot	1
17=	Stefano Modena	1
17=	Christian Fittipaldi	1

Constructors' World Championship

Pos.	Team	Total
1	Williams	164
2	McLaren	99
3	Benetton	91
4	Ferrari	21
5	Lotus	13
6	Tyrrell	8
7=	Footwork	6
7=	Ligier	6
9	March	3
10	Dallara	2
11=	Venturi	1
11=	Jordan	1
11=	Minardi	1

Race Classification

Pos.	Driver	No.	Nat.	Car	Laps	Time/retirement
1	Gerhard Berger	2	A	McLaren-Honda	81	1h 46m 54.786s
2	Michael Schumacher	19	D	Benetton-Ford	81	1h 46m 55.527s
3	Martin Brundle	20	GB	Benetton-Ford	81	1h 47m 48.942s
4	Jean Alesi	27	F	Ferrari	80	
5	Thierry Boutsen	25	B	Ligier-Renault	80	
6	Stefano Modena	32	I	Jordan-Yamaha	80	
7	Mika Häkkinen	11	SF	Lotus-Ford	80	
8	Aguri Suzuki	10	J	Footwork-Mugen	79	
9	Christian Fittipaldi	23	BR	Minardi-Lamborghini	79	
10	Gianni Morbidelli	24	I	Minardi-Lamborghini	79	
11	Nicola Larini	28	I	Ferrari	79	
12	Jan Lammers	16	NL	March-Ilmor	78	
13	Johnny Herbert	12	GB	Lotus-Ford	77	
R	JJ Lehto	21	SF	Dallara-Ferrari	70	Gearbox
R	Emanuele Naspetti	17	I	March-Ilmor	55	Gearbox
R	Bertrand Gachot	29	B	Venturi-Lamborghini	51	Engine
R	Riccardo Patrese	6	I	Williams-Renault	50	Fuel pressure
R	Ukyo Katayama	30	J	Venturi-Lamborghini	35	Differential
R	Andrea de Cesaris	4	I	Tyrrell-Ilmor	29	Fuel pressure/fire
R	Nigel Mansell	5	GB	Williams-Renault	18	Hit by Senna
R	Ayrton Senna	1	BR	McLaren-Honda	18	Collision with Mansell
R	Mauricio Gugelmin	33	BR	Jordan-Yamaha	7	Crashed/brakes
R	Erik Comas	26	F	Ligier-Renault	4	Over-revved engine
R	Michele Alboreto	9	I	Footwork-Mugen	0	Accident
R	Pier-Luigi Martini	22	I	Dallara-Ferrari	0	Collision with Grouillard
R	Olivier Grouillard	3	F	Tyrrell-Ilmor	0	Collision with Martini

Fastest lap: Schumacher, on lap 68, 1m 16.078s, 111.144 mph/178.869 km/h (record).

Non Qualifiers

None. Only 26 cars present.

Non Pre-Qualifiers

No pre-qualifying session held due to the absence of the Brabham, Andrea Moda and Fondmetal teams.